In this innovative book Dr Morris seeks to show the many ways in which the excavated remains of burials can and should be a major source of evidence for social historians of the ancient Graeco-Roman world. Burials have a far wider geographical and social range than the surviving literary texts, which were mainly written for a small elite. They provide us with unique insights into how Greeks and Romans constituted and interpreted their own communities. In particular, burials enable the historian to study social change. Yet hitherto they have been conspicuously under-studied. Ian Morris illustrates the great potential of the material in these respects with examples drawn from societies as diverse in time, space and political context as archaic Rhodes, classical Athens, early imperial Rome and the last days of the western Roman empire. The methods and arguments used have relevance for historians, anthropologists and sociologists of other cultures and societies, and it is one of Dr Morris' and the series' major aims to enable interdisciplinary exchange of ideas across conventional academic frontiers.

KEY THEMES IN ANCIENT HISTORY

Death-ritual and social structure in classical antiquity

KEY THEMES IN ANCIENT HISTORY

EDITORS

Dr P. A. Cartledge
Clare College, Cambridge

Dr P. D. A. Garnsey
Jesus College, Cambridge

Key Themes in Ancient History aims to provide readable, informed and original studies of various basic topics, designed in the first instance for students and teachers of Classics and Ancient History, but also for those engaged in related disciplines. Each volume will be devoted to a general theme in Greek, Roman, or where appropriate, Graeco-Roman history, or to some salient aspect or aspects of it. Besides indicating the state of current research in the relevant area, authors will seek to show how the theme is significant for our own as well as ancient culture and society. By providing books for courses that are oriented around themes it is hoped to encourage and stimulate promising new developments in teaching and research in ancient history.

Other books in the series:

Literacy and orality in ancient Greece, by Rosalind Thomas

DEATH-RITUAL AND SOCIAL STRUCTURE IN CLASSICAL ANTIQUITY

IAN MORRIS

Associate Professor, Departments of History and Classics,
University of Chicago

CAMBRIDGE
UNIVERSITY PRESS

Published by the Press Syndicate of the University of Cambridge
The Pitt Building, Trumpington Street, Cambridge CB2 1RP
40 West 20th Street, New York, NY 10011-4211, USA
10 Stamford Road, Oakleigh, Melbourne 3166, Australia

First published 1992
Reprinted 1994

Printed in Great Britain by
Woolnough Bookbinding Ltd, Irthlingborough, Northants.

A catalogue record for this book is available from the British Library

Morris Ian, 1960—
Death-ritual and social structure in classical antiquity / Ian
Morris.
p.   cm. – (Key themes in ancient history)
Includes bibliographical references and index.
ISBN 0-521-37465-0 (hardback). – ISBN 0-521-37611-4 (paperback)
1. Civilization, Classical.   2. Burial – Greece.   3. Burial Rome.
I. Title.   II. Series.
DE61.B87M67   1992   91-330669   CIP
393′.0938 – dc20

ISBN 0 521 37465 0 hardback
ISBN 0 521 37611 4 paperback

For Kathy

Contents

Figures

Tables

Preface

Nine years ago, I started a Ph.D. thesis about Early Iron Age Greece. I knew that very little literary evidence survived, but it came as something of a shock to discover that there was in fact almost nothing to work with except for brief descriptions of graves. At the first social function for new graduate students, I tried to explain to one of my neighbours, a specialist in Anthony Eden's German policies in the first six months of 1936, what I was planning to write about. He looked confused, and then asked me what a lot of graves had got to do with history. After a long delay I have found an answer, and this book is it.

I believe that burials allow us to go far beyond the limits of textual and iconographic evidence in the study of ancient ritual, and that by studying all aspects of death rites as integrated parts of ritual statements about the actors' perceptions of the world we can reach a new understanding of ancient social structure. The disconcerting experience of having nothing to study but graves turned out not to be such a bad thing after all; I argue that burials provide information of a kind which no other sources provide, and that even in the best documented periods of classical antiquity historians cannot afford to neglect them. I try to make this point with a series of examples drawn from 1,500 years of Greek and Roman history. There will be much for specialists to disagree with in each specific case, but overall I hope that there will be more which stimulates research and proves useful to social historians. The book is aimed at lay and undergraduate audiences in ancient history and archaeology, and at professionals. There is an increasing interest in using archaeological evidence to overcome the small numbers and inherent problems of Greek and Latin texts, but there have been few systematic guides to its interpretation. I hope to fill part of this gap.

I wrote the book between April 1989 and March 1990, beginning

xiii

it at the University of Chicago and completing it as a Junior Fellow at the Center for Hellenic Studies in Washington DC. I wish to thank the Senior Fellows and Director of the Center for electing me to this Fellowship; everyone in and around Washington who had a hand in making the year so enjoyable; and several divisions, departments and committees at the University of Chicago for granting me a year's leave and providing further financial support. Access to books in the Library of Congress, the Joseph Regenstein Library, Georgetown University, the British School at Athens, the Classics Faculty at Cambridge, the Seminary Co-op and Olsson's bookstores was also much appreciated. I am also grateful to Cambridge University Press for all their help in the difficult process of getting the manuscript ready for publication, and for tolerating last minute changes. I have avoided quoting ancient authors in the original languages, since the texts are easily available. Translations are my own unless marked otherwise.

Because I have ventured into fields far beyond those I have previously written about, I have picked the brains of many people. All of them improved this book; none of them agrees with all of it, and most of them are probably horrified by at least something in it. I want to thank Carla Antonaccio, John Bodel, Steve Dyson, Mike Jameson, Elizabeth Meyer, Josh Ober, Richard Saller, Brent Shaw, Barry Strauss and James Whitley for allowing me to read unpublished papers; Anna Maria D'Onofrio, John Humphrey and John Lenz for suggesting reading to me; Sue Alcock, Steve Dyson, David Gill, Herbert Hoffman, Rick Jones, Ed Laumann, David Mattingly, Elizabeth Meyer, Josh Ober, Simon Price, Kathy St John, Brent Shaw, Anthony Snodgrass, Zeph Stewart, Barry Strauss, Sophia Voutsakis, James Whitley and Greg Woolf for commenting on some or all of the manuscript; and particularly Paul Cartledge, Peter Garnsey and Richard Saller, who read the whole text in several versions and were exemplary editors, commentators and friends. Finally, I would like to thank the officers of Cambridge University Press for their part in preparing the book for publication.

Valparaiso, Indiana

Abbreviations

AA	Archäologischer Anzeiger
AAA	Athens Annals of Archaeology
AArchHung	Acta Archaeologica Hungaricae
AD	Arkhaiologikon Deltion
AE	Arkhaiologiki Ephemeris
AHB	Ancient History Bulletin
AHR	American Historical Review
AION ArchStAnt	Annali di Istituto Universitario Orientale, Sezione di Archeologia e Storia Antica
AJA	American Journal of Archaeology
AJAH	American Journal of Ancient History
AJPA	American Journal of Physical Anthropology
AJPh	American Journal of Philology
AM	Mitteilungen des deutschen archäologischen Instituts, Athenische Abteilung
Am Ant	American Antiquity
AMT	M. Schiffer, ed., Advances in Archaeological Method and Theory (New York 1978–)
Anat St	Anatolian Studies
Anc Soc	Ancient Society
Annales ESC	Annales, économies, sociétés, civilisations
Ann Rev Anth	Annual Review of Anthropology
ANRW	Aufstieg und Niedergang der römischen Welts
Ant Cl	L'antiquité classique
AntK	Antike Kunst
AQ	Anthropological Quarterly
AR	Archaeological Reports
Arch Belg	Archaeologia Belgica
Arch Hom	Archaeologia Homerica
ArchJ	Archaeological Journal

ASAA	*Annuario della scuola archeologica di Atene*
BAR	*British Archaeological Reports*
BARS	*British Archaeological Reports*, International Series
BASOR	*Bulletin of the American Schools of Oriental Research*
BCH	*Bulletin de correspondance hellénique*
BSA	*Annual of the British School at Athens*
CA	*Current Anthropology*
CAH	*Cambridge Ancient History*, 2nd edn
CBA	Calendar for British Archaeology
CEG	*Carmina Epigraphica Graeca Saeculorum VII–V*, ed. P. A. Hansen (1983)
CIL	*Corpus Inscriptionum Latinarum* (Berlin 1863–)
CJ	*Classical Journal*
C & M	*Classica et Mediaevalia*
Cl Ant	*Classical Antiquity*
CP	*Classical Philology*
CQ	*Classical Quarterly*
DHA	*Dialogues d'histoire ancienne*
Diss Arch Gand	*Dissertationes Archaeologicae Gandenses*
EMC/CV	*Échos du monde classique/Classical Views*
G & R	*Greece & Rome*
GRBS	*Greek, Roman and Byzantine Studies*
HSCPh	*Harvard Studies in Classical Philology*
HTR	*Harvard Theological Review*
IC	*Inscriptiones Creticae*, ed. M. Guarducci (Rome 1935)
IG	*Inscriptiones Graecae* (Berlin 1873–)
ILCV	*Inscriptiones Latinae Christianae Veteres*, ed. E. Diehl (1925–31)
Ist Mitt	*Mitteilungen des deutschen archäologischen Instituts, Istanbuler Abteilung*
JAS	*Journal of Archaeological Science*
JBAA	*Journal of the British Archaeological Association*
JdI	*Jahrbuch des deutschen archäologischen Instituts, Athenische Abteilung*
JFA	*Journal of Field Archaeology*
JHE	*Journal of Human Evolution*
JHS	*Journal of Hellenic Studies*

JIH	*Journal of Interdisciplinary History*
JMGS	*Journal of Modern Greek Studies*
JMH	*Journal of Modern History*
JRA	*Journal of Roman Archaeology*
JRS	*Journal of Roman Studies*
MAAR	*Memoirs of the American Academy at Rome*
MEFRA	*Mélanges de l'école française à Rome. Antiquité*
MIGRA	*Miscellanea Graeca*
NSc	*Notizie degli Scavi*
OJA	*Oxford Journal of Archaeology*
Op Ath	*Opuscula Atheniensia*
P & P	*Past and Present*
PBA	*Proceedings of the British Academy*
PBSR	*Papers of the British School at Rome*
PCPhS	*Proceedings of the Cambridge Philological Society*
PdP	*Parola del Passato*
PEQ	*Palestine Exploration Quarterly*
PPS	*Proceedings of the Prehistoric Society*
RA	*Revue archéologique*
RDAC	*Report of the Department of Antiquities, Cyprus*
REA	*Revue des études anciennes*
REG	*Revue des études grecques*
RivArchCrist	*Rivista di Archeologia Cristiana*
Röm Mitt	*Mitteilungen des deutschen archäologischen Instituts, Römische Abteilung*
SEG	*Supplementum Epigraphicum Graecum*, vols. I–xxv ed. J. J. E. Hondius and A. G. Woodhead; xxvi–xxxii ed. H. W. Pleket and R. S. Stroud (Leiden 1923–86)
SIA	*Supplementum Inscriptionum Atticarum*, ed. A. N. Oikonomides (1976–86)
SIG	*Sylloge Inscriptionum Graecarum*, ed. W. Dittenberger, 3rd edn (Leipzig 1915–24)
SIMA	*Studies in Mediterranean Archaeology*
TAPhA	*Transactions of the American Philological Association*
WA	*World Archaeology*
ZPE	*Zeitschrift für Papyrologie und Epigraphik*

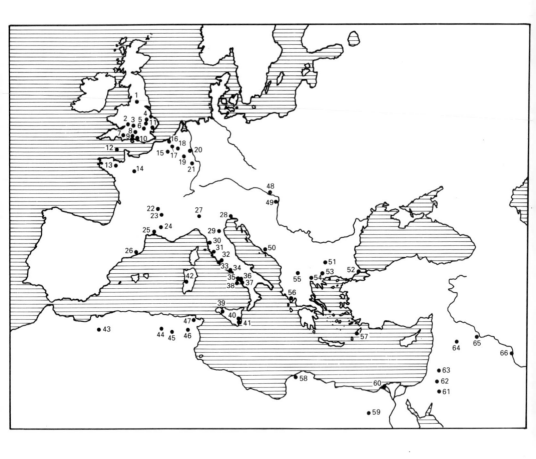

1. York	18. Blicquy	35. Baiae	51. Panagyurishte
2. Birdlip	19. Tongres	36. Puteoli	52. Selymbria
3. Cirencester	20. Bonn	37. Pompeii	53. Drabescus
4. Lynch Farm	21. Goeblingen-Nospelt	38. Pithekoussai	54. Derveni
5. Baldock	22. Lyon	39. Segesta	55. Trebenishte
6. Welwyn	23. Vienne	40. Megara Hyblaea	56. Actium
7. Poundbury	24. Arles	41. Syracuse	57. Vroulia
8. Winchester	25. Lattes	42. Cornus	58. Cyrene
9. Owslebury	26. Ampurias	43. Altava	59. Dakleh Oasis
10. Chichester	27. Milan	44. Castellum	60. Alexandria
11. Lexden	28. Aquileia	Celtianum	61. Petra
12. Guernsey	29. Sarsina	45. Lambaesis	62. Jericho
13. Frénouville	30. Vada	46. Sufetula	63. Qumran
14. Jublains	31. Settefinestre	47. Carthage	64. Palmyra
15. Arras	32. Rome	48. Gerulata Rusovce	65. Dura Europos
16. Oudenburg	33. Ostia	49. Tokod	66. Babylon
17. Tournai	34. Gaeta	50. Salona	

1. Map of sites in the Roman empire discussed in this book.

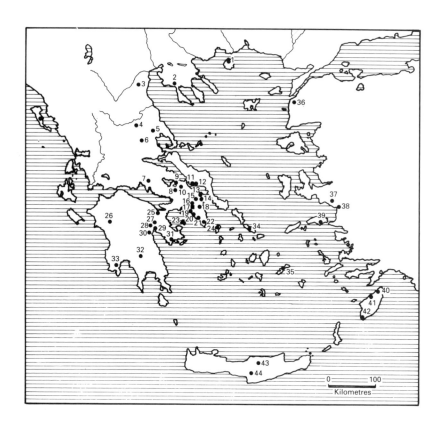

1. Thasos	16. Chalandri	31. Hermione
2. Olynthus	17. Athens	32. Sparta
3. Vergina	18. Draphi	33. Nichoria
4. Krannon	19. Phaleron	34. Tenos
5. Pherae	20. Ano Voula	35. Amorgos
6. Pharsalus	21. Anavyssos	36. Troy
7. Delphi	22. Thorikos	37. Colophon
8. Thebes	23. Aegina	38. Ephesus
9. Rhitsona	24. Ioulis	39. Samos
10. Tanagra	25. Corinth	40. Ialysos
11. Lefkandi	26. Olympia	41. Kameiros
12. Eretria	27. Mycenae	42. Vroulia
13. Rhamnous	28. Argos	43. Knossos
14. Marathon	29. Tiryns	44. Gortyn
15. Spata	30. Lerna	

2. Map of sites in Greece discussed in this book.

CHAPTER I

The anthropology of a dead world

This book is about how a particular sort of evidence, burials, can be used to write a particular sort of history, that of the social structures of classical antiquity. Most of what I say is based on a simple proposition: a burial is part of a funeral, and a funeral is part of a set of rituals by which the living deal with death. All very obvious, perhaps, but it has one major consequence for the historian. Whether we look at graves with religious, economic, social or artistic questions in mind, the analysis of burials is the analysis of symbolic action.

My argument is as follows. In rituals people use symbols to make explicit social structure, an interpretation of the meaning of daily life. Such structure should be central to any attempt to write social history, but on the whole ancient historians have neglected it. This is largely due to the nature of the written sources, which encourages other approaches. Burials are difficult to interpret, but they can be used to augment the written record, giving us for the first time a dynamic account of social structure and how it changed in antiquity.

These are big claims to make in a small book. Most works of ancient history take little account of graves; even the excellent collection *Sources for Ancient History* only gives seven pages to the topic.[1] When historians do look at burials, it is usually in a 'bits-and-pieces' manner, picking out the spectacular or the supposedly 'typical' to illustrate arguments based on texts. It is widely assumed that the rigour which philological historians bring to their sources is only required by archaeologists for dating and classifying material. I hope to overturn such assumptions. I set out the argument in this first chapter, which is rather abstract and theoretical,

[1] Crawford, ed., 1983: 150–2, 166, 179–81, dealing mainly with chronology.

but it is worth taking the time to make the premises clear. It used to be said (and perhaps still is in some quarters) that social history is real history with the politics left out, and there can be a grain of truth in this, since without methodological rigour we quickly descend into fuzziness and platitudes. We have an ever-growing body of evidence, emanating from wider social and geographical groups than those who produced the surviving texts. I believe that it has the potential to transform the way we do ancient social history, but it requires careful handling and constant reflection.

I begin by saying what I mean by social structure and then move on to discuss how rituals create it. 'Create' is a strong word. I use it deliberately, to distinguish my argument from two other approaches to ancient rituals. Both might be called 'common-sense' perspectives, but both, I think, miss much of the potential of ritual evidence. The first is that ritual can only be analysed as part of religious belief, and that this in turn has little to do with 'external' phenomena such as power, conflict, class, ideology and so on. The second is that rituals somehow 'reflect' an underlying social 'reality'. In a famous essay published twenty-five years ago, Clifford Geertz suggested that in rituals people not only set up models *of* proper roles and relationships but also models *for* them.[2] That is, we interpret ritual as a model *of* the world through the prism of our own experiences, and interpret our own experiences through the prism of ritual as a model *for* the world. It was through ceremonies such as funerals that Greeks and Romans constructed and debated the meanings of their worlds.

I wrote this book not just because a lot of graves have been excavated and we need to do something with them, but because social structure is crucially important for the ancient historian. Consequently some ways of using burials are treated only briefly, if at all. My emphasis is on 'total' analysis of burials as part of a ritual system. The core of the book consists of five chapters, grouped loosely around two topics, the body and display. I could have chosen other topics and written different chapters, but these seem to me to provide the most useful introduction. In each chapter I take a specific type of evidence – disposal methods, skeletal remains, grave goods, grave markers, tombstone inscriptions – and

---

[2] Models of and for, Geertz 1973 (1966): 63–4. Debates over meaning in rituals, e.g. Kertzer 1988: 31, 44, 71–2, 102–50.

examine what can be done with it. My method is to provide concrete examples rather than programmatic statements, and my
argument in each case is that no single feature of burial evidence
can be isolated and treated on its own. In chapters 2–6 I emphasise
the 'big picture', looking at how large samples of data contribute to
central questions in social history. In each case I discuss ways to
identify patterns and to relate them to other aspects of the evidence,
and ways not to use the material, although I try not to waste time
on straw men. In chapter 7 I give an example of the kind of nitty-
gritty detailed empirical analysis of burials that I am advocating as
the key to ancient social structures, with a close study of the archaic
Greek site of Vroulia on Rhodes. To begin with, though, I will
explain more carefully what I mean by social structure and why it
is important, before going on to discuss how burials can help us
understand it.

SOCIAL STRUCTURE

This is why poetry is more philosophical and more serious than history:
poetry speaks rather of the universal, history of the particular. By universal I mean the sorts of things that a certain type of person will probably or
necessarily do or say ... the particular is about what Alcibiades did or
what happened to him. (Aristotle, *Poetics* 1.1451b5–11)

This is no book of verse, but, like Aristotle, I am uncomfortable
with accounts of the world that look only at the individual actor.
We are social animals, and truly free beings doing whatever they
want have only existed in the dreams of philosophers. Everyone is
born into a more or less structured world, and is socialised in its
ways. It is often hard to predict how people will act, but with
hindsight even the most unexpected events can turn out to be
comprehensible. From the mass of experiences which rush by each
day, nearly everyone is able to pick out a pattern of how the world
around them works. These unverbalised models are the essence of
my subject matter. Social structure, in the sense that I use it,
consists of taken-for-granted norms about the roles and rules which
make up society – relationships of power, affection, deference,
rights, duties and so on. I do not mean a metaphysical 'collective
consciousness' or an undifferentiated 'mentality'; nor Aristotle's

monolithic and static *koinos logos*, 'that which everyone agrees is right' (*Rhet.* 1.1368b7–9). Ideas of social structure vary from individual to individual and from day to day. No two points of view are the same, but there is enough overlap for an observer to be able to distil an abstraction which can be called an Athenian or Spartan social structure at this or that particular moment in time; while there is sufficient difference that we can break these generalisations down along age, sex, class, race or many other lines, depending on the level of detail we wish to work at.[3]

The first question to ask is what social structure *does*. Only after we have decided what we are looking for can we try to find it. Many of the giants of social theory have butted heads over this. To some, social structure is merely a shorthand way to summarise 'real', empirically observable events; to others, it is an almost Platonic ideal form with a purer kind of reality than everyday happenings. Some of the debates are mutual misunderstandings, and others rapidly move off into the terrain of the philosopher; but how we answer the question has important consequences for social history.[4]

From the 1920s to 1950s, the social sciences were dominated by a school of thought called functionalism, nowadays normally used as a pejorative label. The true functionalist (if such a creature ever existed) took a strong view of social structure: it not only existed 'out there' as well as in the scholar's head, but it also provided the glue which held society together. Society was seen as a system which tried to maintain its own stability. Equilibrium was explained by dividing life into subsystems – economic, religious, and so on – which operated checks and balances to keep the whole on an even keel. Threats from outside the system or 'pathological' disorders within (like food riots, labour unrest or racial conflict) would be met by adjustments to the relevant subsystems, again to the benefit of the whole. Paradoxically, the 'vulgar' forms of Marxism popular in this period took a similar position. Instead of the functionalists' beneficial invisible hand, Marxists found sinister 'ideologies' which were straitjackets on thought and action; but the mechanisms which created stability were essentially the same for

---

[3] Mentality, Vovelle 1990. Levels of generalisation, Ober 1989a; Hunt 1989: 15–16.
[4] E.g. Radcliffe-Brown 1952: 9–11, 188–204; Lévi-Strauss 1953; E. R. Leach 1954; Gellner 1958; Kelly 1974; Bloch 1977; Asad 1979.

both groups.[5] Gellner's summary of functionalism applies equally well to pre-war Marxism:

The idea was that a tribal society has a certain structure or organisation, each part of which imposed such pressures and sanctions on the individuals within it as to ensure that they behaved in a way that sustained that structure, and so on forever, or at any rate for quite a long time. Structure was important, a matter of serious concern for men (inside the society or among investigators). Culture, on the other hand, was relatively ephemeral, accidental, epiphenomenal, and altogether suitable for women (inside the society or among investigators). Structure was, for instance, whom one could marry; culture was what the bride wore. (Gellner 1985: 135–6)

In the sixties and seventies, culture struck back. Functionalist analyses were increasingly seen as tautologous or just plain silly. Perhaps saying that Hindus refuse to eat cows and the Kwakiutl burn their blankets as adaptive mechanisms to maintain equilibrium does not tell us much after all. Structure in this crude sense lost much of its appeal. In a 1981 survey of British social anthropologists, 52.5% of those born before 1925 gave social structure as their primary research interest, while only 21.5% of those born after 1945 gave this answer. Most of the loss went to various forms of cognitive anthropology, which rose from 13% among the older group to 32% among the post-war generation. Anthropologists and historians were rejecting the need to explain rituals, speech acts or texts in terms of underlying social structures. Michel Foucault, one of the most influential writers of the 1960s, argued that we should discard the very idea of 'total' social history as an organising scheme for human experience, and instead write general history, abandoning 'an overall shape' in favour of 'the space of dispersion' (1972: 9–10). The term social history began to carry some of the same taint as functionalism, and a new wave of cultural historians increasingly sought inspiration in literary theory, not sociology. One result has been an 'inability to move toward any overarching interpretation ... even more significantly, rather than there being vigorous competition between schools, each confidently pressing

[5] Marxism and functionalism, Asad 1979; Abercrombie et al. 1980: 7–58; Bloch 1983: 95–140.

the claims of its own scheme, potential contenders seem to be in the process of breaking down' (Novick 1988: 457–8).[6]

Over the last ten years there have been attempts to find a middle ground, and these provide the best way for the ancient historian to think about social structure. Anthony Giddens has developed what he calls a 'theory of structuration', the process by which people create a social structure which is neither a fiction made by sociologists nor a mystified 'spirit of the age'. The social structure we are born into and socialised within is a set of assumptions about what we should say, do and even think in given situations, but it does not determine our behaviour. Everything we do is informed by learned social structure, but the structure itself is only transmitted through time and space by real people as they repeat what they themselves have learned, or react against it. It has no independent, extra-human existence. Our own input into this process will affect it, perhaps ever so little; but in the course of just a few years completely new ways of thinking about society may appear. Alternatively, the pace of structural change may be glacially slow, but in either case it is the combination of pre-existing rules and individual actions based on them which transmits and transforms structure through time. Marshall Sahlins explains it in a neat turn of phrase: 'the historical process unfolds as a continuous and reciprocal movement between the practice of the structure and the structure of the practice' (1981: 72). That is, each event puts social structure into practice and recreates or challenges it, while social structure simultaneously gives form and meaning to events. Geertz's definition of culture sums up the way I want to use 'social structure': 'Though ideational, it does not exist in someone's head; though unphysical, it is not an occult entity ... the question as to whether culture is patterned conduct or a frame of mind, or even the two somehow mixed together, loses sense' (Geertz 1973: 10).[7]

[6] Cows and blankets, M. Harris 1974; 1985. Survey, Kuper 1983: 206–10. Breakdown, Ortner 1984; Novick 1988: 415–629; Hunt 1989. Challenge to total history paradigms, Furet 1983; Stearns 1985; Hunt 1986. Pejorative use of 'social history', La Capra 1983; 1985. Literary criticism as a model, Kramer 1989. These changes are often linked to the rise of post-modernist epistemics: see Marcus & Fischer 1986: 7–44; Connor 1989a; Gallagher 1990; Manville 1990: ix–xi.

[7] Structuration, Giddens 1981: 26–68; 1984, with excellent comments in Thompson 1984: 48–72; Karp 1986; Cohen 1987; Lloyd 1986: 306–17. On the relationship between 'culture' and 'structure' in the functionalist sense, Geertz 1973: 142–6. Debates, Silverman 1990, with an extensive bibliography, to which add Chartier 1985; 1989; Darnton 1986; Bloch 1987; Biersack 1989; Pecora 1990.

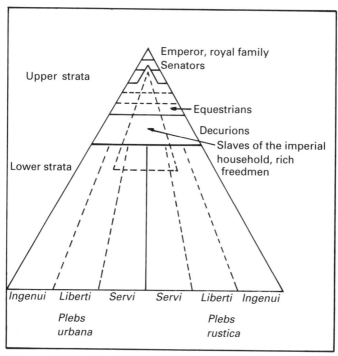

3. Alföldy's model of social relations at Rome in the first two centuries A.D. (after Alföldy 1985: fig. 1)

As an example of what I am talking about, we might take Alföldy's model of Roman society in the first two centuries A.D. (fig. 3). This is a well thought out diagram showing stratification by wealth and power and the way status groups and personal ties crosscut class lines. I will observe certain shortcomings in the next section; but it seems to capture the implicit assumptions of men like Cassius Dio and Aelius Aristides, who describe their world in similar terms, stressing fixity and the boundedness of the orders. Yet we now know – perhaps better than the Romans did – that these orders were anything but rigid. Senatorial families disappeared and were replaced at a rate of 75% per generation, and the equestrian order was still more fluid. The reasons were both social and biological. Roman law gave rich families the potential to secure their status in the next generation and to conform to this ideal model through adoption and trusts; yet on the whole they chose not to. This situation, where people seem to say one thing and do another, is

often called the 'Nuer paradox' after a Sudanese people famous for
the gap between their strongly articulated principle that life is
based on rigid clans and the fluidity of their actual kinship patterns. But if we look at social structure in the sense described
above, the paradox disappears. Social structure is neither a catalogue of marriages nor an ideal of *pietas*; the interaction between the
two 'levels' provides the field of structuration, and we have to work
at both to understand social structure.[8]

But this is easier said than done. One reason why so few ancient
historians have tried to study social structure is because it is so
difficult to generalise to broad patterns from the individualised
literary and epigraphic sources. Even in contemporary settings,
identifying the structures of an unfamiliar world is no walkover –
'as graduate students ... have found to their cost, it is not all that
easy to see or hear bits of social structure in the stream of events
which the anthropologist witnesses' (Bloch 1977: 286). Next, we
must consider how we can reach ancient social structure.

RITUAL

Bloch lets his student in on the game: *it is rituals which make social
structure*. '[O]nce the bewildered fieldworker has realised that it is in
this type of behaviour, and in this type of behaviour alone, that he
needs to look for social structure, the problems disappear and the
task is made strangely easy' (ibid.). Well, not quite that easy.
Ritual is one of those words where we all know what it means but
no one can define it. Most would agree that ritual involves action,
and is governed by rules of who should do what. It should be
repeatable, but ritual and custom are not the same. Nor is just any
regularised behaviour ritual, although all activity may be said to
have ritual aspects. At the margins, observers and participants may
dispute what is or is not ritual, but in any culture there is a central

---

[8] Aristides, *To Rome*; Dio 51.19.1–4; cf. Pliny, *Letters* 9.5; *Paneg.* 88.1–2. Structure, Alföldy
1985: 146–56; Garnsey & Saller 1987: 112–25; Saller, forthcoming. Replacement, M.
Hammond 1957; Hopkins 1983: 120–200, with criticisms in Hahn & Leunissen 1990.
Trusts, Johnston 1988; Saller 1991. Nuer paradox, Evans-Pritchard 1951; Schneider 1966;
Kelly 1974: 290–8. I am grateful to Richard Saller for allowing me to read two unpub-
lished papers.

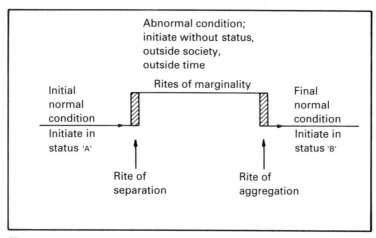

4. The tripartite structure of the rite of passage (after E. R. Leach 1976: fig. 7)

field where all intuitively know they are in its presence.[9] And rituals say something, even if those taking part or watching do not agree what it is, or cannot put it into words at all. One of the most influential analysts of symbolism, Dan Sperber, suggests that rituals 'evoke a picture of the world that, were it made explicit, could only itself be put in quotes' (1975: 140). Ritual action is not a code or a defective language, but produces its own kind of symbolic knowledge. Social structure, as a set of internalised but constantly renegotiated roles and rules, is an artefact of this knowledge.[10]

I will come back to the ambiguities of ritual action later on. First, though, we should look at how we can analyse funerals. Customs vary enormously around the world, but eighty years ago Hertz and Van Gennep drew attention to a consistent pattern underlying them. In almost all cases, the actions can be broken down into a three-stage pattern known as a *rite of passage* (fig. 4). The biological death of an individual sets off a more prolonged social process of

[9] To some people 'ritual' implies external actions carried out without any commitment to the values and ideas they express. Our pejorative use of ritualist is largely a product of the sixteenth-century Reformation; but even if we think ancient rituals were 'ritualised' in this sense, they are still significant. Luther himself noted this in words which uncannily echo modern writings: 'ceremonies are to be given the same place in the life of a Christian as models and plans have among builders and artisans' (*Christian Liberty* (Grimm, ed., 1957: 38)).

[10] G. Lewis (1980: 6–38) gives the richest discussion. See also Goody 1961; La Fontaine 1985: 11–18; Kertzer 1988: 8–12.

dying. The first stage, the 'rite of separation', is a ceremony which moves those involved out of their normal conditions of life into the second stage, a liminal status. Some of the survivors take on the role of mourners, while the deceased moves from being a person to a corpse and some kind of soul is usually liberated from the body. These transitions may happen at the moment death is announced, or at some later point; all at once, or more gradually. The actors are often secluded and polluted, and reverse much of their normal behaviour. The mourners may wear very formal clothing, or may be dishevelled; they may be solemnly silent, or they may cry hysterically; they may combine all these acts. In some places these statuses last only moments; in others, years. Their length and intensity vary according to who is involved. The third stage, the 'rite of aggregation', restores normalcy. The mourners return to social life, but without the deceased; the corpse is finally laid to rest; and the soul joins the ancestors. This tripartite rite-of-passage sequence is prominent in ancient descriptions of funerals, and the rituals effecting these changes in status repeatedly remind all involved of the relationships they are involved in, through the inversion and affirmation of norms.[11]

The next question must be how we can study ancient rituals. We might construct a hierarchy of sources.

1. Direct observation/participation in the rituals
2. Verbal testimony, oral or written, describing or explaining the rituals
3. Artistic representations of the rituals
4. The material remains of rituals

This is the obvious way to rank the materials, but in practice their value gets mixed up. The first class is unavailable. The second is undeniably the most informative, but its scarcity makes it difficult to use. There are two broad responses to the shortage of texts. The first is the 'synchronic' method. Often sources allude only to parts of rituals, and to create a fuller picture we have to stitch together

[11] Hertz 1960 (1907); Van Gennep 1960 (1909). The literature on funerals and rites of passage is immense. I find E. R. Leach (1976), Huntington & Metcalf (1979), G. Lewis (1980), Bloch & Parry, eds. (1982) and La Fontaine (1985) among the best. The rite-of-passage structure of funerals is described for Greece by R. Garland (1985), and for Rome by Scheid (1984) and Maurin (1984).

texts spanning long periods of time. At best, we can describe 'the' ritual, but lose all chance of analysing how it changed through time or how different groups used it; at worst, we create a 'composite' ritual bearing little relationship to the actual experiences of actors at any stage in its history. For some scholars this is not a problem, and several studies of 'Greek' marriage, myth and initiation throw together sources from different states and centuries. But moving from dynamic, constantly recreated social structure to stable long-term mentalities is a step backwards, albeit one which the fragmentary sources encourage. There have been some excellent reconstructions of the ritual setting of Athenian drama, but as Connor shows, it is difficult to fix the chronology of the various features of the festivals, and the dates *do* make a difference to how we understand the rituals. Similarly, Loraux's work on Athenian funeral orations is powerfully persuasive when treating the texts (dated *c.* 440–322 B.C.) as a single body or comparing 'the' Athenian ideology of death with 'the' Roman, but much less so when looking at changes through time.[12]

The second method is the 'one-off' analysis of a single episode. The problem here is how to extrapolate from one event – for example, Agrippa's funeral as discussed by Fraschetti – to wider patterns of ritual action. Strauss shows both these methods at their best in a paper providing a composite picture of the rituals of the Athenian assembly spanning the whole fourth century B.C. and a study of a 'one-off' procession to the acropolis in October 403. The two examples are revealing and complement each other, but only allow us to talk about *normative* practices. It would be as if an ethnographer watched a single marriage or funeral and then came home to write a monograph about ritual. Recent studies of the regulations for seating in Roman amphitheatres run into the same problems. We get a glimpse into the hierarchy of the orders, but it is static, rather like Alföldy's model. We can learn that the Spanish town of Irni kept its own seating order, but we cannot observe how these rules were renegotiated in ritual practice. We can compare it with the classical Athenian theatre, with its more democratic layout; but in both cases we see a single, stable picture. Temporal and

---

[12] Statements of the 'synchronic' method in ancient Greece come from scholars as diverse as Detienne (1979: 6–7) and Burkert (1985: 6). Drama, Cartledge 1985; Goldhill 1987; 1988; Winkler & Zeitlin, eds. 1990. Orations, Connor 1989b; Loraux 1986; cf. R. Thomas 1989: 206–21 (see also ch. 5 below). Loraux draws on Polybius 6.53–6 for Roman ideology.

regional contrasts disappear, along with disputes over meaning within communities. Again, we get 'the' Athenian and then 'the' Roman mentality. We need to enter into actual practices, reconstructing the variations between ritual performances as well as the constants. But even in the exceptional cases where this can be done, as with the hundred or so lawcourt speeches from fourth-century Athens, historians find it difficult to avoid treating the whole corpus as a single group. Ober and Strauss have argued persuasively that similar principles of analysis can be applied to the speeches and to drama, allowing us 'to extend the study of Athenian political culture on an ideological plane from the later fourth century ... back into the early or mid-fifth century' (1990: 269–70), but we are still only able to lengthen the period to which the static model is relevant, rather than to study a constantly evolving ritual structure. Beard's paper on the Acta of the Arval Brethren is a rare case where change through time is more apparent. She draws fascinating conclusions about the symbolic significance of the inscribing of these texts, but their very peculiarity limits their value. Hopkins responds to the source problem boldly with empathetic imagination, but abandoning evidence altogether is hardly satisfactory.[13]

The third class of evidence, images, can be used to flesh out the textual evidence or studied in its own right, but to some extent this material has to be treated in the light of the fourth class. The debate over whether the sculptural scenes on imperial Roman sarcophagi were 'religious' or 'profane' illustrates the problem: much of our artistic evidence was itself created for the very rituals we wish to understand. Sarcophagi only became common around A.D. 200, when the Latin parts of the empire adopted inhumation. Ideas of what this change 'meant' necessarily colour perception of the iconography (see ch. 2).[14]

[13] Agrippa, Fraschetti 1984. Athens, Strauss, forthcoming. I am grateful to Barry Strauss for sending me a copy of this paper. Social structure and change through time in Roman rituals, North 1976; 1989; Liebeschuetz 1979; Beard 1987; 1989, esp. pp. 45–7; Eck 1984; Price 1984; 1987; Zanker 1988; papers in Beard & North, eds., 1990, esp. Gordon 1990a. Seating regulations, Seutonius, *Aug.* 44; *Claud.* 21.3; Tacitus, *Ann.* 13.54; 15.32; Dio 60.7.3–4; Kolendo 1981; Polacco 1982; Gonzalez 1986; Williamson 1987; Rawson 1987; Zanker 1988: 147–53. Athenian theatre seating, Pickard-Cambridge 1968: 269–72; Ober 1989b: 152–5. Athenian legal evidence, R. G. Osborne 1985a; Humphreys 1986; 1988; Ober 1989b. Synchronic approach, Ober 1989b: 36–8. Problems, J. K. Davies 1978: 165–87. Arval Acta, Beard 1985. Empathy, Hopkins 1983: xv.

[14] There are excellent studies in Bérard, ed., 1989. Sarcophagi, Turcan 1978; Froning 1980; Koch & Sichtermann 1982; Wrede 1989.

Fine work has been done on representations of death and the afterlife on Athenian painted pottery, the most abundant class of evidence, but the vases only rarely come from a well-documented context, and (as we will see in chapter 4) this is a major problem. Snodgrass stresses that almost all the earliest figured scenes, dating from about 750 B.C. and often showing funerals, come from a single cemetery. We cannot understand these paintings without explaining why they entered the archaeological record here and hardly anywhere else: and that can only mean a detailed study of burials. Similarly, many sixth-century Athenian vases were found in tombs in Etruria. Any interpretation of them must begin with Etruscan burial practices.[15]

The final class of evidence, material remains of actual rituals, lets us reconstruct the variability of symbols in concrete actions, and follow this as far through space and time as archaeological fieldwork has been taken. Ritual action created much of the patterning in the archaeological record. I am not claiming that archaeological evidence is somehow 'better' than written or pictorial evidence, or that it constitutes an alternative source. It can be used to augment the surviving texts, and it has two great virtues: there is a lot of it, and we can find a lot more still. But it has equally great drawbacks, stemming from the fact that it is only part of the death ritual, and not necessarily even the most important part. Only certain aspects of that part of the burial process itself produce a recognisable material residue. In a famous story, Homer (*Od.* 19.141–7; 24.131–7) has Penelope weave, and secretly unwind, a fabulous shroud for her father-in-law; but this would not normally survive in the Greek soil.[16] Textiles and the number and noise of mourners were probably crucial aspects of ritual statements in at least some periods, but cannot be excavated. This obviously casts some doubt on archaeologists' attempts to infer much from their finds, and general

[15] Vase painting, e.g. H. Hoffmann 1977; 1986; 1988; 1989; Vermeule 1979; Burn 1985; Sourvinou-Inwood 1987; R. G. Osborne 1988; Lissarrague 1988; Baldassarre 1988. Kurtz (1984) surveys the themes. R. G. Osborne (1989) argues for the priority of pictures over the fourth class of evidence, but pays little attention to contextual problems. Eighth-century vases, Snodgrass 1987: 146–67; Whitley 1991. Etruria, Vickers 1985/6; 1987; Arafat & Morgan, forthcoming; cf. d'Agostino 1989. Some recent studies of Athenian funerary sculpture (e.g. D'Onofrio 1982; 1988; Vedder 1988) show great sensitivity to context.

[16] Shrouds do sometimes survive, as in the 'Homeric' burial at Lefkandi, of *c.* 1000 B.C. (Popham et al. 1982).

laws trying to do away with our uncertainties are not convincing.
Bartel, for example, optimistically proposes a rule of symbolic
redundancy, that any archaeologically invisible ritual act will be
paralleled by one meaning much the same thing which we *can* see.[17]
Pader is more explicit, suggesting that 'as burial is indeed an
integral part of the ritual, and therefore consists of largely non-
random behaviour which makes sense in terms of what came before
and what comes afterwards, it is a viable unit of study' (Pader
1982: 42). Both claims are partly true, but require a leap of faith if
they are to be applied in any particular case. We cannot 'retrodict'
the relationship between what we find and what we do not; but
neither do we have to throw our hands up in despair. In a study of
three Plains Indian groups, O'Shea shows that 'our perception of
social organisation derived from the analysis of mortuary remains
may be distorted, but distorted in a regular and predictable manner' (1981: 52). He offers methods for treating the problem at the
empirical level, not by theoretical propositions. Uncertainty will
always be with us, but it can be controlled. Sometimes we will have
to concede that we really cannot learn much from a specific set of
burials or aspect of the ritual (as on p. 107 below). But often we can
detect patterns in the residues of ancient rituals, and unless these
were caused by accidents or by post-depositional disturbance, we
can learn something from them. In chapter 7, for example, I describe the burials found at Vroulia on Rhodes. The only trace of
most of these rituals is an ash layer about 10 cm thick. But all the
same, certain unmistakable patterns emerge. There is a direct relationship between the age at death of children and the shape of pot
used to hold their bones; a clear division between adults and children; a strong tendency to place relatively rich objects (compared
to those found in the settlement) with the first adult cremation in
each adult tomb, but not to use grave goods with his or her descendants; and a striking spatial distribution in the depth of tombs and
the emphasis on descent as the organising principle of ritual. Certainly we have lost much information, but the fact remains that we
do have some evidence here for what the Vroulians did in their
rituals, and we can use this to catch at least a glimpse of the social
structure which they wove around themselves. Not knowing every-

---

[17] Theories, Bartel 1982. See also O'Shea 1984: 302. I discuss the sort of background
necessary for analysis in Morris 1987: 44–54, 211–12.

thing that originally happened does not mean that we are powerless – if it did, we would have to give up history-writing altogether.

STRUCTURE AND BELIEF

Different observers of a funeral come away with different impressions of what it was all about. The 'meaning' of any ritual is within certain limits open for interpretation by the observer, from the most cynical to the most romantic. We might range types of interpretation along a spectrum, from the functionalist (already discussed) to the intellectualist. Both can be reductionist: functionalism producing what Gellner (1985: 135–6) calls a 'solid, earthy, blokey ... somewhat Philistine' attitude to ritual, ignoring its content, and intellectualism seeing it as a form of philosophical speculation on the cosmos, concentrating on personal and psychological content rather than social context.

Most ritual studies in classics have been intellectualist. Price (1984: 10) even argues that the perspective is 'covertly Christianizing'. It is not difficult to see why. Around the turn of the century the 'Cambridge School' forged close links between classics and the anthropology of religion, but these were short-lived. Paul Shorey probably spoke for many in the 1920s in condemning 'the anthropological Hellenism of Sir James Frazer, the irrational, semi-sentimental, Polynesian, free-verse, sex-freedom Hellenism of all the gushful geysers of "rapturous rubbish" about the Greek spirit' (quoted in Finley 1975: 102–3). The parting of the ways was abrupt. The British and American functionalist schools took their inspiration largely from Durkheim's *The Elementary Forms of the Religious Life*, which appeared in 1912, and by the time Radcliffe-Brown and Parsons came to dominate the scene, classicists took little interest in social theory.

Much fine work has come out of this tradition in classics, but it draws a sharp line between 'religious' and 'social' explanations of rituals, instead of seeing them as complementary. Religion becomes an independent field with closer links to theology than to social history, and it is sometimes felt that changes in sacrificial or burial practices should be explained solely in terms of this specialism. Some historians of other periods reject this approach out of hand: Watson, for instance, distinguishes in his analyses of Chinese rituals between orthodoxy, correct beliefs about death, and orthopraxy, adherence to socially acceptable patterns of ritual behaviour. The latter, he argues, was more important than the former; and Geary suggests that the point is also valid in the highly charged religious world of medieval Christianity. But even taking a more conservative position, religion must be seen as being as much a part of social structure as status or kinship. To say that Christian beliefs influenced burial in the later Roman empire is not to say that we cannot learn about population movements, economic changes and social structure (see ch. 6) from graves. No sensible historian would deny that the coming of Christianity was itself part of a far-reaching transformation of society in this period; but when moving from texts to artefacts, many historians lose sight of the complexity of factors that affect culture.[18]

Religious historians often lock their subject away and examine it in isolation. The classic case is sixteenth-century Calvinism. Few would accept without qualification Max Weber's thesis trying to explain the rise of capitalism in terms of the Protestant Reformation, but fewer still would deny that Calvin's *Institutes of the Christian Religion* can be read as a social as well as a theological document. In a recent study of the phrase *hiera kai hosia* in classical Athens, Connor has shown that the Athenians did not draw a sharp distinction between secular and sacred; the two were intimately linked. To Athenians, the definition of status and role in funeral rites would have required both 'sociological' and 'religious' analysis. Thus when Vernant criticised Moulinier for refusing to seek a logic behind Greek purity beliefs, it was not a matter of one of them being right and the other wrong. They simply adopted different standards of explanation, with Moulinier concentrating on pollution as a discrete category, and Vernant looking at a wider system of thought. MacMullen (1984: 3) says 'we must decide ... whether our object is history or theology', but I think it is more a matter of deciding what kind of history we want to write.[19]

I have already made it clear what kind of history I want to write. My analyses of burial fall towards the 'social' end of the scale. Intellectualist readings of the same events could be equally valid, and my concentration on social structure as defined above is not in

[18] Orthopraxy, Watson 1988: 10. Christianity, Geary 1979; P. Brown 1981: 19.
[19] Calvinism, Weber 1976 (1904/5); Giddens 1976; Gellner 1988: 100–12, with references. *Hiera kai hosia*, Connor 1988a. Greek purity, Moulinier 1952; Vernant 1980: 110–29; Parker 1983.

principle a criticism of 'religious' treatments. But in practice most intellectualist readings of archaeological data are unconvincing, because they take a naïve view of symbolism.

The anthropologist would like to identify and interpret the symbolism in ritual. But this is often the hardest part of his work, the part he least understands and only after much effort and learning. He does not witness a performance and say to himself, 'Ah! this stands for that, and this for that, etc. Therefore these are symbols, therefore I have seen a ritual performance.' What he says is more likely to be, 'This is odd. This is ritual. Why do they do it like that? There is more to this than meets the eye. I must try to find out what.' (G. Lewis 1980: 7–8)

Lewis shows us two ways to interpret symbolism, which I will call 'direct' and 'linguistic' interpretations. The first is simple: action A signifies idea B, etc. Symbolism is just a code. We find out what A means, and our job is easy. This is a well-established tradition. Cumont's work is the best example in classics of the reduction of symbolic analysis to a series of equations: the snake means death, the olive means life, the egg is a sign of rebirth and so on. Grave goods are used because the deceased will need them in the next world; libations at the grave are to nourish the dead. Intellectualist interpretations in archaeology depend almost exclusively on these one-to-one associations.[20]

I am not saying that direct interpretations are wrong, only that they are more complicated to apply than most practitioners seem to realise, and that they can be a dead end. Even when we have texts, we can rarely assign 'the meaning' to an action, or assume that it really had such a meaning independent of its context of use. The best example is a handful of fourth- and third-century B.C. graves from South Italy, Crete and Thessaly containing small gold leaves bearing inscriptions about the afterworld. In one remarkable case our knowledge is due only to the sharp eyes of Petros Themelis, who spotted that a 'log' in the cremation pyre was in fact a burned papyrus roll, the now famous Derveni *Theogony*. All other aspects of these graves were typical of local burial customs, even though the

---

[20] Cumont 1922; 1942; 1949. Cumont's work is perceptively discussed by Nock (1946) and Gordon (1975); for a more detailed attack on this logic in archaic Greece, see Morris 1989a.

texts tell us that these people looked forward to an afterlife entirely different from that in 'official' Greek religion. The texts were originally thought to be Orphic; Pythagoreans or Dionysiacs are nowadays more favoured. But that is not important here. The cremation of the body and the placing of pottery and jewellery in the grave meant radically different things to these people, whatever their sects, than to other contemporaries. The objects themselves have little inherent meaning; their expressive force comes from their ritual context, and unless we know that this is Dionysiac (or whatever) to begin with, we cannot make direct interpretations of the symbolism.[21]

The second approach stresses the role of ritual action as part of a system of relations analogous to a language. Leach summarises thus:

The indices in non-verbal communication systems, like the sound elements in spoken language, do not have meaning as isolated but only as members of sets. A sign or symbol only acquires meaning when it is discriminated from some other contrary sign or symbol. (E. R. Leach 1976: 49)

This leads to a form of analysis just as complex and lacking in explicit certainties as ritual action itself seems to be. We cannot barge in and assign meanings, even on the authority of ancient texts; we must move within *systems* of practice, looking at *all* the evidence.

It also makes our task much harder. Even small shifts through space or time, or from one group of observers to another, can totally transform the symbolic systems. For example, in a small cemetery at Eretria of about 700 B.C., adults were cremated with their ashes in bronze urns, while children were inhumed in wooden coffins. This has led to great excitement about the opposition between burning and rotting, with the adult, a creature of culture, being sent off in flames while the child, a creature of nature, decomposed. But just fifty miles away at Anavyssos near Athens, adults were being inhumed in pit graves while children were cremated and their ashes put in wine jars. Going another fifty miles to Corinth, we find both adults and children being inhumed.[22] No single set of

[21] So-called Orphic graves, Makaronas 1963; Zuntz 1971: 277–393; Cole 1980; West 1983: 98–101; Tsantsanoglou & Parassoglou 1987; Merkelbach 1989. Cf. Burkert 1987: 22–7.
[22] Eretria, Bérard 1970. Mrs Angeliki Andreiomenou (personal communication 1983) advises me that initial reports that child cremations in jars have been found in the town of Eretria were inaccurate. Anavyssos, Themelis 1973/4. Corinth, R. S. Young 1964.

meanings can be attached to these symbols outside the particular rituals where they were used. Different symbols were being used to 'say' much the same things in these three places. This possibility was already clear to Herodotus:

> Darius, during his own rule, called together some of the Greeks who were in attendance on him and asked them what they would take to eat their dead fathers. They said that no price in the world would make them do so. After that Darius summoned some of those of the Indians who are called Callatians, who *do* eat their parents, and, in the presence of the Greeks (who understood the conversation through an interpreter), asked them what price would make them burn their dead fathers with fire. They shouted aloud, 'Don't mention such horrors!' These are matters of settled custom, and I think Pindar is right when he says, 'Custom is king of all'. (Herodotus 3.38; tr. D. Grene)

The extreme form of the linguistic approach is parodied by Gellner, who imagines an archaeologist of the future excavating a casino at Monte Carlo. His fantasy (or nightmare?) is worth quoting at length:

> [He is] a very happy archaeologist indeed. As the language in which the croupier kept his record has not yet been mastered ... he does not know what those signs, like 'odd' and 'even' or 'red' and 'black', actually mean. But that does not worry him one little bit. In fact, it gives him pleasure ... Extraneous reference of a symbol is not a thing of great moment. It is the system of which it is a part that matters ... it has that binary polarised quality that brings joy to his heart. Here is a system oscillating neatly between the polarities 'red' and 'black', 'odd' or 'even'. Whatever these terms refer to (and to hell with that), they clearly were the polar concepts entering into the construction of that world, indicating its limits, expressing its vital tensions. (Gellner 1985: 140)

No doubt such an interpretation would have its merits, but it does rather miss the point. Cumont and others are right that signs are not wholly arbitrary. When Romans saw ships' prows on coins or on tombs in the late first century B.C., they probably understood them as allusions to Actium and the 'restored Republic'. A tall woman in an aegis 'meant' Athena in sixth-century Athens, to an extent which amused Herodotus (1.60) a century later. When a body was burned at Eretria or Anavyssos, the use of fire was more than a symbolic reversal of rotting; it triggered off a whole set of associations connected with the use of fire in sacrifice and the preparation of food.[23] Ian Hodder gets to the core of the problem:

In the construction of the cultural world, all dimensions (the height or colour of pottery for example) already have meaning associations. An individual in the past is situated within this historical frame, and inter-prets the cultural order from within its perspective. The archaeologist seeks also to get 'inside' the historical context, but the jump is often a considerable one. (Hodder 1987a: 7)

So where do we stand? Direct interpretation is unworkable and simplistic. In practice we have to proceed by methods closer to Leach's model, but we must try to link actions and ideas by setting the burials into context. Skinner's approach to political language provides a good model, moving from individual expression to ideol-ogy, conflict and change through the careful elaboration of context. Partner speaks of a 'language-model epistemology', which has been 'smuggled out of linguistics and philosophy departments ... and lobbed like grenades into unsuspecting history departments' (1986: 95); similarly the linguistic analogy in archaeology creates new uncertainties, but the gains justify it. As White says, 'It would appear that the question confronting contemporary historians [and archaeologists] is not whether they will utilize a linguistic model to aid them in their work ... but what kind of linguistic model they will use' (1987: 188–9). Hodder's own work on Neolithic Europe is a good example. Dissatisfied with recent theories reducing mega-liths to ritual markers legitimising a lineage's claim to the land, Hodder started from within the ritual system. He identified eight points of significant similarity between long barrows and central European houses, and argued that the tombs and houses evoked each other. He saw this ritual symmetry as part of a discourse naturalising relations between men and women as well as between lineages at a time of rapid social change.[24]

This is a far cry from Cumont. Once we abandon the specious

---

[23] Herodotus, Humphreys 1987. Ships' prows, Zanker 1988: 82–5. Athena, Connor 1987: 42–7. Fire in Greece, Vernant 1989: 38–43, 63–8; Furley 1981; Burkert 1983: 9–11, 274–84; 1985: 60–4. Burkert's derivation of funerary rituals from hunting and sacrifice (1983: 48–58) is, however, unnecessarily limiting.

[24] Linguistic turn, Toews 1987; in archaeology, Hodder 1988. Tilley (1990: 65–74) and Hodder (1990) discuss the limitations of structuralist analysis in archaeology and the problems of finding meaning. Tully 1988; Hodder 1984a.

security of direct interpretation, intellectualist analysis becomes very difficult. Maybe graves can tell us about religion in a narrowly defined sense, but it is not the only way to use them; and if I avoid the purely religious aspect in this book, it is because at present I see no way to approach it without making a series of indefensible assumptions. If I may be permitted a little armchair psychologising, we can see why so many classicists have not taken this point. Snodgrass, following Liam Hudson, distinguishes between *converging* and *diverging* intellects. The convergers excel at finding the right answer to questions when there is a right answer to find, while divergers do better with open-ended problems. Classicists tend to come from the extreme converger end of the scale; but in the analysis of ritual action, to find one answer is usually to find a bad answer.[25]

The theoretical base of this book is now in place. I seek to examine social structure, the essence of ancient society, through the medium of ritual. The textual evidence does not allow this without reducing dynamic structure to stable mentality; only burials give enough evidence that can be studied in fine detail. We cannot assign meanings to specific practices without long and careful thought; and much of the time, we have to treat the evidence as an abstract system without guessing at the formal messages attached to different symbols by the observers.

DIALOGUES WITH THE DEAD

But how do we do it? No rules cover all cases, and the skills required only become clear in actual analysis. I will spend the rest of the chapter laying out some of the principles I find most useful, even though methods described in separation from substantive research can appear trite. Their value must be judged from chapters 2–7.

The problem is how to move from the brute evidence of excavated graves to the ethereal level of theories about social structure. The first serious attempt to go beyond direct interpretation was in the 1960s, when the self-styled 'New Archaeologists' challenged more traditional styles of analysis. Burial was a main battleground. In a classic paper, Ucko had showed the danger of the haphazard

---

[25] Snodgrass 1987: 10–11, drawing on Hudson 1966.

bits-and-pieces analogies common in prehistory. Many New Archaeologists stressed an alternative, where hypotheses could be
tested against cross-cultural regularities which might provide laws
– or at least highly probable generalisations – of the relationships
between behaviour and material culture.[26]

But this is no solution. In spite of the great contributions of some
New Archaeologists, they lost sight of the basic fact that the evidence is created in rituals. Binford's classic paper 'Mortuary practices: their study and their potential' illustrated this. Binford
offered the hypothesis, which he examined against a sample of forty
non-state societies, that 'there should be a high degree of isomor-
phism between (a) the complexity of the status structure in a socio-
cultural system and (b) the complexity of mortuary ceremonialism
as regards differential treatment of persons occupying different
status positions' (Binford 1971: 18). Cutting through the jargon,
Binford claimed that the variability of a culture's burials is a function of social differentiation. He leaves no room for ritual statements: we move straight from graves to social complexity (defined
by Binford in terms of food production). Others added more cross-
culturally 'tested' propositions, such as Saxe's (refined by Goldstein) that the emergence of formal, bounded cemeteries reserved
for the dead indicates the appearance of unilineal descent groups
monopolising access to some vital resource (usually the land).
Once the new paradigm was safely established, still others
provided a battery of quantitative techniques so we could measure
just how differentiated customs were, or just how formal a cemetery
was. Societies could then be placed on a ladder of social complexity.[27]

I oversimplify a complex and still unfolding intellectual history,
but the main points hold true. Problems of symbolism were circumvented by being ignored. Cross-cultural tests against ethnographic
data replaced context-dependent analysis as the standard of valida-
tion, and the experience of individuals within a society was neg-

---

[26] Ucko 1969. The unofficial manifesto of the New Archaeology as a whole is probably
Binford 1968, with comments in S. J. Shennan 1989; for burials, J. A. Brown, ed., 1971;
Chapman & Randsborg 1981; Chapman 1990: 2–6. For appraisals of the developments of
the 1960s, see Hodder 1982a; Meltzer et al., eds., 1986; Trigger 1989: 289–328; Gibbon
1989; Lamberg-Karlovsky, ed., 1989; Pinsky & Wylie, eds., 1989.

[27] Binford 1971; Saxe 1970: 119–21; Goldstein 1981, with comments in Morris 1987: 37–8,
52–4; 1991. Social evolution, Johnson & Earle 1987. Quantitative methods, Tainter 1975;
1978; O'Shea 1984.

lected in favour of pigeon-holing into modern categories. The subject matter of most social historians was ruled out of court as 'uninteresting'. The behavioural programme of the New Archaeology would be impossible if real people acting within and transforming their social structure, rather than an all-powerful functionalist system, created the archaeological record. Saxe (1970: 235) noted the possibility of 'egalitarian ideology flying in the face of social fact', but looked at this as an irritation, not as the essence of the inquiry. But as Hodder observes, 'in archaeology *all* inference is via material culture. If material culture, all of it, has a symbolic dimension such that the relationship between people and things is affected, then *all* of archaeology, economic and social, is implicated' (1986: 3). We must face up to the complexities of the rituals in which our evidence was created: 'burial ritual is not a passive reflection of other aspects of life. It is meaningfully constructed ... In death people often become what they have not been in life' (Hodder 1982b: 141, 146).

Imposing the same rules of evidence on all societies will not work. Hodder and his students have identified the core of their conflict with the New Archaeology in differences over the use of analogy. They distinguish between relational analogy, where we argue from context A to context B because we can show A to be relevant, and formal analogy, where practices are taken out of context and imposed on other cultures without good reasons. Cross-cultural checklisting is rejected in favour of looking at the evidence in the terms of the people who produced it *as well as* in the terms of the modern observer. Once again, burial is a major area of debate.[28]

At the most fundamental level (although this probably never happens in reality) we assume as little as possible, and simply look for patterns in the burial record. This is in itself subjective, since we have to decide what features are worth looking at. Prehistorians tend to assume that the treatment of the body, the provision and placing of grave goods, the use of markers, the spatial arrangement

---

[28] Analogy, Hodder 1982b: 11–27; Wylie 1985; cf. Wylie 1989. Debates, Hodder 1982a; 1984b; 1985; 1986: 18–33, 171–8; Binford 1982; 1983: 15–18; 1987; Yengoyan 1985; Earle & Preucel 1987; Hodder et al. 1988; Watson & Fotiadis 1990. Burials, Hodder 1982c: 163–70; Parker Pearson 1982; Morris 1987: 29–43, 211–12; Shanks & Tilley 1987: 42–5; Cannon 1989; Chapman 1990: 2–6. Pader (1982) presents a very fine account of burial symbolism.

of cemeteries and so on are worth investigating, while the number of grains of soil in the fill of a grave or a difference of one or two centimetres in grave lengths are normally not. The ancient historian can be a little more confident since the literature from Homer to Procopius and beyond suggests that many of our expectations about what actions would carry meaning are valid. But, as I argued above, we cannot assume anything about what the patterns mean.

Once we think we have a pattern, we should try to define it statistically. Classical archaeologists do not usually get as agitated as one American historian, who damned forever all who 'worship at the shrine of that Bitch-goddess QUANTIFICATION',[29] but they are often uncomfortable with numbers. However, all that quantification does is provide tools to give precision to the kind of statements that we make all the time. We say that aristocratic tombs became more ornate in late Republican Rome, but just how much more? Did the escalation affect all tombs, or only a certain proportion? Grave goods may have declined in the later empire, but just how much? Was it just the quantity that changed, or did their distribution change too? Vague impressions are useless; only accurate quantification will do. Sometimes statistical tests will show that the patterns scholars thought they saw are not really there at all, but quantification is not a substitute for historical thought: it is a method to clarify it.

I suggest five axes along which we can range the evidence in searching for patterns and their significance. In practice, we look along all axes at once. The results are cumulative; the richer the context into which we set the burials, the more powerful the interpretation will be.[30]

1. *Typology*

This is both the beginning and the end. We can only select the important dimensions of the evidence as problems come to mind; but at some point in the analytical process, we will need a detailed study of all the burial evidence, breaking it down and identifying its salient features. This must be a two-way process. Presuppositions

---

[29] Carl Bridenbaugh in *AHR* 68 (1963) 326, quoted by Novick (1988: 384).
[30] Hodder (1987a: 5; 1987b) suggests four similar lines of attack.

about typology will restrict the range of patterns we can see, and so we have to be ready to modify what originally seemed like perfectly good classifications of our data in the light of the other axes of analysis. Often finding a suitable typology is the last as well as the first stage of a study.

2. *Time*

To determine how social structures change through time is the goal at the theoretical level; and at the practical level, change through time is a crucial methodological tool. Static patterns cannot be interpreted easily. We need to identify points at which patterns change, and the precise nature of the changes. However, where chronology is poor, time and typology become confused, as we cannot tell whether we are dealing with a single phase of varied burials, or several phases of homogeneous burials. After all, archaeological dating is based on typology; our dependence on datable objects compounds the problem. These items are not a neutral yardstick, but are themselves parts of the rituals. Our neat, abstract time-frames may distort complex social practices. Analysis is easier in some periods than in others, but time can be both the most important and most complex of our axes.

3. *Contexts of deposition*

We must also compare burials with other classes of evidence. Again, subjectivity shapes decisions about what is relevant; and we need to demonstrate rather than to assume links. For example, around 750 B.C. grave goods more or less disappear at Corinth. This coincides with a vast increase in the use of many of the same objects as sanctuary dedications, which strongly suggests that the two processes are connected. Some people began to have larger houses around this time, and there is a definite increase in the monumentality of public buildings. Treated in isolation the decline in grave goods would not be easy to explain without the arbitrary assignation of meaning. We might say that people got poorer, but the larger houses and the objects found in them suggest otherwise. Perhaps they became more rational about the conservation of wealth; but its lavish use as votive offerings counts against this. Or maybe ideas of the afterworld changed. Obviously this is true insofar as grave goods are part of death rites, but put in context, it seems to be part of a reordering of the whole ritual system, and the sort of questions we need to ask start to change.

4. *Space*

This is crucial in two ways. First, the spatial relationships between contexts of deposition may change. In Corinth around 750, we find a separation of the dead from the living, whereas previously graves had been among the houses. At about the same time, we find greater spatial demarcation of sanctuaries, and the walling-off of settlement space. This encourages us to return to context, in its literal sense of 'with the text'; the literary sources hint that rules about pollution were changing to reinforce the divisions between gods, men and the dead. We can also exploit spatial analysis by widening the geographical context to find the scale of the patterns we are observing. We find the same patterns of change in many parts of Greece between 750 and 700 – fewer grave goods, richer votives for the gods, monumental temples, bigger houses, extra-mural cemeteries and city walls; plus the adoption of writing, new figured art styles, the expansion of the settlement pattern, changes in warfare ... the list could go on. This means we have to change the focus of our inquiry once again. Now we are looking for two things: we need a panhellenic explanation, as relevant to Argos, Eretria and Athens as to Corinth; but we also need to examine in detail the differences between the regions, to see what was peculiar to each. For instance, at Athens we find a switch from cremation to inhumation around 750, followed by a reversion to burning around 700. At Corinth, inhumation was the norm throughout. How important is this? Should we treat disposal of the corpse as an arbitrary signifier, useful only as yet another indication of sudden symbolic change, or does it need to be a central feature of our historical interpretation?

5. *Demography*

The age and sex of burials can within limits be established, so one recurring question is how changes relate to age and sex. At Corinth, adults and children are treated much the same as each other and buried together after 750, although before then children often had richer grave goods. At Argos, adult graves are moved outside the settlement around 700 but the children stay on and continue to have some grave goods, while adults usually get none. At Athens, things are still more complex. Before 725 it is unusual to find child graves at all; from 725–700 they start to be common in formerly adult cemeteries; and after 700 they usually have their own cemeteries. Lack of sexed skeletons makes it hard to say much about gender, but both before and after 750 the richest grave goods and markers may have been going to women, especially adolescents. The more complex houses of the seventh and sixth centuries probably facilitated the separation of men and women, but this does not spill over strongly into burial. The generally better treatment of women and children in death is unlikely to mean that they were richer or better off in life than men; it might be better to say that, whatever the changes in rituals in the eighth century mean, they had less effect on the social representations of women and children than they did on those of men.[31]

By contextualising the initial problem of a decline in grave goods, we completely transform it. Now we need to explain the relatively sudden overhaul of the ritual system, varying from place to place, but in one way or another affecting most of the Greek world. This was the question which first drew me into the analysis of burials. I believe that the rituals of the late eighth century were part of an entirely new social structure, emphasising a community of adult male citizens in place of the structure divided into elite and commoners which had existed in the Dark Age. The relationships of all groups – gods, spirits, heroes, men, women, children, the dead – were questioned and reordered in this time of flux. The new pattern remained in place, albeit with considerable regional and temporal variations and always under pressure from competing models of what the community should be, for the next 500 years.[32]

You may have noticed, though, that I have said nothing about *why* the social structures evoked by rituals changed. By recognising that burials only tell us about the rituals which created them, we have to face the fact that we cannot also use them to tell us about more mundane processes like demography, trade, war and so on.

---

[31] This material is treated more fully in Morris 1987: 185–96; 1989a. Whitley (1991) provides the best analysis of gender.
[32] Morris 1986a; 1987; 1988; 1989b.

There is a danger of being trapped within the rituals themselves, unable to do more than identify patterns and describe them: in short, to be forced into a position like Foucault's (see p. 5 above), where we do not even try to link symbolism to more material forces. As Hodder puts it, 'The separation of symbolic and social ... will be hard to maintain' (1990: 3).

The drift towards formalism is common to all structuralist methods. In a previous intellectual incarnation, Hodder tried to stop it with an interesting cross-cultural generalisation. If the patterning of material culture is largely formed in ritual statements through which people define themselves, then greater elaboration should represent greater interest in drawing boundaries. Basically, the more pressure there is on a group, the more emphatically they mark themselves off symbolically from their neighbours and rivals, in what we can call 'style wars'. Periods of rapid change in the archaeological record, Hodder suggested, can be read as times of 'stress', when competition intensified. Childe had floated a similar idea, arguing that 'in a stable society the gravegoods tend to grow relatively and even absolutely poorer as time goes on' (1945: 17), with periods of very rich burial showing the instability of elites and their need to legitimate their position. The 'stress hypothesis' has been cleverly deployed by Parker Pearson to interpret the Danish Iron Age as a series of cyclical crises interspersed with periods of stability. Miller, in a more complex study, explained changes in modern Indian pottery design in terms of competitive emulation of the styles of elites by the non-elite, with the former adopting new styles to continue to define themselves.[33]

We could, then, identify a lot of 'stress' in eighth-century Greece. But what would it be? Leach criticised Hodder's stress as being 'highly abstract' and lacking explanatory power. Hodder (maybe wisely) left it rather vague, apparently covering a wide range of economic, social and psychological unpleasantness. The idea is, after all, a return to the New Archaeology style of 'middle-range theory' which can be fitted to any set of data, and Hodder has himself retreated from this position. When he gives an example of his contextual archaeology at work, in an account of why the Ilchamus decorate their calabashes more elaborately than the other groups who live around Lake Baringo in Kenya, he explicitly

[33] Hodder 1979; 1982c: 186–90; Parker Pearson 1984; 1989; D. Miller 1985.

rejects this idea. Instead he enters into Ilchamus aesthetics. *Reading the Past* is informed throughout by a reading of Collingwood, and Hodder at times urges an empathetic approach rather like Hopkins' (see p. 12 above), and open to the same criticisms: the kinds of evidence required simply do not exist. Cannon has proposed a different answer to the problem, but sharing Hodder's interest in internally generated aesthetic values. He sees the kind of cycles which Parker Pearson identified in Danish burials as resulting from the logic of artistic processes, what he calls 'expressive redundancy'. When display reaches a certain level, it ceases to have the same impact on viewers, and is abandoned, only to return when restraint is no longer impressing people. This also cuts graves off from earthy matters like class conflict or status dissonance.[34]

Greek and Roman historians have a great advantage in that the textual evidence might narrow down the range of plausible interpretations of ritual changes without relying on questionable cross-cultural logic or leaps of faith. Nevertheless, moving from structure to process remains difficult, and these difficulties will surface again and again in the chapters that follow. The stress hypothesis, for all its theoretical problems, sometimes provides a compelling explanation for changes; and in other cases, expressive redundancy is a useful concept. The archaeological evidence is just one more sort of historical evidence, to be evaluated and interpreted by traditional historical methods of judgement.

CONCLUSION

By minimising our assumptions about what practices 'mean' until we have broken the evidence down along these five axes, and eschewing the bits-and-pieces approach in favour of large-scale empirical analysis, we can illuminate social structures in all periods. But the proof of the pudding is in the eating. No one starts with a specific method in mind and then looks for places to apply it, or with a set of graves and then looks for historical problems to unleash them on. Usually in studying the social structure of a particular time and place some feature of the archaeological record grabs our attention, and we combine and recombine various ways

[34] E. R. Leach 1979: 121; Hodder 1986: 105–17 (Ilchamus), 90–102 (on Collingwood (1946)); Cannon 1989. I discuss Cannon's theories in more detail in chs. 5 and 6 below.

of looking at the data to examine how the rituals work. In chapters 2–6, I look at two major aspects of Greek and Roman burials and outline ways in which they can be used in this kind of structural history. The first of these is the body. In chapter 2, I look at disposal practices, and especially the switch from cremation to inhumation in the Roman empire. In chapter 3, I discuss the physical remains, sketching some of the techniques available. The next three chapters are about display in rituals. Chapter 4 looks at grave goods, and chapter 5 at monuments over graves. Both concentrate on classical Athens. Chapter 6 examines inscribed tombstones, this time dealing mainly with imperial Rome. In all cases the emphasis is on examining the particular type of evidence within its total ritual context. The chapters can be read independently, but I have not really tried to write a handbook. They are meant to have a cumulative effect, linking up to form a general introduction to the historical analysis of burial. Chapter 7 is an example of such analysis in action, exemplifying the limits and strengths of this class of evidence. The final chapter sums up the arguments.

CHAPTER 2

'Mos Romanus': cremation and inhumation in the Roman empire

Tacitus tells us that Nero, a bad-tempered emperor at the best of times, killed his wife Poppaea in A.D. 65 by kicking her in the stomach when she was pregnant (or maybe by a less dastardly dose of poison). He goes on: 'The body was not consigned to the flames, as is the Roman custom (*mos Romanus*), but following the practice of foreign kings it was embalmed with spices' (*Ann.* 16.6 (written *c.* A.D. 115)). Three hundred years later, though, Macrobius could say that cremation was the sort of thing that people only read about in books (*Sat.* 7.7.5). Two interesting stories, to be sure. There are strict limits on what we can do with them, but they hint at the biggest single event in ancient burial, the change in 'the Roman custom' from cremation to inhumation. This involved tens of millions of people across the whole western part of the empire.[1]

This is the first of two linked chapters dealing specifically with the body. The body is a uniquely powerful medium for ritual communication, furnishing a set of 'natural symbols', as some would call them. Intuitive awareness of this led early ethnologists to seek pan-human explanations for burial customs. After observing one funeral, Frazer claimed that 'Heavy stones were piled on his grave to keep him down, on the principle of "sit tibi terra gravis"' (a little Latin humour here, reversing the common Roman epitaph 'sit tibi terra levis', 'may the earth be light upon you'). Küsters suggested that crouched burial in fireplaces meant that 'People did not know yet what death was and therefore tried to warm up the body', or better still, that exposure of the corpse in trees 'can be explained by

---

[1] There are a few other sources, such as Pliny (*NH* 36.131) who perhaps represents sarcophagi as exotic items, although his amazement may be due more to the special properties of the stone in this case; and Petronius (*Satyr.* 111.2) who describes inhumation in a hypogeum as 'graeco more' ('in the Greek manner'). The Theodosian Code (9.17.6) refers to both rites in 381, but the overall fact of the change is clear.

the fact that people originally lived in trees' (all quoted in Binford 1971: 7, 13). We need not bother with this sort of 'explanation', but from Homer's account of Patroclus on, ancient authors assume that the body's treatment evokes powerful responses. Disposing of the corpse is in one sense the main task of burial ritual, but I want to make a point which I think is even more important, and which applies to all the topics covered in this book: *no one feature of burial customs can be privileged over the others in analysis.* Yet this is precisely what has happened in this case. A tradition of analysis has grown up which is a sort of academic grave-robbing. The corpse is torn from its ritual context and interrogated with intellectualist questions. But the dead refuse to answer.

Tacitus' main concern in the passage quoted above seems to be to present Nero's actions as being inappropriate. Even though there is no hint of religious scruples here or in the other early references to inhumation, the change in rites has usually been taken as evidence for what MacMullen would call theology (see p. 16 above). We could in turn argue that there was a religious factor by suggesting that since Poppaea was interested in Judaism, Nero's remorse led him to bury her in accordance with her beliefs. But probably not. Embalming was not a Jewish custom, nor was it part of western inhumation. Consequently, neither Judaism nor Christianity (which could hardly have been so potent so early) is usually evoked. Instead, Cumont, largely followed by Turcan and Audin, saw the spirit being moved by Oriental mystery religions, bringing inhumation in their wake. Toynbee proposed that a kinder, gentler afterlife emerged, and with it less harsh treatment for the corpse. Sixty years ago Nock showed the weakness of such claims, but this has deterred few. In a remarkable piece of intellectual gymnastics van Doorselaer showed that Cumont and Nock were both right, and that Christianity and Judaism were also both crucial.[2]

The easternness of 'oriental' religions, the extent to which they really won followers and what it meant to be a convert have all

---

[2] Poppaea, Jos. *AJ* 20.195. Jewish burial, Hachlili & Killebrew 1983. Embalming in Rome, Lucr.3.891; Toynbee 1971: 41–2. Early growth of Christianity, Frend 1984. Cumont 1949: 387–90; Turcan 1958; Audin 1960; Toynbee 1971: 33–41; Nock 1932; van Doorselaer 1967: 29–86. More (similar) theories of inhumation, Richmond 1950: 19; Macdonald 1977: 37; Wrede 1978; Merrifield 1987: 60–1; Parmeggiani 1985: 208. De Visscher (1963) continues to argue for Christianity as the prime mover. Koch & Sichtermann (1982: 23–30) present a balanced overview of the competing theories.

been questioned,[3] but my main concern is with the methodological problems which the burials raise. Rick Jones comments
that 'It is remarkable to realise that such an apparently substantial
and significant shift in practice should not have been discussed at
length in English for nearly half a century' (1981: 15). But is it
really so surprising? The intellectualist concerns of those who have
tackled the problem make the archaeological record itself rather
irrelevant. The question is reduced to one of finding out what
cremation and inhumation 'meant', and extrapolating to explain
the transition. The graves become merely illustrative material.

I offer little to those who want to know whether inhumation was
part of a new religion. No amount of evidence is ever going to help
us answer that. Those who pursue that question must stick to the
few tangentially relevant texts, and to guesswork. But this does not
mean that this profound change in rituals has no interest. To some
extent my conclusions are like Nock's, who sixty years ago dismissed it as a matter of 'fashion'. At Rome the change was one of
form only: it led to changes in the form of other parts of the ritual
system to preserve the overall structure, but inhumation in the
third century said much the same things about the dead as cremation had done in the first. Yet this is not the end of the matter.
Ritual fashions are the stuff social structure is made of. Outside
Rome the evidence is fuzzier, but the spread of inhumation is often
part of a complete overhaul of the burial system. It was caught up
in the complex events which we call the 'third-century crisis'.

I argue that we have to do two things – to embed the change in
body treatment in its ritual context, and to fragment the process by
working at several geographical levels. Stressing detailed variation
over broader patterns – deliberately looking for the trees rather
than the wood – can be an excuse for not reaching a conclusion, but
this is not my intention. When we make generalisations, they must
be at the best level. We need a mosaic of local understandings as
well as a Rome-based view of how a rite swept across Europe and
as it did so was redefined in countless small-scale ritual systems. I
do not see how the graves can tell us about the popularity of
mystery cults, but they do show a massive cultural homogenisation
of the Roman world at a time when political and economic regionalism was increasing, which in some ways is far more interesting.

---

[3] Burkert 1987; MacMullen 1981: 112–30; 1984a; cf. Gordon 1990b: 245–55.

Where do we start? I choose a point not in the Roman empire but in our own recent history. The Roman evidence has been used poorly because we have asked bad questions. Anthropologists applying for grants to do fieldwork among the Ik, Tiv or whoever often claim that 'out there' they can see social processes more clearly than in the dulling familiarity of their own surroundings. I want to turn this round. By seeing the limitations inherent in the direct interpretation of our own symbolism, the problems of analysing ancient society become clearer, and we can ask more realistic questions, looking at both the *forms* and the underlying *structure* of rituals.

FROM INHUMATION TO CREMATION: EUROPE SINCE 1900

In 1885, only three cremations are known to have taken place in Britain. By 1909, thirteen crematoria were operating; and since 1945, the use of cremation has increased at a steady annual rate of 1–2%. In 1976, 62% of all corpses were cremated, with 218 crematoria burning 413,712 bodies. The changes in twentieth-century disposal practices in parts of northern Europe and some of its overseas colonies (see table 1) are the only example in world history on a larger scale than those in Rome.[4]

Those in search of direct interpretations have abundant primary sources. Cremation often was, and sometimes still is, seen as incompatible with the Christian idea of the judgement of the dead, and it was seized on as an anti-clerical symbol at the end of the nineteenth century, as mass popular parties challenged more traditional forms of liberal government and offered radical critiques of bourgeois society. Take the motto of the Austrian Workers' Funeral Association: 'A proletarian life, a proletarian death, and cremation in the spirit of cultural progress.' But cremation was not only a symbol in the class struggle, and explanations which start from materialist premises soon come to involve more intellectual factors. It was initially most popular among the free-thinking elite, and as

---

[4] Curl 1972; Cunnington & Lucas 1972; Polson & Marshall 1972; Lerner 1975; Cannadine 1981; Parker Pearson 1982. 1976 figures, Thalmann 1978: 140. The adoption of cremation by 10–30% of the population of China between the tenth and fourteenth centuries A.D. involved large numbers of people over a huge area; but as Ebrey's study (1990) shows, intellectualist and direct interpretations are no more convincing in that case than they are for modern Europe.

Table 1. *The use of cremation, 1976 (after*
Thalmann 1978: 140)

	Percentage of the dead being cremated
France	0.5
Belgium	2.2
Luxemburg	3.2
USA	7.3
Finland	9.1
Austria	11.9
Hungary	13.7
West Germany	16.8
Netherlands	28.2
Norway	28.4
Switzerland	43.3
Australia	44.9
Czechoslovakia	45.5
Sweden	46.2
Denmark	50.1
Rhodesia (Zimbabwe)	50.2
United Kingdom	62.6

late as 1977, one Cambridge undertakers' firm reported that 70% of its (undefined) upper-class customers wanted cremation, as against 50% of lower-class patrons. Plenty of good Christians also burned their dead, often championing the ritual as one which cut wasteful spending on funerals. In 1899 one writer suggested that cremation marked a welcome shift in Christian thought from the afterlife to this life.[5]

Similarly, accounts beginning at the 'religious' end have to be tied to larger social processes. The case of Catholicism and cremation is striking. The Church ruled that cremation was pagan in 785, but only felt the need to ban the rite in 1886, just as it was gaining popularity. This ban remained in force until 1963; by 1966 some 10% of practising Catholics dying in England were already being cremated. Rome's ban on cremation was part of its general stand against radical politics and modernism, what Larkin calls its

---

[5] Beginnings of cremation and social change, Hobsbawm 1987: 112–41, 264–7; Jacob 1899. 1977 proportions, Parker Pearson 1982: 103.

'devotional revolution', and control over funeral rites was a crucial part of this. The change in the 1960s belongs to a general shift in dogma, with internal belief being privileged over the external referents of symbolic acts (shades of Luther!). Even abstinence from meat on Fridays was abandoned as hollow ritualism. The speed with which Catholics adopted cremation suggests that while theology provides a necessary condition for change, it is not a sufficient explanation. Table 1 shows that the Protestant countries of western Europe tend to cremate far more than the Catholics; but the preference for inhumation in Luxemburg and Belgium must have as much or more to do with French cultural influence as with religious belief. In Catholic Italy, inhumation is still overwhelmingly dominant; but it is interesting to see that this is also true in the special *acattolico* cemetery at Rome, which since 1800 has been used mainly by foreign Protestants. The excommunicated Antonio Gramsci was cremated and buried here in 1937, probably at the wishes of his family; but he was always a special case. Other non-Catholics (including many British and Germans) continue to assimilate themselves to the local tradition, as do the Catholics in cremating countries.[6]

Another motive was suggested by the Africanist Geoffrey Gorer (1965: 45) after a survey in Britain: 'In many cases, it would appear, cremation is chosen because it is felt to get rid of the dead more completely and finally than does burial.' The same factors may be behind a parallel rise in the number of people leaving their bodies to science. Gorer and many others see here a pathological modern tendency to deny the very fact of death. Explanations for this range from the intellectualist to the materialist. Some speak of a crisis in organised religion leading to fear of death and despair over what comes next. Others stress demographic changes, with death becoming something that only happens to the old. Death is marginalised and ignored. The institutionalisation of medicine is also invoked: in Britain in the 1970s, some 60% of all deaths were in specialised facilities. Medical professionals' attempts to preserve their status perhaps accelerate the removal of death from the domestic context. The dying person is reduced to a puppet with no control over his or her fate, and death becomes horrific. Others

---

[6] Schnitzer 1934; Ucko 1969: 274; Douglas 1970: 65–73; Larkin 1972, discussing Ireland; cf. L. J. Taylor 1989: 180. *Acattolico* cemetery, Rahtz 1987; Randsborg 1989: 94–6.

still, developing Freud, see the world wars, the holocaust and the nuclear threat as devaluing death in European thought.[7]

These are all direct interpretations of symbolism. They look for what cremation 'means', which then explains why it has ousted inhumation. The theories all work in one way or another, but they are vulnerable to the criticisms discussed in chapter 1. Widening the spatial context shows this. Most of the explanatory factors invoked apply even more strongly to the USA than to Britain, but although the first American crematorium was opened in 1876, as late as 1920 only 1% of the dead were burned, and in 1976 the figure was still only 7.3%. Since the 1860s virtually all bodies have been embalmed and then inhumed, a practice which has made little impression in Europe.[8]

The normative practices of western Europe and the USA are as different as could be, but if we look beyond the forms of symbols to their functions in the rituals, embalming does much the same job as cremation. Undertakers have the technology to preserve the corpse almost indefinitely, but customers do not want this. Instead, embalming merely postpones putrefaction, allowing Americans to focus ceremonies around 'viewing' the corpse in the home or funeral parlour. Direct interpretations of the symbolism are as varied as those of European practices, but imported ideas are generally given more weight. Some stress the influence of the Irish Catholic wake, which is of roughly the same antiquity; Bernal emphasises the revival of interest in Egypt. But whatever the origins of the particular forms of symbolism, the burial itself and the cemetery declined as ritual foci. European cremation accomplishes the same thing by accelerating decay; the soft tissues are purged in the flames to leave stable ashes, with ritual again being private and familial, centring on scattering the ashes or putting an urn within the home. Both leave still less scope for the cemetery than in the

---

[7] See Wahl 1959; Gorer 1965: 23–9, 171–2; Kübler-Ross 1970: 5–8; E. Becker 1973; Lerner 1975; Huntington & Metcalf 1979: 210–11; Ariès 1981: 559–614, esp. 577–8; Cannadine 1981; Parker Pearson 1982: 111; Giddens 1987: 194–7; Palgi & Abramovich 1984; Richardson 1988: 258–60.

[8] Dempsey 1975: 180; Pine 1975; Farrell (1980) with a fascinating account of cremation vs. embalming at pp. 164–9. Irion (1968) explains the American refusal to consider cremation as a result of discomfort with the idea of death (cf. Bowman 1959), the same factor that Gorer uses to explain its popularity in Britain. Embalming in Britain, Mitford 1963: 161–76; cf. Huntington & Metcalf 1979: 187–9. However, Parker Pearson (1982: 110) reports that 75% of inhumations in London and 30% in Cambridge were being embalmed in 1979.

USA. In the *Iliad*, the heroes had the best of both worlds when the gods intervened to protect Patroclus and Hector from decay; after an American-style viewing, the body was reduced to ashes in a European manner.[9]

Both rites can be seen as parts of systems minimising display and competition. The uniformity on each side of the Atlantic is remarkable, with people adhering closely to norms of decency. As Huntington and Metcalf note, 'Americans feel that [embalming] is the sort of thing that *ought* to be required by law' (1979: 198); and, in spite of those who see the whole thing as a devilish plot foisted onto a dazed public by profit-seeking morticians, they point out that 'In general, the impression is of a striving to find the *correct* level of expenditure in funerary accoutrements, rather than the most *impressive*' (ibid.: 192).[10]

Studying the structure of British funerals, Parker Pearson (1982) suggested that they function as part of a capitalist ideology, legitimising inequality by disguising it. The archaeologist of the future excavating a British settlement would find enormous variety in lifestyles. Wealth and power lie in a few hands, and age, sex, class and race conflict are widespread. Yet the funeral reduces all this to equality. As in the state rituals for the war dead, divisions disappear in the funeral, creating an ideal national consensus transcending social and local struggles. Huntington and Metcalf interpret the American funeral in a similar way, again emphasising the link with national death rituals. The funeral is the core of a civil religion binding together a very disparate society. They ascribe great symbolic importance to Abraham Lincoln. This is particularly interesting, since embalming first won prominence through its use to preserve his body on its epic journey from Washington to Springfield in 1865. 'In humbler rites across the country', they suggest, 'a nation still grieving its war dead tried to capture in its funerals some of the peace written upon Lincoln's face' (1979: 206).

---

[9] On embalming, see Habenstein & Lamers 1955: 321–52; Huntington & Metcalf 1979: 190–201; Farrell 1980: 157–69, 202–6. Irish wake, Turner 1989: 183. Egypt, Bernal 1987: 267–8, although calling US customs 'mummification' and cremation 'the Greek form' are both exaggerations. On 'Egyptianising' tendencies, see Farrell 1980: 162–70. Curl (1982: 153–72) describes the spread of Egyptian styles in funerary monuments in the USA and Europe in the mid- and late nineteenth century. Bloch (1982) gives a powerful account of the ideological functions of rotting, with useful comments on Homer.

[10] Diversity in American funerals, K. Jackson 1989: 48–63; R. Meyer 1989. Jordan (1982) laments the decline of ethnic variation in Texan cemeteries.

Cremation and embalming seem to function similarly in Britain and the USA. All become equal in rituals which deny corruption and decay, uniting the nation-state through the combination of private and public funerals. But Parker Pearson's neo-Marxist critique of capitalist ideology may be misplaced, since Soviet and Chinese funerals of the 1970s worked in much the same ways. It might be better to look beyond political ideologies, to see the funerals as promoting a social structure suited to the (post-)industrial nation-state, creating potentially interchangeable citizens freed from binding ties to region or kin, and denying real boundaries within the national group. Cultural and political borders coincide; as Huntington and Metcalf realise, burials mark off nations from one another, rather than class groups within the nations. The emergence of these structure-bearing rituals in the 1890s and their dominance since 1945 offer interesting avenues of research into the modern state; and comparing the individual–egalitarian–nationalist model with the rites of states with different histories and structures opens further possibilities. In modern Greece, for example, traditional rural practices where 'the ossuary is a powerful symbol of the unity of the village dead' (Danforth & Tsiaras 1982: 56) are now giving way to new rituals, but ones emphasising the differences in wealth between individuals and a town/country distinction. Similar trends have been noted in Communist China, where the official promotion of cremation since 1949 'emphasize[s] ... that one's status in society during life and afterward is dependent fundamentally on one's place and contributions in the bureaucratic pecking order, with minimal mediation by family or kin' (Whyte 1988: 312–13), although it has simultaneously opened a new ritual division between the cities and the villages (table 2).[11]

This structural approach gives new perspectives and shows up

[11] Civil religion, Bellah 1967; Bellah et al. 1985: 219–49. On the interaction of state and family rituals, see Neville 1989 (Selkirk, Scotland) and Ryan 1989 (parades in nineteenth-century America). Burial in the USSR, Fried & Fried 1980: 246–51; C. Lane 1981: 82–6. C. Lane (1981: 255–60) also offers an interesting comparison of Soviet, American and British rituals. Interestingly, state attempts to impose cremation as the appropriate way to dispose of the dead in a socialist society have made little headway in either the USSR (Fried & Fried 1980: 247) or rural China (ibid.: 253–4; Whyte 1988; Wakeman 1988; Ebrey 1990: 406). This model of 'industrial' social structure owes much to Gellner (1983: 19–38), Giddens (1987) and Hobsbawm (1990: 163–83). As Giddens shows (1987: 137–47), the distinction between 'capitalism' and 'industrialism' as categories for understanding modernity is not very helpful. Modern Greece, Hirschon 1983; Bennett 1988; Dubisch 1989.

Table 2. *Cremation in the People's
Republic of China*

Period	Percentage of the dead being cremated	
	Urban	Rural
1949–65	38	7
1966–74	85	13
1983	90	15

Source: Whyte 1988: 303–4. Figures are
not easy to come by; other sources
suggest an overall decline in cremation
since Mao's death, from 37% of all
burials in 1978 to 30% in 1983 (ibid.:
301)

distinct weaknesses in direct interpretations. Waugh's and Mitford's famous satires on American funerals achieve their effects
through a systematic refusal to see the rituals on their own terms.
This could be put down to upper-class British snobbishness, but it
is less easy to excuse Ariès' reactionary critiques of both European
and American attitudes toward death, wallowing in nostalgia for
an imagined past. Nineteenth- and twentieth-century funerals
make sense when we look at how they functioned; it is wrenching
them out of context which reduces them to nonsense. Similarly,
those who lament the decline of ritualism in the twentieth century
seem oddly out of touch with their own times. Modern funerals
create a modern social structure; a structure of no structure, as it
were, where all are free to fulfil their potential as citizens.[12]

So what have we learned? Two points come out of all this. First,
even where primary sources are plentiful, direct/intellectual interpretations only provide a partial reading. Even at the best of
times, participants' verbalised explanations of the symbols they use
obscure as much as they reveal. And ancient historians do not deal
with the best of times. There was no Geoffrey Gorer carrying out
opinion polls in second-century Gaul. Our evidence is fragmentary,
has been pre-selected by transmission processes we cannot control,
and is unevenly distributed in time and space. Constraints of genre

[12] Waugh 1948; Mitford 1963; Ariès 1981; Douglas 1970.

shape the expression of emotion in complex ways. The closest thing we have to an interpretation of the 'meaning' of rites comes from Lucretius, writing at Rome in the first century B.C.:

If it's terrible to be mauled by the jaws and teeth of wild animals when you're dead, I don't see how it could not be unpleasant to be laid down in fires and shrivelled up in hot flames; or to be packed in honey and suffocated; or to grow stiff with cold, lying on a slab of freezing marble; or to be buried and squashed under a mass of earth above you. (*de rer. nat.* 3.888–93)

What a choice! With him as a guide, we might despair of saying anything at all about the selection of disposal methods. The only description we have of a decision to inhume rather than to cremate is that of Domitian's secretary Abascantus in Statius' collection of poems called the *Silvae*, published about A.D. 100. Abascantus 'could not bear the smoke of burning and the clamour of the pyre', and so inhumed his wife Priscilla in a marble tomb instead (5.1.226–7). We simply cannot generalise from such limited and complex sources to a process involving half a continent.

The second point is that the purely 'relational' approach is also limited, reducing the symbols themselves to arbitrary signifiers generated in historical accidents like the rhetoric of nineteenth-century socialism or the need to get Lincoln's body from the east coast to Illinois. In spite of the similarity in the functions of burial rituals in the USA, USSR, China and western Europe, the specific rites stop at national frontiers; and looking at the differing symbols against the background of their shared structure we see a crucial point, that culture underwrites the nation-state as the all-embracing way of life in the twentieth century. If we cannot assume a single meaning for a rite across vast areas in these days of global communications, *a fortiori* it is even more of a problem in the Roman empire. When inhumation swept the West it subsumed a huge number of intensely localised burial systems, and detailed regional studies are needed. Further, concentrating on a 'transitional' period from about 150 to 250 is too narrow; we need to look at continuous processes spanning the first century B.C. to the fourth century A.D. The relational and direct approaches have to be combined, and in what follows I ask two questions: first, how far changes in the *form* of symbols were also changes in the *structure* of rituals; and second, what the purely formal aspects can tell us. I have to be impressionistic, picking examples from the huge mass of data rather than tackling it in all its bewildering complexity; but I hope to show the potential for more rigorous studies.

FROM CREMATION TO INHUMATION: THE ROMAN EMPIRE

The obvious place to start is Rome. Cicero (*Laws* 2.57, *c.* 50 B.C.) and Pliny (*NH* 7.187, *c.* A.D. 77) comment that with Sulla's death in 78 B.C. even the ultra-conservative Cornelii gave up inhumation, implying that cremation was by then the norm for the wealthy. However, no actual burial of this period survives from the 'super tombs' around Rome: the bodies of the very rich are lost, and we cannot add nuances to the picture. So too with the poor. Literary sources mention huge pits called *puticuli* which were used as mass graves, but in spite of Lanciani's excavation of 75 of these there is little agreement on what they were. Bodel's interpretation seems best, that the Esquiline hill was used for the casual disposal of the poor in pits, without cremation, in the third and second centuries B.C. Early in the first century B.C. the Senate had the area buried under a massive dump of rubble. A new site next to it was then used for a while, and was probably the boneyard mentioned by Horace (*Sat.* 1.8); and the whole area was finally bought up and reorganised as a garden by Maecenas in 35 B.C. Bodel goes on to argue that similar informal inhumation cemeteries existed outside other Italian towns in the second and first centuries B.C., being replaced by mass cremation in the first century A.D.[13]

Consequently, there are few direct traces of the poor. The second-century B.C. cremation cemetery outside the Porta Romana at Ostia had no elaborate markers, but in the next century more impressive tombs appear here, and it may be that even before 100 B.C. we are dealing with a well-off group. This is clearly the case in the Pian di Bezzo area at Sarsina and the Street of the Tombs at

---

[13] Eisner (1986) catalogues 110 tombs around Rome (not including smaller tomb types like the *columbaria* and chamber tombs or finds since 1978); the only burial is a third-century Vestal Virgin (pp. 110–11). *Puticuli*, Varro, *de lang. lat.* 5.25; Horace, *Sat.* 1.8; Festus, s.v. *puticuli*. Interpretation, Bodel, forthcoming, ch. 4. I am very grateful to John Bodel for allowing me to read his manuscript in advance of publication. See also Lanciani 1888: 64–5; Pinza 1914; Le Gall 1980/1; Albertoni 1983. Coarelli (1979: 202) suggested that the *pozzi funerari* at Fregellae may be the same as the Roman *puticuli*, but this seems unlikely.

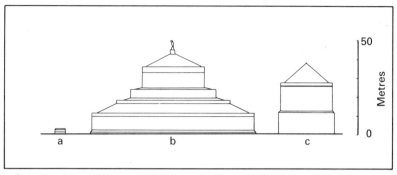

5. Relative sizes of funerary monuments at Rome: (a) public tomb of the consul
A. Hirtius, died 43 B.C.; (b) mausoleum of Augustus, died A.D. 14; (c) mausoleum
of C. Metella, probably *c.* 30 B.C. (after Zanker 1988: fig. 58)

Pompeii, where all the first-century B.C. burials are cremations. At
Rome itself, cremation is almost the only rite in the published
tombs of 'middling' type, in which the inscriptions mainly name
freedmen. There are hints of interesting patterns, as in Via Caelimontana tomb 1, where the three original owners were inhumed,
while four of the five later burials were cremations; but there is just
not enough evidence to explore the relationships between the rites
in detail. It looks as if cremation predominated for the well-off in
Rome throughout the first century B.C., although the very poor may
well not have been burned before burial in mass graves.[14]

The lack of evidence for the spread of cremation in the first
century B.C. is most unfortunate given that after 100 B.C. Roman
nobles began erecting very lavish tombs and statues which borrowed heavily from the Hellenistic East. The interest of this is that
inhumation was the normal rite everywhere in the East Mediterranean; studying the interaction of rite and monument could add
greatly to our understanding of the complex processes often lumped
together under the heading of 'Hellenisation', as well as to their
resolution in what Zanker calls 'the Augustan program of cultural
renewal'. Augustus' huge mausoleum (fig. 5) seems to have redefined lavish burial display as appropriate for his family alone. From

---

[14] Ostia, Squarciapino 1958: 11–60; Meiggs 1973: 455–70; Boschung 1987a: 111–14. Sar-
sina, Ortalli 1987. Pompeii, Toynbee 1971: 119–30; Borelli et al. 1983; Kockel 1983;
Kockel et al. 1985; 1986; d'Ambrosio & de Caro 1987. Via Caelimontana, Fornari 1917;
Toynbee 1971: 117–18; Zanker 1975.

30 B.C. on, the very rich began to use much simpler family tombs organised around modest funerary altars, typically adorned with new symbols of *pietas*, such as garlands, torches and branches. However, around A.D. 115 great differences between the tombs of the rich and the poor were still taken so much for granted by Tacitus that he could use them as a simile: 'just as the nobly born are distinguished in the mode of their burial from the vulgar dead, so, when history records their end, each shall receive and keep his special mention' (*Ann.* 16.16).[15]

The typical surviving early imperial tomb type in Rome is the *columbarium*, a Latin word (meaning 'dovecot') chosen by modern scholars to describe barrel-vaulted brick and masonry tombs with walls lined with niches to hold cremation urns. The earliest example dates from *c.* 50 B.C. and comes from the Esquiline Hill (near the *puticuli*), but they only become common in the 40s A.D. The Ostian examples get bigger and bigger as the first century wears on. One found at Rome in 1726 held 3,000 urns, but 50–100 urns was more normal. There were virtually no exceptions to the rule of cremation in these and other kinds of 'house tomb'. Only one inhumation (*c.* A.D. 50) was found among the thousands of burials at Pompeii (destroyed in A.D. 79), and none at all in the first-century A.D. Porta Laurentina cemetery at Ostia.[16]

'The poor always ye have with you', says the good book (John 12: 8); but not their graves. *Columbaria* were expensive, and inscriptions suggest that they were built by the rich or by *collegia*, co-operative funeral clubs in which members contributed to a joint tomb. Not everyone could afford *collegium* fees or find a rich patron, as indicated by the emperor Nerva (A.D. 96–8), who tried to curry favour with the poor by giving everyone a burial allowance. But we do not know what proportion of the population ended up in *columbaria*, nor (with any confidence) the fate of those who did not. Eck asserts that the master-slave psychology was such that family slaves filled no small part of the *columbaria*. Inscriptions from the family tomb of the Volusii show that this certainly could be true,

[15] Cultural renewal, Zanker 1988; Wallace-Hadrill 1989: 163–4. Late Republican tombs, Eisner 1986. Early imperial tombs, Boschung 1987b; Sinn-Henninger 1987; Kleiner 1987; 1988. Mausoleum of Augustus, Platner & Ashby 1929: 332–5; Nash 1968: 38–43.
[16] *Columbaria*, G. Davies 1977: 17; Boschung 1987a: 120–3; Hopkins 1983: 216. The Roman tombs are summarised in an excellent article by von Hesberg (1987a), with von Hesberg 1987b and von Hesberg & Pfanner 1988. Ostia and Pompeii, see n. 14 above.

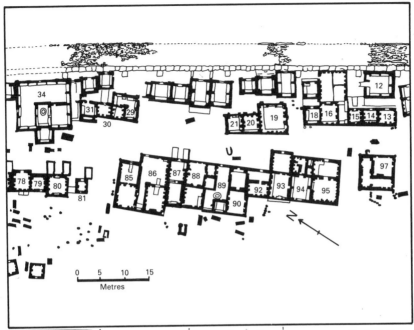

6. Part of the second- to third-century A.D. Isola Sacra cemetery at Ostia (after Toynbee 1971: fig 3)

but we cannot know how common it was to include so many slaves; and in any case, we are more concerned with the much larger group of the free poor and slaves attached to lesser households, who might not themselves have had a *columbarium*. Purcell (1987: 39) suggests that only 'a group a few hundred or a few thousand strong' used *columbaria* at Rome, meaning less than 1% of the population. My feeling is that this is too low, but there is no good evidence either way. In the second-century A.D. Isola Sacra cemetery at Ostia 160 graves were found scattered between the big tombs (fig. 6). These make up at most 7% of the cemetery's population, and probably much less. Similarly, in the Vatican cemetery the tile graves can only be a tiny fraction of the number of burials in built tombs. The poor probably had separate cemeteries, so we cannot argue from this that the bulk of the population had access to *columbaria*; but we can note that 121 of the Isola Sacra 'poor' graves were definitely cremations. Only one of the 39 'barrel tombs' (*tombe a cassone*) was opened, and it too held a cremation in an urn. I would conclude that cremation was probably virtually the only rite used at Rome in the first century A.D.[17]

This uniformity is important. Augustus' mausoleum was a turning point. In contrast to his self-presentation in his *Res Gestae*, this monument set him and his line off from the rest of the nobility, who more or less gave up competing in their burials, at least at Rome itself. Munatius Plancus, who in 27 B.C. had proposed that Octavian should be given the title Augustus, showed equal tact in putting his own huge tomb (*c.* 20 B.C.) safely out of the way at Gaeta; from then on only marginal figures built great tombs at Rome itself. Part of the humour of Trimalchio's planned tomb (Petr. 71) is that no rich man of taste would want such an overblown memorial any more. Eck argues persuasively that senatorial competition shifted from Rome to the Italian towns in this period, with Augustus effectively monopolising display in the capital city.[18]

Recent studies of Roman 'streets of tombs' emphasise how the cemeteries vary, but the similarities still outweigh the differences. The observant visitor to a cemetery would notice wide status distinctions in inscriptions or expressed through the form, location and painting of niches within *columbaria*, but the overwhelming impression was of solidity and stability: of Rome restored. Funerary portraits of freedmen illustrate this well. The sculptures began before 50 B.C., but the vast majority date *c.* 30 B.C.–A.D. 5. Stylisation reaches the point of monotony, especially for women; Kleiner suggests that 'The freedmen are represented as simple people in a simple manner' (1977: 185). Simultaneous changes in painting, domestic architecture and epigraphic formulae reinforce the impression of a new ritual order emerging in the 20s B.C. In the tombs of Ostia, according to Calza, 'still more noteworthy [than variations] is the evident architectural dignity, the nobility and decorative grace of the tombs, when compared to the social rank of the deceased, who belong to the more humble class of citizens' (1940: 48). Much of this uniformity was planned from the begin-

---

[17] Expense, Hopkins 1983: 211–17; Purcell 1987: 34–8. Prices for funerary altars, Kleiner 1987: 25–6. Slaves, Eck 1988: 136–8. Saller & Shaw (1984: 127–8) suggest that *collegia* were much more open. Tomb of the Volusii, Buonocore 1984. Inscriptions, Saller & Shaw 1984: 125–8; Eck 1986; 1987; 1988. Nerva, Degrassi 1962: 697–702. Isola Sacra, Calza 1940: 44, 53–4, 78–80. Vatican, Toynbee & Ward-Perkins 1956: 142–53.
[18] Munatius Plancus, Fellmann 1956. Augustus and the scale of tombs, Zanker 1988: 15–18, 72–7, 274–8, 291–5. Italian towns, Eck 1984.

ning, as in the Porta Laurentina area at Ostia, which was almost entirely used by freedmen.[19]

Hopkins suggests a functionalist interpretation of *columbaria*, as a response to rising land prices at Rome, the need to dispose of huge numbers of corpses, and the desire to preserve individuality. This is plausible, but there is a more symbolic aspect too: the new tomb types created a social structure with a solid, unified and respectable well-off class, embracing citizens, freedmen and even slaves. The use of cremation even for those who could not get into *columbaria* extended to all the fundamental unity of this vision of Rome, while still admitting major divisions between free and slave and decent elements and those less so. It is sometimes said that the *columbarium* reproduces the feeling of the crowded apartment blocks of Rome, with individuals submerged in a collective mass, but the orderly structure evoked by the tombs contrasts sharply with the bustling chaos and the extremes of luxury and misery in the cities. The interplay of the madding crowd of the living and the serene order of the dead created a Roman social structure which was highly appropriate for the capital of a world empire.[20]

The relationships between this evolving system and the rest of the empire are complex. From about 475 to 200 B.C. inhumation had been normal in western Europe, but as time goes on it becomes harder for archaeologists to find graves, and hardly any are known from the second century. Exposure of the dead, leaving few material traces, was probably widespread. When burials reappear in the first century B.C., the whole area from Poland to England is characterised by cremation, but even these are few and far between, and there is strong regional variation. The English Aylesford–Swarling Culture, just a small part of the cremating area known as the North Gallic Culture, typifies this. At Owslebury ashes were scattered in the grave fill, while at Welwyn they were in canvas bags. Elsewhere pedestalled urns, open bowls, buckets and wooden boxes were used. Human bones are quite common on

[19] Variations, von Hesberg & Zanker, eds., 1987: *passim*. Portraits, Kleiner 1977; Zanker 1988: 292–5; Dyson, forthcoming, ch. 6. Painting, E. W. Leach 1982. Architecture, Wallace-Hadrill 1988. Inscriptions, Eck 1984. Porta Laurentina, Boschung 1987a: 116–18.

[20] Hopkins 1983: 211–17. Other interpretations of the *columbarium*, Purcell 1987: 34–40. Contemporary settlement evidence, Packer 1967; Scobie 1986; Stambaugh 1988; Wallace-Hadrill 1988.

settlement sites, and skulls found in the River Thames probably belong to this period. Despite the general paucity of grave goods, cremation in the North Gallic Culture separated a small elite from the bulk of the population. Around the edges of this region, contracted inhumations occur. Further west, at sites like Birdlip, extended inhumations are the norm; and on Guernsey, bodies are inhumed in stone cist graves.[21]

Given such patterns, it is not surprising that cremation functioned very differently from place to place, and that we need different 'answers' to why inhumation took over, depending on what we are looking at and where from. Colin Haselgrove's work on Belgic Gaul is a good example of analysis at a detailed level. Although Caesar (*BG* 6.19) commented on the lavish scale of pre-conquest Gallic funerals, the archaeological evidence suggests that truly rich graves only began *c.* 50 B.C. in the Rhineland, spreading westwards to reach Britain around 10 B.C. Haselgrove suggests that Caesar's conquest of Gaul drained off the wealth through which local elites had defined themselves and won followers, especially in their votive practices (cf. Suet. *Div. Jul.* 54.2; Strabo 4.1.13).[22] He argues that competition for status moved from sanctuaries to cremations, which continued to be reserved for the notables, and which

must be seen as projecting the desirability of the alliance with Rome and the benefits of acculturation on the part of a class who owed their position to the relationship. At burial sites such as Goeblingen-Nospelt the message is reiterated in everything from large-scale wine consumption to the cremation rite; the power and continued success of the ruling groups was indissolubly linked to the Roman alliance. (1987: 116)

Large cemeteries of cremations in urns emerged suddenly in the first century A.D., at the beginning in northern Spain, around the middle in Gaul and towards the end in Britain and the Danube provinces. In the second century cremation was displacing inhumation in North Africa too. The historian looking through the eyes of Rome-based writers might see a simple index of Romanisation: the extension of Augustus' creation of a uniform set of images, part of the package of cities, Latin, baths and togas through which,

[21] Collis 1977a; 1984: 126–57. British burials and remains from settlements, Whimster 1979; L. Walker 1984. River Thames, Bradley & Gordon 1988. There is similar variability across northern Gaul (Wightman 1985: 14–25; Galliou 1989: 16–18).
[22] See Collis 1977a: 10–11; M. Millett 1986. On Caesar's impact, see also Roymans 1983; M. Millett 1990: 29–35.

according to Tacitus (*Agric.* 21 (published A.D. 98)), the Romans made willing slaves out of the Britons. Tizzoni makes a good case for treating cremation in Lombardy in this way. The Romans penetrated the area in the 190s B.C. and set up colonies in the 180s, but the unusual local inhuming tradition only yielded gradually. By the late second century B.C., men were being cremated. The Cisalpines were granted Latin status in 89 B.C. and full Roman citizenship in 49. By then warrior burials had stopped, and Tizzoni concludes that 'After the years 25/20 B.C. it is impossible to distinguish the Gaulish from the Roman graves'. He sees the length of this process as a result of its being a 'cultural instead of military penetration' (1985: 43).[23]

In discussing the cult of the emperors in the western provinces up to A.D. 150, Fishwick (1988: 93) draws a distinction between 'wild, uncivilized territories' and areas 'already integrated within the empire', pointing out that the cult grew most quickly in the former regions. The same is true of cremation in urn cemeteries. But while Garnsey and Saller can write that 'the provincial cult of the emperor was first employed as an instrument for the promotion of the military and political might of Rome' (1987: 165), it is hard to see burial customs in such a light, and local initiative rather than central government action must be the crucial factor. The main agent in disseminating urn cemeteries was probably the army rather than imperial propagandists, which again might explain the geographical pattern, with the more military provinces adopting the rite first. The spread of this cemetery type can give us a very different sort of information from that of more 'controlled' manifestations like urbanisation or the 'Capitoline triad' of Jupiter, Juno and Minerva.[24]

Cremation may have been thought of as a sign of allegiance to Rome, but the variations in its use suggest that it had other meanings too. In Gaul, for example, all the first- and second-century graves found at Jublains were cremations, and 87% of them were in urns; while at Blicquy all the classifiable graves dating *c.* A.D. 50–200 were also cremations, but the proportion in urns was never more than 36% (see table 3). At nearby Tongres about 30% of the

---

[23] Spain and Gaul, see nn. 25 and 26; Africa, Gsell 1901: 396–412; Février & Gaspary 1966/7; Février & Guéry 1980.
[24] See the excellent discussion in Gordon 1990b: 240–5.

Table 3. *Cremation at Blicquy and Jublains*, A.D. 50–200

(a) Blicquy (data from de Laet et al. 1972)

Cremation type	Period 50–100	100–150	150–200
Urn cremation in pit grave	36%	20%	20%
Primary cremation in pit grave	61%	73%	68%
Other types*	3%	6%	12%
Number of graves	139	74	25

* Urn and primary cremation in wood- and stone-lined pits.

(b) Jublains (data from Bousquet 1971)

Cremation type	Period 50–200
Urn cremation in pit grave	87%
Primary cremation in pit grave	10%
Cremation in wooden box	3%
Number of graves	123

first- and second-century graves were inhumations. At Vienne, 19 of the 31 excavated second-century graves were inhumations, and finds of sarcophagi at Arles suggest a strong South Gallic inhuming tradition through the first century A.D. No single meaning for either rite can be imposed on the whole province.[25]

Roman-style monuments were exported to some regions along with urn cremation; the walled plots at Aquileia and Salona hardly differ from those at Pompeii, and the 'garden cemeteries' which Rome took over from Alexandria spread as far as Britain and Gaul. But other markers subvert the possible Romanising messages

[25] Jublains, Bousquet 1971: 249. Blicquy, de Laet et al. 1972. Tongres, van Crombruggen 1962. Vienne, Leglay 1971: 426; Pelletier 1988: 45–6. Arles, Hatt 1951. Rivet (1988) describes southern Gallic urbanisation and the location of cemeteries. Types of Gallic cremation grave, van Doorselaer 1967: 100–11. Van Doorselaer (1967: 87–217) and R. F. J. Jones (1977) provide overviews of Gaul, and Galliou (1989: 39–50) of Armoricum. Laubenheimer (1987: 361) says that recent work shows that inhumation was important in many parts of Gaul in the first century A.D. I have not seen *Nécropoles à incinération du Haut-Empire* (Lyon 1987) to which he refers. Hatt (1951) argues that inhumation was a 'survival' from prehistory in Gaul, van Doorselaer (1967: 50–86) that it was introduced in the first century A.D. by oriental traders.

of cremation. At Ampurias in Spain, the cremation cemetery of Las Corts begins *c.* 200 B.C., with the incorporation of the area under Roman rule, but many of the urns are placed under 'Iberian' markers typical of the pre-Roman styles. Similarly, the frontier areas of the empire – Britain, the Rhine and Danube provinces – have many first- and second-century cremations under tumuli. Holloway made a good case for believing that all the round tombs of Roman Italy ('gasometers', as Toynbee called them) dated after 28 B.C. were modelled on Augustus' mausoleum, and this is often extended to explain the revival of provincial mounds. The mausoleum was, after all, originally known as the 'tumulus Iuliorum'; and to a Roman soldier or governor the new custom may well have looked like imitation of Rome. But Koethe long ago showed the similarities between the Roman-period barrows and those of the Late Bronze Age, seeing the revival as a native reaction to the Roman conquest. Gauls, Thracians and others lived in a landscape dotted with prehistoric mounds, which must have held meaning for them; we should assume that provincials would interpret their mounds in the first century at least as much in terms of their own history as of official Roman symbolism. In Armoricum, the natives even reused Neolithic tombs. Once again, two levels of analysis are needed, allowing room for the reinterpretation of the same ritual action by different viewers in different contexts.[26]

The use of tumuli varied as much as the use of cremation. In Britain mounds were heaped over single inurned cremations, and secondary burials were almost unknown; in Pannonia they contained larger numbers of cremations, both with and without urns; and in Thrace they were used mainly for extremely rich burials. Detailed local studies are as important with mounds as with cremation, but it is certainly tempting to see them working at one level as a form of symbolic resistance to imperialism.[27]

[26] Roman-style tombs, Gabelmann 1979; 1987; Andrikopoulou-Strack 1986. Aquileia, Brusin 1941; Reusser 1987. Salona, Cambi 1987, with other Dalmatian cemeteries reviewed on pp. 273–9. Ampurias, Almagro 1953: 251–390; 1955; R. F. J. Jones 1984b. Chronological problems of Las Corts, Jones 1984b: 238. Augustus, Holloway 1966; Koethe 1939. Walled cemeteries and tumuli, Jessup 1959; 1962; Amand 1960; van Doorselaer 1967: 174–9, 193–5, 205–8; Toynbee 1971: 91–100, 179–88. Armoricum, Galliou 1989: 31.

[27] Regional studies of mounds, Amand 1965; 1987; 1988; Galliou 1989: 30–1. The picture in Britain is especially complex (Foster 1986: 188–98). On the problems of the archaeology of resistance, see Gledhill 1988; D. Miller 1989; van der Leeuw & Torrence, eds., 1989. Wrede (1987) makes interesting suggestions about symbolic resistance to the emperors in first-century funerary altars. Generally, see Pippidi, ed., 1976.

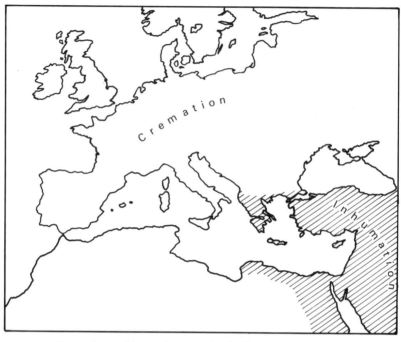

7. Cremating and inhuming areas in the Roman empire *c.* A.D. 60

THE COMING OF INHUMATION

By A.D. 60, when Petronius (111.2) called inhumation a 'Greek custom', the empire can be roughly divided into a western/cremating/Latin part and an eastern/inhuming/Greek part (fig. 7). Even where Romans established colonies in the East, inhumation continued. Twenty-eight graves in the North Cemetery at Corinth date between its refoundation as a *colonia* in 44 B.C. and *c.* A.D. 100; only four are cremations. Knossos was also planted as a new colony, some time after 67 B.C. The settlers may have introduced rock-cut chamber tombs to the area, but all of the hundreds of burials are inhumations. Philopappos, a Syrian, whose grave marker still dominates the Pnyx at Athens, was about as Romanised as an aristocrat could get (he was suffect consul in A.D. 109); but he did not adopt the rulers' burial rite. Similarly, for all the regional and chronological variety in the great cemeteries at Dura Europos, Palmyra and Petra, inhumation was the absolute rule. In second-century B.C. Alexandria many cremations took place with the ashes buried in pots known after the main cemetery as Hadra hydriae. Spectroscopic analysis shows that the pots came from central Crete, and it is widely assumed that they hold the remains of Greek mercenaries, traders and ambassadors rather than resident Egyptians. Whatever the merits of these direct interpretations (after all, cremation was not a Greek rite), by the time the Romans arrived, cremation was once again extremely rare.[28]

Hellenistic culture flourished at Rome in the second century A.D. Orators, architects and artists took part in a 'classical revival' of Greek influence under Hadrian; and between the 130s and 300 inhumation spread from the Hellenised to the Latinised areas. But we cannot operate with the simplistic *ex oriente lux* model of diffusion so favoured by an earlier generation of archaeologists. Gruen, speaking of the Republic, puts it well:

The success of Greek culture in Rome came in part because it could serve certain public purposes – whether in a positive or a negative fashion. Roman leaders were attuned to the possibilities. They engaged in adaptation, modification, and manipulation – not merely reaction. Posturing and symbolic activity hold a more central place in Roman civic life than has generally been recognised. And the serviceability of Hellenism in that context merits special attention. (Gruen 1990: 1)

This is just as true for the empire, but with the added complication that by A.D. 150 the imperial household played a crucial part in cultural change at the highest levels. 'Greek' customs were actively reconstructed, not passively absorbed. The details of how inhumation caught on at Rome itself are therefore crucial.[29]

---

[28] A century after Petronius, Lucian (*On Mourning* 21), called cremation a 'Greek custom', perhaps basing himself in the literary tradition going back to Herodotus 3.38, quoted on p. 19 above, rather than in current practice, which just goes to show the problems in the anecdotal sources. Corinth, Palmer 1964: 294–300. Knossos, Hood & Smyth 1981: 22–6, with references; Carrington Smith 1982; cf. Davaras 1985. Philopappos, Kleiner 1983: 43–4. Greek sarcophagus styles changed several times (Heldejürgen 1981). Dura, Palmyra and Petra are described with references in Toynbee 1971: 167–71, 191–9, 219–34; Negev 1986: 69–97. Egyptian cremations, B. F. Cook 1968/9; Callaghan & Jones 1985.

[29] Classical revival, Bowersock 1969; Strong 1976: chs. 8, 9; Walker & Cameron, eds., 1989. See Renfrew & Cherry, eds., 1986; Rowlands et al., eds., 1987; Champion, ed., 1989, on the problems of diffusion as a form of explanation, and more sophisticated alternatives.

Nock suggested that inhumation began in the second century among lesser mortals and was only later taken up by the emperors. Recent archaeological work has shown that inhumation came into vogue outside the emperors' circles even earlier than Nock thought, but the evidence for the emperors themselves is far from clearcut, and must be discussed at some length. All that we can really say is that the richer classes at Rome, from the emperors down to wealthy non-magistrates, probably all took up the new rite within the space of a generation or so, between about 140 and 180; the lower orders apparently took to it rather more slowly, as did those outside Rome. But even this much is highly significant.

The literary accounts of emperors' funerals are full of problems. Our best source for the second century is Xiphilinus' summary of Dio, which says (69.2.3) that Trajan was cremated in 117, but only that Hadrian was buried, *etaphē*, in 138 (69.23.1). This offhandedness might mean that Hadrian was inhumed; this was the normal custom in Dio's time, and hence perhaps not worth detailed comment. However, we are relying on a Byzantine summary, not Dio's original words, and such inferences may be unsafe. Two passages in the *Historia Augusta* say that Hadrian's remains were carried from Baiae to Rome and buried in the gardens of Domitia (*Ant. P.* 5.1; *Marc. Ant.* 6.1), while a third (*Had.* 25.7) says only 'sepultus est', again simply 'he was buried', at Puteoli. This unreliable source is our main guide for the emperors and their appointed heirs who died between 161 and 193, and who, apparently, were consistently inhumed. But when Septimius Severus died in 211, it seems that he was cremated. The elder of his two sons, Caracalla, murdered the younger, Geta, in 211; Geta was probably inhumed, and Caracalla was cremated in 217. After this, inhumation was normal, although the *Historia Augusta* remains our main, and increasingly fantastic, guide. Turcan suggests that Severus and Caracalla were cremated in line with North African family traditions, but cremation was no commoner there than anywhere else; the rites may be due to unusual circumstances – Severus died at York with the army and had to be got back to Rome without decomposing, and in the early third century Tertullian (*de res. carn.* 1) treats crem-ation as the normal rite in military camps. Dio (79.9.1) says that Caracalla was so hated that his remains had to be sneaked into Rome at night for burial. The choice of cremation may have been made to protect his body from outrage, and in both cases contingencies rather than a vaguely defined 'tradition' may be behind the choice of rite.[30]

Price uses inscriptions and coins to argue like Nock that 'emperors continued to be cremated throughout the second and third centuries' (1987: 96). His main evidence is that the pyre grew more important in accounts of the emperors' consecrations as the second century went on, eventually becoming synonymous with it in the decrees of the Arval Brethren; and that the pyre is featured on coins as late as 270, and again from 310 to 313. Price suggests that as inhumation came to dominate at Rome 'The emperor was buried in a way that increasingly marked him out from the élite and indeed from the rest of his subjects' (1987: 97). In the 240s, however, Herodian (4.2.2) observed that the emperor would be buried 'according to the custom of men' (*katathaptousin anthrōpōn nomōi*), by then definitely inhumation, while an elaborate wax image of him would be placed on the second layer of a five-storey pyre and burned a week later (4.2.2–11). The use of a wax image alongside the real body went back to the first century (Tac. *Ann.* 3.5). The increasing emphasis on the pyre was perhaps a way to link emperors to the past, not part of a growing ritual gap between emperor and noble. The pyre motif on coins spoke of the emperor's legitimacy, and need not mean that emperors actually continued to be burned.[31]

The archaeological evidence is just as difficult to use. Trajan's ashes were placed in a gold urn in a niche at the base of his famous column in 117, but the remains of other second-century emperors have not been found. Hadrian's mausoleum, completed in 139, probably held urns and sarcophagi. It is unsafe to assume that since Hadrian's burial was the earliest he must have been cre-

---

[30] Nock (1932: 325) gives an important warning that we cannot rely on the accuracy of the terminology about funerals; this is especially true of the Byzantine epitomes of Dio. Deaths 161–217: SHA, *Marc. Ant.* 7.10; 20.1; *Verus* 11.1; *Comm.* 17.4, supported by Dio 73(74).2.1; *Did. Jul.* 8.10. Severus, Dio 76(77).15.3; Her. 4.2.2; SHA, *Sev.* 24.1, with Turcan 1958: 325–8. Caracalla, Dio 79.9.1; Aur. Vict., *de Caes.* 21.6. Geta, Dio 79.24.3; SHA, *Geta* 7.2. Generally, see Arce 1988: 59–123.

[31] Price's observation (1987: 96) that *katathapto* and *sōma* in Her. 4.2.2 could refer to either rite is indisputable, but I think that the rest of the sentence, stressing the emperors' adherence to the *nomos anthrōpōn*, lessens the relevance of this point. It is also difficult to reconcile with Price's claim of increasing ritual separation for the emperors, except in the more limited sense of the growing symbolic association between emperors and the old-fashioned pyre. Chantraine (1980) offers a different interpretation of this passage in Herodian and other texts.

mated, with inhumation coming in later; but there is equally little reason to accept the tradition that a porphyry sarcophagus taken from here to be reused as Pope Innocent II's tomb in 1143 was originally Hadrian's. Antoninus Pius, who died in 161, was also buried here, and a group of enclosures excavated in 1703 near his memorial column is usually seen as the pyre on which he and his heirs were cremated. However, there is no evidence for this, and it is more likely that it was an altar to him. A similar structure found near the column of Marcus Aurelius in 1907 may have been used to burn that emperor in 180, but the site was only partially excavated and once again there is no good evidence for its function. No inhumation of the imperial household has been found. An early second-century sarcophagus might be from Augustus' mausoleum, but it probably only got there in a sixteenth-century art fraud. Even the sarcophagus said to be that of the emperor Balbinus (died 238), widely thought to be the only certain attribution, is not above question. Anyway, putting our faith in a sarcophagus or two would be to fall into the same trap as Audin, who takes the stories about Poppaea and Priscilla as serious evidence that the imperial household switched to inhumation before A.D. 100.[32]

Inhumation, then, may have begun to be used for emperors as early as 138; or cremation may still have been normal in 238. On balance, I prefer to adopt what seems to me the most natural reading of the *Historia Augusta*, following Boatwright in interpreting the structures near the columns of Antoninus Pius and Marcus Aurelius as altars: that is, that by 161 inhumation was normal for the emperors, except in unusual circumstances. Admittedly, 'unusual circumstances' arose rather frequently, but the important thing, I think, is that by the mid-second century inhumation was probably taken for granted at the very highest levels in Rome.

There is much more evidence for those wealthy Romans who were not at the very pinnacle of society. Baldassarre's excavations beneath the floors of the tombs in Ostia show that inhumation was common by 160, but as fig. 8 shows, the sudden change to building

[32] Trajan, Boni 1907: 361–404. Hadrian, Platner & Ashby 1929: 336–8; Nash 1968: 44–8. Antoninus Pius and Marcus Aurelius, Hülsen 1889; Vaglieri 1907: 527–9; Mancini 1913; Platner & Ashby 1929: 545; Nash 1968: 487–9; Vogel 1973: 30. The identification of the structures as second-century *ustrina* is effectively destroyed by Boatwright (1985; 1987: 161–81). Second-century sarcophagus, Toynbee 1927. Fittschen (1979) accepts the identification of Balbinus' sarcophagus; Price (1987: 97, n. 81) queries this case too. Audin 1960.

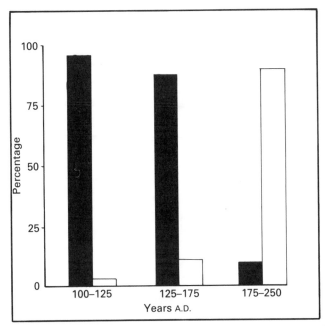

8. Proportions of spaces in new tombs at the Isola Sacra cemetery, Ostia,
allotted for cremations (solid bars) and inhumations (hollow bars), A.D. 100–250
(data from Calza 1940)

tombs primarily or solely for inhumations only came in the 170s. In
the Vatican cemetery (fig. 9), tomb D was designed solely for urns;
tomb B almost solely for them; and tombs C and E very largely for
them. Tombs A–E probably date *c.* 125–60. Most of the later tombs
were built for both rites. By the time we get to tomb Φ, inhumations outnumber cremations, and in tombs Q and z there were
probably no cremations. Five tiles used in tomb Q bore stamps we
can date to 147–61, suggesting a date for the tomb in the 150s or
160s. Φ and z must be later than A–E, and perhaps belong in the
170s, as does F (fig. 10). In area P several early inhumations in tile
graves were found. Gr. θ included a stamped tile dated 115–23,
although the grave itself could of course be much later. The most
interesting case is gr. γ, which, from its position, must be earlier
than gr. θ (fig. 11). Toynbee and Ward-Perkins suggested that the
mosaic pavement sealing the area provides a *terminus ante quem* of
140–160 for both graves.[33]

[33] Ostia, Calza 1940; Baldassarre 1984; 1985; 1987. Vatican, Toynbee & Ward-Perkins
1956: 30, 32–4, 37, 41, 49, 51, 55, 61 n. 33, 72, 82; Mielsch & von Hesberg 1986.

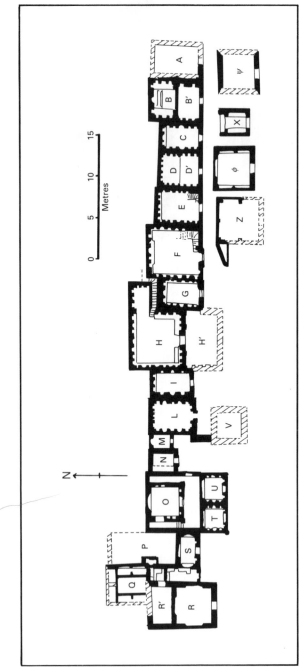

9. The cemetery under St Peter's on the Vatican hill, Rome (after Toynbee 1971: fig. 4)

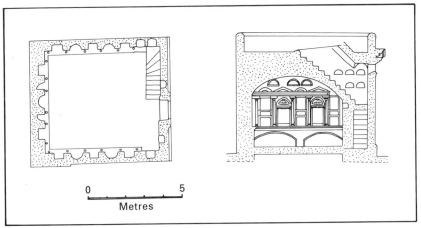

0   5

Metres

10. Mausoleum F in the Vatican cemetery, probably 160s A.D. Note the presence of niches for urns and beds for sarcophagi (after von Hesberg 1987a: fig. 11)

This could be evidence for the poor adopting the new rite before the rich, but it probably is not. Gr. γ, a child's burial, had an elaborate marker of tiles, bricks and marble, and the position of the graves, beneath the later shrine of St Peter, makes it possible that the buriers were indeed Christians following Jewish traditions. A simple shrine to St Peter was probably erected in area P around 170. As often happens, the best preserved evidence may be the least typical. But nothing is clear about this unique site. We are on firmer ground with a tomb at Ostia where inscriptions tell us that the dependants of a rich household continued to be cremated with their ashes placed in urns in the enclosure outside the tomb while their betters were inhumed within it.[34]

Rather than quibble over inadequate sources, we should simply say that in a very short space of time – perhaps just two or three decades – the imperial household and the wealthy but less elevated folk who were buried on the Vatican hill and at Ostia (the inscriptions name no Roman magistrates) went over to inhumation. Given the high status of Greek culture among the Roman elite in the second century, and the philhellenism of emperors like Hadrian and Marcus Aurelius (who even wrote his *Meditations* in Greek), conscious borrowing from the East seems very likely, whether

[34] Vatican tile graves, Toynbee & Ward-Perkins 1956: 142–53; Kirschbaum 1959: 102–19. Shrine, Kirschbaum 1959: 63–94. Ostia, Calza 1928: 147.

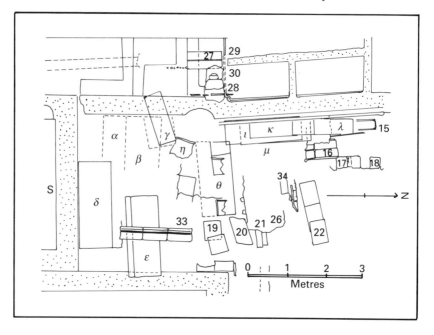

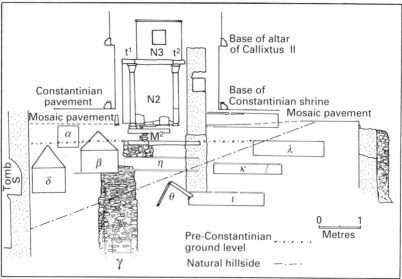

11. Area P of the Vatican cemetery (a) in plan (after Kirschbaum 1959: fig. 20) and (b) in section (after Toynbee & Ward-Perkins 1956: fig. 12). Note the lack of stratigraphic recording, which greatly complicates attempts to interpret the burials

begun by the emperors themselves or by Hellenised nobles, comfortable in the knowledge that the ruler would view their actions with approval. No excavation will ever prove or disprove either view, but perhaps it does not matter so much. The origins of the custom are less interesting than its functions. The imperial household defined and circumscribed symbols and competition. By, say, 200, anyone still cremating at Rome would probably have been seen as distinctly odd – or dangerous. Inhumation was one more symbol to be used by the elite in positioning themselves within imperial culture.

The most obvious impact of the new rite on the structure of the ritual system was that tombs could not hold as many inhumations as cremations. At Ostia, the average number of receptacles for burials per tomb declined from 15.1 (*c.* 100–25) to 14.4 (125–75) to just 8.5 (175–250). A tomb built after 175 would inevitably emphasise a narrower kin or professional group than previously. Some believe that there were important changes in upper-class ideas of the family in this period, but this is questionable (see p. 160 below), and in any case the two phenomena could not be linked in any significant way. It would have taken a decade or two for the new tombs to be filled; and already by 200 new tomb types were emerging, particularly catacombs, which allowed more inhumations to be placed together, preserving the older cemetery structure. Contrary to popular belief, the catacombs were not originally a Christian phenomenon, and Pergola points out that in their first phase, *c.* 200–325, catacombs did much the same job as the earlier *columbaria*, even down to having chambers for privileged burials, corresponding to the earlier central niches for special urns (see pp. 169–71 below).[35]

The pattern established under Augustus continued uninterrupted, and the change from cremation to inhumation at Rome must, I think, be seen as one purely of form. In this I agree with Nock, but I find it a much more interesting conclusion than he did. I suggested earlier that although embalming in the USA and cremation in Britain say much the same things about the person being buried, the distribution of the formal symbols tells us a great deal

[35] Ostia statistics based on Calza 1940. Family changes, Veyne 1978, followed by P. Brown 1987: 239–46 and challenged by Saller & Shaw 1984: 134–6; Shaw 1984: 483–3. Catacombs and *columbaria*, Pergola 1986: 185; cf. Pergola 1983; St-Roch 1981; 1983; 1986; Nicolai 1986.

about the nation-state structure of the modern world. The same sort of perspective applies to the Roman empire, where the spread of the rite can provide detailed evidence on how people described their relationship to the centre. Emperors encouraged emulation of Rome, and provincial elites regularly seized on imperial images and reused them. Arguments about whether inhumation spread because of new religions, new philosophies or new fashions are really only about the mechanisms by which symbols were disseminated. The interest of the changes lies in the reinterpretation of centrally defined symbols within local ritual systems.[36]

But once we get outside Italy, two serious problems appear. First, chronology. It took time for inhumation to spread across the West, but just how much? It makes a big difference: much of the West was convulsed by invasions, civil wars and economic problems in the third century, and we need to relate changes in rituals to these events. Italian tombs can be closely dated by architecture, painting and tile-stamps, but in the provinces we have to rely more on grave goods, particularly coins. Even the least spectacular cremations often have a datable urn; but inhumation graves may be completely empty. Unless fixed stratigraphically they may float around in time, and are often lumped together into the fourth century, more out of desperation than anything else. This is very inconvenient. In northern Gaul we can see that inhumation first caught on at the main cities, only spreading into the countryside after 250; in Britain there is no town/country divide, but Jones points out that this may be just a result of poor dating.[37]

Second, sampling. Rome probably produced fifteen times as many corpses each year as did even a major western city like Lyon, but it is much harder to get good samples spanning long periods from the provincial cities. The Italian custom of using one tomb for several generations was very space-intensive, and a large excavation can provide a decent number of burials from both the cremating and inhuming periods (see, for example, fig. 6 on p. 45 above). Where individual graves were normal, as in the West, cemeteries simply took up a lot more space, and if excavation has been restricted to

---

[36] Ruler cult in the West, Smadja 1985; Fishwick 1978; 1988. In the East, Price, 1984: 53–77. See also R. R. R. Smith 1987; 1988a; 1988b.

[37] Problems in dating fourth- to eighth-century graves, Rahtz 1968; 1977; Wilson 1968. Gallic inhumation, van Doorselaer 1967: map 6. Town and country in Britain, R. F. J. Jones 1981: 16.

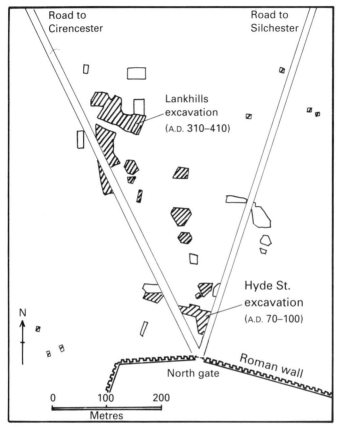

12. The growth of the North Cemetery at Winchester. The Hyde Street
excavation found graves dated mainly *c*. A.D. 70–100; Lankhills dates *c*. A.D. 310–
410. Hatched areas represent finds of graves (after Clarke 1979: fig. 2)

just one area our samples may have chronological biases. The extensive excavations in the cemeteries at Winchester over the last century (fig. 12) illustrate the spatial problem. At some sites we hit
early Roman cremations, and at others late Roman inhumations;
but simply throwing all the finds from different locations together to
contrast 'the' cremating pattern and 'the' inhuming pattern would
lose the very evidence of local variations which we are looking for.

We are left with two useful types of cemeteries: those few cities
where there has been large-scale digging, and rural sites with small
cemeteries. Some of the urban cemeteries suggest that the coming
of inhumation was part of a wider set of changes in burial rituals

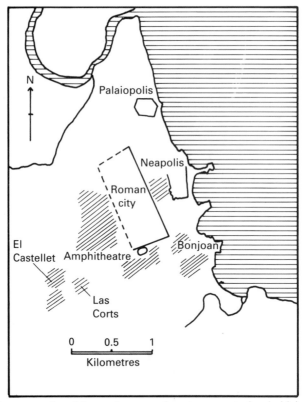

13. The cemeteries of Ampurias, second century B.C. to (probably) seventh century A.D. (after R. F. J. Jones 1984b: fig. 1)

than was the case at Rome. At Ampurias in north-east Spain, for example, Jones' cluster analyses show a distinct contrast between the first-century A.D. cremations, where relatively undifferentiated graves are grouped around nuclei of richer and more complex burials, and the later inhumations, which are uniformly poor, with almost no variation except for the tower tomb in the El Castellet cemetery (fig. 13). This is interesting; the excavator placed this group in the third century, which might suggest a sudden equalisation of display with the coming of inhumation, followed by a further gradual decline over the next few centuries.[38]

Could this be part of a new kind of social structure? It is certainly

---

[38] Cluster analyses, R. F. J. Jones 1984b. On tower tombs, see Toynbee 1971: 164–72. Interpretation, Almagro 1955: 289–94.

possible; some historians see legal distinctions between different groups among the poor, which had been of considerable significance earlier, declining in the third century. In 212 Caracalla extended citizenship to the whole free-born male population of the empire, which provides a convenient indicator that the old status system was disappearing (see also pp. 168–9 below). A new legal distinction began to emerge in the mid-to-late second century between the *honestiores*, a privileged group, and a rather homogeneous lower order of *humiliores*. A 'dual-penalty system' exposed the *humilior* to harsher sentences than the *honestior*, as well as to flogging, torture and inequality in access to legal processes. Another late second-century phenomenon, the decline of the class of well-off provincial burghers, the *decuriones*, also reached alarming proportions by 250. Such men had to be compelled to shoulder a ruinous burden of taxation and compulsory public services. The largest single entry in the Theodosian legal code is section XII.1, 'On *decuriones*', containing 192 provisions dating from 332 onwards. During this period the very rich became even richer and the poor got much poorer. There is further evidence for the third century as a time of momentous change in ritual activity, with a massive decline in erecting both inscriptions (see ch. 6) and monumental buildings, and of major artistic developments.[39]

But when we come back from grand constructs to Ampurias, there are difficulties. The El Castellet graves could be as late as the fifth century, and most of the other groups of inhumations cannot be pinned down between 200 and 600. Ballesta inhumation gr. 2 contained a coin dated 140–3 and Bonjoan inhumation gr. 3 a second-century coin, but both were badly worn from long use, and the graves themselves are probably much later. Although Ampurias has been under excavation for decades (it even has its own journal), sampling is still problematic. The settlement has not been thoroughly explored. The city may have been abandoned in the second and third centuries, only to be resettled in the fourth, in which case contrasts between the cremations and inhumations are not very helpful.[40]

---

[39] See A. H. M. Jones 1964: 724–63; Ste Croix 1981: 456–74; Alföldy 1985: 157–85; and especially Garnsey 1970; 1974. On *decuriones*, cf. MacMullen 1988: 44–51. Buildings and inscriptions, Mrozek 1984; Jouffroy 1986.

[40] Chronology, R. F. J. Jones 1984b: 243. Graves with coins, Almagro 1955: 90, 281. Jones (1984b: 239) assumes from the coins that inhumation had begun here by 150, but the degree of wear on the coins seems to me to suggest a later date.

A number of other sites reveal a similar decline in variation when inhumation appears, but they have their own problems. At Chichester and Baldock, for example, we are dealing with a tiny number of third-century inhumations in areas of the cemeteries which had had their main use in the late first century. The fact that these inhumations were made in an old and all but disused part of the cemetery, at a time when the vast majority of burials were taking place elsewhere, suggests that there may be something special about these graves. After all, there had to be a reason for burying these people away from everyone else; and it may be a mistake to draw conclusions from comparing 'normal' first-century graves with 'abnormal' third-century ones.[41]

We are on firmer ground with small cemeteries for farms or hamlets, though few have been studied. At Owslebury, the inhumations are much more complex and differentiated than the cremations. Collis (1977b: 34) argued that a wider range of status distinctions was appearing, with 'a single "rich" family, and a lower class of labourers or slaves' living there. The latest urn was made in the reign of Hadrian (117–38), and stratigraphic evidence placed one inhumation no later than the third century and another no later than the fourth. Collis put the transition in the second century, but it could easily be a century later, as at Lynch Farm and Bradley Hill. It is tempting to suggest that urban and rural cemeteries were developing differently in late Roman Britain, but the evidence is complicated, and I will return to it in the next chapter.[42]

Different parts of the empire had very different experiences of the 'third-century crisis', and not surprisingly we can document a wide range of processes. At Tournai, for example, excavations since the 1960s have produced large samples, and inhumation rituals were just as varied as the earlier cremations; while at Gerulata Rusovce there is actually an increase in differentiation. Here all the coins dated either to the early second century (all from cremations) or the early to mid-fourth century (all from inhumations). The excavator saw a break in the cemetery in the third century, followed by a new group of people arriving, bringing inhumation with them.

---

[41] Chichester, Down & Rule 1971 (9 inhumations and 317 cremations); Baldock, Westell 1931 (about 15 inhumations and over 300 cremations).

[42] Dating, Collis 1977b: 26. Lynch Farm, R. F. J. Jones 1975. Bradley Hill, Leech 1981. More generally R. F. J. Jones 1987.

Clarke has challenged this, pointing out that only 22 of the 155 graves contained coins at all, and that there are other indications of continuity. If he is right, then we have a clear case of the change in rites being part of a larger ritual transformation. The use of oil lamps as grave goods is particularly striking: 34 of the 84 cremations held at least one lamp, while none was found in the 71 inhumations.[43]

At other sites (e.g. Curroux, large parts of the Rhône valley), though, there may indeed be a gap between the latest cremations and the earliest inhumations. Historians working from aerial photographs have suggested that in these turbulent times many of the sites were temporarily abandoned. At best, this would make the transition between rites difficult to excavate; at worst, sites could be reoccupied by entirely new populations, including Germanic invaders coming from a different ritual tradition.[44]

Sampling problems may account for some of the variation from place to place; in the huge cemetery at Poundbury, we can see an early phase of inhumations which is characterised by variation in alignment, grave forms and wealth of grave goods, followed in the fourth century by a uniform East–West alignment and extreme evenness and scarcity of offerings.[45] A smaller dig might find only one phase, leading us to interpret a chronological pattern as spatial variability. However, this is clearly not the case at some sites, as we will see in more detail in chapter 3.

The switch from cremation to inhumation is, at the highest level of generality, a diffusion from the Greek East to the Latin West, but that tells us little. The crucial point is that the new rite was first taken up by the top circles in Rome: after that its Hellenistic or Asiatic connotations probably faded into the background for all but an educated few. It was the Roman, not the Greek custom by the time it reached Tournai or York. I argued that within the Italian burying pattern, at sites like Aquileia as much as at Rome, the change-over was a matter of competitive emulation, with the mighty jumping to copy the emperors (or possibly the reverse), and

---

[43] Different responses to third-century crisis, King & Henig, eds., 1981; MacMullen 1988: 15–35. Tournai, Hubert 1963; Mertens & Remy 1972; Dumas 1975; Brulet & Coulon 1977. Gerulata Rusovce, Kraskovská 1976, with Clarke 1978.

[44] Curroux, Martin-Kilcher 1976. Rhône valley, R. F. J. Jones 1977. Aerial photography, Agache 1975. Germanic invaders, Agache & Agache 1978: 156.

[45] Green 1977; 1982, giving Christianity as the explanation for the later pattern.

the rest of the population following suit within a couple of generations. Outside Italy there are chronological problems, but inhumation clearly took some time to spread. Cremation was still dominant in many places in the 230s, when the 'third-century crisis' is
normally said to begin. By the end of this period, fixed in political
terms by Diocletian's accession in 284, inhumation was far more
common. The new rite thus became involved, outside Italy, in a set
of complex processes which differed enormously from place to
place. Some areas were unaffected; other communities were destroyed or settled by invaders, while others still did rather well out
of supplying the army. It is no surprise that inhumation often
appears as part of a large-scale change in rites, nor that the direction of the changes varied so much. Thorough empirical analysis of
the way these changes worked will add enormously to our understanding of the third century.

But some empire-wide generalisations are also possible. The dis-
solution of the East/West burning/burying boundary created for
the first time a real *mos Romanus*. This is important. The third
century was a time of powerful centrifugal forces. Empires of the
Gauls and Palmyrenes broke away, barbarians breached the frontiers, and economic systems became more regional and self-suf-
ficient. Yet as the empire seemed to fall to bits – the ancient authors
agree on this, if little else – a new ritual united it.[46]

It may be overreading the evidence to say that people con-
sciously sought to create in their rituals a social structure which
provided a cohesiveness which the real world could no longer offer;
but this certainly was a *consequence* of the shift. There was a homogenisation of Roman culture, tying the world together in a time of
crisis. From York to Petra, the forms of disposal of the dead spoke
of a system more perfect in its universality than even Aristides' ideal
Rome, although the details of the rituals divided communities from
each other and within themselves, with Roman models being
remade to suit local needs. And for all the weaknesses of theories
which make Christianity the prime mover, it can hardly be denied
that this ritual unity and its fortuitous overlap with the Jewish
customs which the Christians favoured must have aided the spread
of the new faith.

[46] Contemporary views, Alföldy 1974; de Blois 1984.

CONCLUSION

Huntington and Metcalf close their impressive book *Celebrations of Death* with a bold claim: 'The vitality of a culture or ideology', they assert, 'depends upon its ability to channel the power of such mordant symbols as the corpse' (1979: 211). But natural symbol or not, the importance of the treatment of the body can only be interpreted by seeing it in its context. To do this properly for the Roman empire would require a whole book, but I hope I have made clear the need for and the potential of large-scale empirical analyses by investigators who are aware of historical problems. The current tendency for archaeologists to write dry-as-dust monographs on tomb architecture and for historians to dip into the evidence in a bits-and-pieces manner to illustrate other theories helps no one.

This is just one example, albeit the most striking one, of this kind of problem. There are plenty of others. I could have looked at how and why the Egyptian upper classes used mummification with such consistency throughout antiquity; or why a few places, like Athens or the Crimea, changed disposal types so often; or why the Greek world generally went over from multiple to individual burial around 1100 B.C. This is a particularly interesting case, since simplistic theories that collective tombs went out of use because of invasions, the re-emergence of a 'Minyan' consciousness or just the unsettled conditions of the times can now be evaluated against a series of detailed studies of the reuse of earlier tombs, the declining size of new tombs and the piecemeal introduction of cremation after 1200.[47]

Disposal of the body, then, can only be treated in the light of other kinds of evidence from the burials; and the other evidence from the burials can only be treated in the light of the way the body is disposed of, as will become clear in the next chapter.

[47] See Paidoussis & Sbarounis 1975; Cavanagh and Mee 1978; 1990; Mee & Cavanagh 1984; Cavanagh 1987.

CHAPTER 3

'Dem bones': skeletal remains

For the layman it may seem almost incredible that so full a picture can be built up on so slight a foundation, but modern methods of laboratory research now enable archaeologists to speak with an assurance that would have astonished their predecessors. Lack of space prevents us from describing the complicated and laborious methods of enquiry employed by the Professors and we can only summarise their conclusions. The occupant of the grave was, it appears, a local chieftain, middle-aged, five foot seven in height and markedly dolichocephalic. He was married, but not happy in his home life, suffered from stomach ulcers and an impacted wisdom tooth and died as a result of a sharp blow over the left ear. He had probably fallen on his head as a child and was certainly devoted to his dog, a cross-bred mastiff eight hands in height with a badly damaged tail...[1]

This chieftain of the Draynflete Culture, the Via Hernia and Professors Spiggot and Hackenbacker were all products of Osbert Lancaster's wicked sense of humour, but truth, as they say, is stranger than fiction. On 1 August 1984 the appropriately named Andy Mould pulled from a bog in Cheshire a 2000-year-old foot. The police handed the matter over to the archaeologists. Five days later a complete body, now known as Pete Marsh or Lindow Man, was in their hands. How would Lancaster have reacted to the news that one day in March or April in the first century A.D. this tormented soul was stunned by two blows to the head, stabbed in the chest, garrotted and had his throat cut? That he was about five foot seven (like the Draynflete chief), had shaved with shears a few days before his ritual murder, and had neatly manicured fingernails? That he was infested by whipworm and maw worm, but was not in any discomfort? Or that his last food was probably a small snack of

[1] Lancaster 1984: 88.

burned bread? The bog man gives antiquity almost too much immediacy.[2]

The 'bits-and-pieces' paradigm is nowhere more apparent than here. The bog bodies on the north-west fringe of the classical world and the mummies on the south-east bring out the worst in historians. Some claim that Pete Marsh is an example of a Germanic practice described by Tacitus around A.D. 100 (*Germ.* 12) where 'cowards, shirkers and sodomites are pressed down under a wicker hurdle into the slimy mud of a bog'. Others link the mistletoe pollen in his gut to the Druids. Both claims could well be right, but they trivialise the archaeological record, giving us nothing more than illustrations for the seedier stories in the ancient literature. And it is not just the well-preserved bodies which get this treatment. Vast numbers of skeletons have been excavated, but it is tales from the dark side which get prominence – human sacrifice and baby-eating in Minoan Crete, and skull cults in Dark Age Argos and Roman Britain.[3]

This is certainly good stuff, but catalogues of quirks and oddities do not get us very far. Once again, the key lies in the systematic study of large samples, armed with sensitivity to ritual context and the formation processes behind the archaeological record. Skeletons can be sexed and aged; we can examine their deformities, diseases and diet. But evidence for demography, pathology and nutrition does not reach us in neat, discrete packages. We only have the ancient bodies because, like most things dug up in graves, someone chose to put them there as part of a funeral. Wide-eyed faith in the wonders of science must not blind us to the transforming power of ritual. Sometimes this is obvious. We cannot know as much about demography or disease in the western Roman empire before A.D. 250 as after, because cremation preserves less evidence. Similarly, if we wrote demographic history using the skeletons recovered from the Kaiadas, a gorge into which the Spartans used to throw Messenian prisoners and various criminals,[4] it would be

---

[2] Brothwell 1986. Date, Gowlett et al. 1989.
[3] Tacitus, bog men and Druids, Ross & Robins 1989. Greece, Wall et al. 1986; Sakellarakis & Sapouna-Sakellaraki 1981; Charles 1965: 67–9. England, Clarke 1979: 372–5; C. Wells 1981; Harman et al. 1981.
[4] Potential of cremations, McKinley 1989. Kaiadas, Thuc. 1.134; Strabo 8.5.7; Paus. 4.17.10–24.3. Themelis 1982; Pritchett 1985a: 58–60. I thank John Lenz for drawing my attention to this site.

very misleading. But ritual also affects the evidence in more subtle ways. As usual, this is both good and bad. Attempts to write a real history from below are hampered by the way rituals only preserve certain kinds of evidence; but sometimes osteology can help us see or explain patterns in ritual behaviour which were otherwise hidden, throwing crucial light on social structure. The last remains of the ancients themselves tell us less about the 'realities' of life and death and more about the buriers' ideas of the world than we might expect.

PALAEODEMOGRAPHY

Age

The inadequacy of the written evidence for the age structures of antiquity is well known. The richest source is Roman epitaphs, but even these are unreliable (see pp. 158–64 below). As a result, historians have turned to life tables compiled for recent non-industrial societies, on the assumption that these might offer good analogies for ancient populations. But there are strict limits on what can be done with this material. Life tables assume a static population: that is, that birth and death rates balance each other exactly, with no immigration, emigration, population increase or decline. No real population ever fits these conditions, and so using a life table involves us in a certain amount of abstraction. In some cases, texts allow us to limit the range of life tables which would be appropriate for our data. For example, the life table with the 'best fit' for Late Republican Rome, where population grew rapidly through immigration and where appalling conditions must have created a mortality rate much higher than the birth rate, would not be the same as that for Hellenistic Boeotia, where population was declining. But even so, a good deal of guesswork would be involved in selecting the best analogy, and most of the time we are dealing with ancient populations about which we can make even fewer limiting assumptions. Consequently, we can only use modern life tables for ancient demography if we are prepared to work at a high level of generality, and not attempt to make fine distinctions between regions or through time.[5]

---

[5] Textual sources: Greece, Grmek 1989: 105–7; R. Garland 1990: 245–8. Rome, Hopkins 1966; 1987. Life tables, Weiss 1973; Coale & Demeney 1983. Conditions at Rome, Scobie 1986. Boeotia, Polyb. 36.17.7; Her. Cret. 1.25; Sallares 1991: 158–60.

Still, judicious application of life tables can have surprising results. For instance, starting from life tables, Saller has been able to shatter many fondly held illusions about the *patria potestas* and the structure of the Roman family, showing in computer simulations that very few Roman men would still have a father alive when they got married and started their own households.[6] He is careful not to make inferences which go beyond the legitimate level of abstraction, and that is what gives his arguments their force; but for a more detailed historical demography we have to turn to the skeletons themselves.

Bodies can be aged quite precisely up to about 25 years from teeth, and between 13 and 25 for girls and 15 and 25 for boys from the 'epiphyseal union', the fusion of cartilaginous areas at the ends of the long bones (figs. 14, 15). Older specimens are harder to age, and the reliability of one of the main techniques, examination of the pubic bone, has been seriously challenged by Bocquet-Appel and Masset. They claim that biases in compiling modern life tables have led to consistent errors in ageing adult skeletons. There have been angry responses, but some medievalists also feel that bone analysis produces average adult ages at death ten to fifteen years too young. Archaeologists respond that the medieval sources are as problematic as the bones, but, as Boddington (1987: 190) concedes, 'when the archaeological data is [sic] compared to the historical evidence the skeletal population has consistently higher mortality rates and the suspicion of under-ageing is hard to dispel'. The Caldwells even suggest that physical anthropologists and demographers have reinforced each others' untested assumptions to the point where few traces of reality can enter into the project. Buikstra warns us that 'Overstating the data base is tempting ... there is frequently pressure upon the osteologist to contribute information concerning demographic parameters ... qualifications are lost as the general models develop and error is compounded as higher levels of inference are reached' (1981: 123).[7]

---

[6] Computer simulations, Saller 1987. *Patria potestas*, Saller 1986; 1988; Garnsey & Saller 1987: 136–41.

[7] Ageing techniques, Ubelaker 1984; Workshop of European Anthropologists 1980; Brothwell 1981: 64–73; Condon et al. 1986; Hillson 1986: 188–201; 1989: 131–2; Samson & Branigan 1987; Cruwys 1989. Criticisms, Bocquet-Appel & Masset 1982. Responses, van Gerven & Armelagos 1983; Buikstra & Konigsberg 1985. On the os pubis, Katz & Suchey 1986. Medievalists, Cayton 1980; Molleson 1981. Problems of life tables, Sattenspiel & Harpending 1983; Boddington 1987; Horowitz et al. 1988; Caldwell et al. 1987.

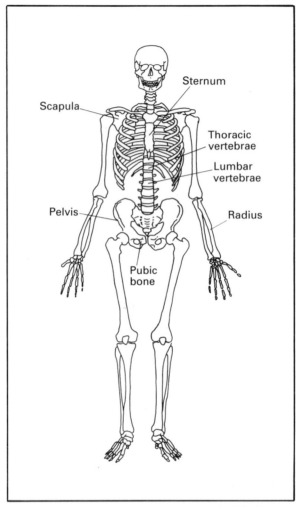

14. Parts of the human skeleton discussed in this chapter

Differential preservation of bones is another obvious problem. The remains of children and the very old decay more rapidly than those of young adults. Powell, in a study of the Moundville site in Alabama, claims that smoothing the data and simplifying the figures for those dying at under one or over fifty years produce usable life tables, but others are less sanguine. Angel, for half a century the leading figure in the physical anthropology of ancient

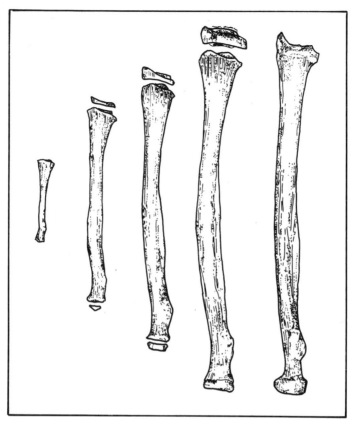

15. Stages of epiphyseal union in the left radius (see fig. 14) from birth to adulthood (after Stirland 1989: fig. 2)

Greece, took a pragmatic line and abandoned life tables and life expectancy at birth as useful statistics, concentrating instead on the average adult age at death (table 4). His data revealed that the average adult age at death rose fairly steadily from 33.6 for men and 29.8 for women in Early Neolithic times to 44.1 for men and 36.8 for women in the classical period, thereafter declining again to 38.8 for men and 34.2 for women by the second century A.D. He also identified a decline in child mortality. In the Mycenaean cemeteries at Lerna, the ratio of infant (0–5 years) to child (5–15) and adult (over 15) burials is 8:5:10; in fourth-century B.C. Olynthus, it improves to 5:3:10. Since all the observations on age at death were

Table 4. Skeletal data from Greece, c. 6000 B.C.–A.D. 600 (after Bisel & Angel 1985: table 4)

	Average adult age at death		Number of diseased teeth per mouth*	Frequency of teeth with enamel hypoplasia	Frequency of vertebral arthritis	Frequency of porotic hyperostosis
	Female	Male				
Imperial Roman	34.2 n = 51	38.8 n = 79	6.1 n = 91	17.9% n = 39	61% n = 36	25% n = 100
Hellenistic	38.0 n = 50	41.9 n = 103	5.2 n = 114	18.8% n = 85	62% n = 40	13% n = 158
Classical	36.8 n = 84	44.1 n = 146	4.1 n = 138	37.9% n = 103	76% n = 71	6% n = 151
Early Iron Age	30.9 n = 90	39.0 n = 105	6.8 n = 106	36.1% n = 83	52% n = 79	7% n = 114
Late Bronze Age	32.6 n = 120	39.6 n = 182	6.7 n = 134	38.6% n = 71	63% n = 79	9% n = 215
Shaft graves (c. 1600 B.C.)	36.1 n = 5	35.9 n = 22	1.2 n = 20	40% n = 20	59% n = 17	—
Middle Bronze Age	31.4 n = 94	36.7 n = 107	6.1 n = 123	52.8% n = 108	65% n = 106	12% n = 169
Early Bronze Age	29.4 n = 206	33.6 n = 184	5.0 n = 202	9.9% n = 111	69% n = 144	12% n = 332
Late Neolithic	29.2 n = 43	33.1 n = 31	2.6 n = 36	23.8% n = 21	45% n = 22	21% n = 63
Early Neolithic	29.8 n = 157	33.6 n = 106	3.5 n = 105	11.1% n = 90	65% n = 66	43% n = 165

* Number of teeth lost or showing caries or abscess. Corrected for loss of alveoli in ground and to age forty, following the method outlined by Angel (1974)

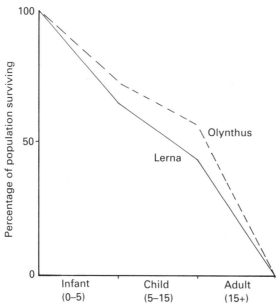

16. Mortality curves for Lerna and Olynthus, plotted by age categories (note that the average age at death for adults was higher at Olynthus than at Lerna)

made by a single scientist, the overall pattern has value, although other anthropologists might not reach exactly the same conclusions on the absolute figures for lifespans. But his demographic profiles for Lerna and Olynthus (fig. 16) are more problematic. The curves would change dramatically if we were to discover cemeteries reserved for specific age groups at either site; or if we learned that the Mycenaeans at Lerna often disposed of the elderly without formal burial; or that the Olynthians treated many infants with equal disregard. Some of these possibilities may be dismissed as unlikely, and the literary sources for fourth-century Greece give us some control at Olynthus, but we cannot pretend to know local customs in any detail. The strongest argument in favour of accepting fig. 16 as representing the actual population is simply that *it makes sense*. Both mortality patterns can be accommodated to our expectations based on modern life tables; in the absence of evidence to the contrary we can afford the luxury of assuming that the fit between the archaeological record and mortality patterns is quite

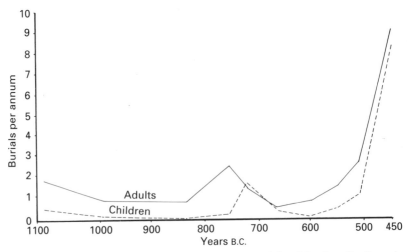

17. Adult and child burials at Athens, 1100–400 B.C. (after Morris 1987: fig. 22)

good at both these sites, although the sort of demography this produces is hardly very satisfying.[8]

But what if the age structure does not make sense? This is when palaeodemography really comes into its own. Fig. 17 shows the frequency of adult and child graves at Athens from 1125 to 400 B.C. In the fifth century, the adult:child ratio is roughly 1:1, which is what modern data lead us to expect for an ancient population. In the Kerameikos cemetery at Athens, 510 of the 1,009 published fifth-century graves belong to youths or adults and 445 to infants or children, with 54 unclear cases. So, when we see from fig. 17 that 90–95% of the excavated burials dated *c.*925–725 are adults, diverging massively from all pre-modern analogies, our suspicions should be aroused. Explaining the small number of children in this period as a result of bone decay is not enough, because when infant numbers suddenly increase to about 53% of the total in 725–700, they are mainly buried in what had previously been adult-only cemeteries. There is no reason to suppose that the soil suddenly began to be kinder to small bones after 725. Nor does sampling

[8] Differential preservation, Walker et al. 1988; Moore et al. 1975. Moundsville, Powell 1988: 89–103. Ages at death, Angel 1972. Greek data, Angel 1945; 1971; Grmek 1989: 99–105. Angel's attempt to quantify fecundity from scars on the pubic symphysis (1939; 1969: 432) is open to serious doubt (Ullrich 1975; Hermann & Bergfelder 1978). The scanty literary evidence is reviewed by R. Garland (1990: 98–9).

error – a consistent failure to locate cemeteries of child graves of the same type as the few that have been found – seem valid, in view of the dense and fairly random pattern of excavations at Athens. Putting the pattern in geographical perspective helps to rule out this possibility: in cemeteries in the Athenian countryside and at Argos, where burial customs were very different, child burials are also very rare down to 725, then suddenly proliferate, leaping from 8% of the total to 59% in Attica and from 12% to 43% at Argos.[9]

In *Burial and Ancient Society* I argued from these observations that treating fig. 17 as evidence for a rapid population growth in the eighth century – at a rate of 4% per annum, which is about as fast as human populations have ever been known to grow – would be a mistake, and that the eighth-century increase in burials was caused partly by changes in burial customs for children. This means that a larger proportion of child graves are known from after *c.* 725 than from before, when they are seriously under-represented. But recently Sallares has tried to rescue the demographic significance of this evidence, suggesting that the pattern does make sense after all. He points out that if an agrarian population grows, it is usually because the birth rate has increased, rather than because people are living longer. He observes that

If a population starts to grow rapidly, the number of adults does eventually increase, but the numbers of infants and juveniles increase much more rapidly, leading to a much lower average age for the entire population, a much younger age distribution pattern, and a younger average age of death (not identical to life expectancy in a population which is not stationary) because infants, with their relatively high mortality rate, come to form a steadily larger proportion of the whole population. (Sallares 1991: 124)

Sallares gives an example of what this might mean for the archaeologist by drawing on one of the most widely used life tables. He sketches a scenario where before the spurt in population growth – say around 800 B.C. – infants and children might make up about 20% of the living population, contributing some 36% of the group's total mortalities. During the period of expansion, *c.* 750 B.C., the birth rate would be higher. Now about 36% of the living population would be in the infant/child categories, providing roughly 68% of the burials. He concludes from this that fig. 17 really does

[9] Morris 1987: 57–62, 101–4, 182–5, 218–21. Pattern of excavation, ibid.: fig. 31.

represent the mortality rates of a population undergoing rapid expansion. However, the evidence does not bear out the increase in child mortality which he proposes on the basis of modern analogies. There are two serious flaws in the argument. The first is comparative: no amount of juggling with life tables can obscure the fact that a 200-year period when infant and child mortality combined never rose above 5–10% is absolutely unparalleled in world history. Such a low rate was first recorded in Sweden after 1900, and Sallares' claim that 'Attica may well have been a healthier place to live in in the earlier period' (1991: 124) than it was in the late eighth century does not alter this. The second problem is empirical, and more damaging: the changes shown in fig. 17 simply do not follow the pattern he suggests. Sallares expects to see a sudden rise in the proportion of burials attributed to children, with numbers of adult deaths catching up later. What we see in the eighth century is precisely the opposite. In 750–725 (Late Geometric I) infants and children actually make up a smaller proportion of the burials (4.5%, compared to 91% for adults and 4.5% unknown) than at any other time. When child burials become common at the end of the eighth century (Late Geometric II) the number of adult burials is already falling, and it continues to decline until the middle of the seventh century.[10]

In the end, then, the 'demographic' trends of fig. 17 do not make comparative sense; no living population could behave in this way. Sallares' argument is a good example of the dangers of the bits-and-pieces approach to burial. By not taking the full range of the evidence into account, he leaves no space for ritual action, and moves directly from excavation to demography. The only reasonable explanation of fig. 17 is that for two centuries the Athenians (and Argives) chose to dispose of dead children with rather little ceremony, in manners which left few easily discoverable material remains. Then, around 725, they changed their ways.

As always, such a conclusion has two implications. The first is negative. We cannot use the graves to document eighth-century population growth (although it did occur), because the rituals which created the burial record 'skewed' it in a fashion which

---

[10] Morris 1987: 57–62. The burials were first used to document population growth by Snodgrass (1977). Sallares (1991: 122–9) uses Coale & Demeney (1983) Model West mortality level 7 (female).

makes it all but useless for the demographer. But what we can do (the second, positive, implication) is to talk about the construction of age categories in death rituals, and why there was a set of major changes in the late eighth century. Before 725, the burial of dead children must have been a very casual matter. This is not to say that children's bodies were simply thrown away; their funerals constituted rites of passage into the next world, just as the funerals of Romans buried in the *puticuli* mentioned in chapter 2 would have done. It is just that they are much harder for the excavator to find because less care was taken over them. Some historians of early modern Europe argue that children were regarded as social 'non-persons', and that parents reacted to their deaths in a casual and detached way to reduce the psychological costs of living with high infant mortality. Plutarch, writing around A.D. 100, interpreted rituals in a similar way:

We neither bring offerings of drink to those who die in infancy nor do we do for them the things which it is customary to do for the dead; for they had no part in this world or in the things of this world; nor are we devoted to their graves and monuments, nor to the laying out of their bodies, nor do we sit by their bodies; for the laws do not allow us to mourn those of such an age. (Plut. *Mor.* 612A = *Cons. ad Ux.* 11)

But we must beware of making direct interpretations of energy expenditure in terms of emotional involvement. Golden argues that the kind of features of child burial which early modern historians see as indicating lack of concern could equally well be taken to show heightened psychological involvement with the young. Saying that parents started to care more about their children around 725 would probably be naïve, and although burial is the only source which even allows us to tackle this question directly, it has not so far proved possible to develop a satisfactory psychohistory.[11]

Sex

Just as there are problems in reconstructing ancient age structures, so too the most obvious use of the sex of skeletons, to quantify the

[11] Early modern attitudes, Stone 1977: 77–87; Pollack (1983) argues against the 'diminished involvement' theory. A group of interesting papers is collected in *Continuity & Change* 4:2 (1989), especially Burton 1989. Involvement in Athens, Golden 1988; 1990a: 80–100. For literary evidence on the category of the child in Greece, see R. Garland 1990: 59–121; Golden 1990a: 1–22. For the elderly, see Falkner & de Luce, eds., 1989. Psychological involvement, Stearns 1985; Cannon 1989. Problems of psychohistory of ancient Greek death, Morris 1989a: 297–9.

sex ratio (the number of males per 100 females), is fraught with dangers. There are some purely technical problems. Anthropologists achieve up to 95% accuracy in sexing adults from the pelvis, but this is not always preserved. The skull, spine, sternum, scapula and long bones can also be used, but they are much less reliable. Cremations are usually impossible to sex, and even well-preserved children may be unidentifiable. Often bodies are sexed by criteria such as 'heaviness of build', and systematic errors can result. Weiss suggests that a bias of up to 12% in favour of males is common, as a result of the greater ease of identifying male characteristics and the tendency of the lighter female skeletons to decompose more rapidly. The analysis of citrates in the bones may be more accurate than physical inspection, but so far it has not been used in classical archaeology.[12]

The sex structure has to be studied in much the same way as the age structure. We must begin with clearly defined assumptions about what we expect to find – in this case, a sex ratio somewhere in the area of 100; and if we find something radically different, we have to eliminate the possibility that it is the burial ritual which is causing the surprise before we go on to make extravagant claims about demography. Many historians think that in some periods female infanticide was one of the main ways Greeks and Romans controlled population growth. Sex ratios should provide the best possible evidence for this, but the utmost caution is needed before deploying them.[13]

The first-century A.D. cemetery at Qumran in Palestine is a good example. The main cemetery contained over 1,000 burials, all male. A few women and children were found around the perimeter. This is not the case at contemporary sites like Jericho and Jerusalem. An explanation is at hand: the Dead Sea scrolls led many historians to believe that Qumran was the home of the Essenes, who put great emphasis on male purity and the defilement caused by women. But such obliging texts are rare, and the explanation of imbalances is usually more difficult.[14]

---

[12] Brothwell 1981: 59–63; Workshop of European Anthropologists 1980; Bennike 1985. Bias, Weiss 1972. Citrate analysis, Dennison 1979.

[13] Infanticide is fiercely debated; see especially Engels (1980; 1984) against W. V. Harris (1980; 1982). Boswell (1988: 3–137), R. Garland (1990: 84–93), Golden (1990a: 86–8) and Sallares (1991: 151–4) are the most recent reviews.

[14] De Vaux 1973: 46–58; Bar-Adon 1977. Normal pattern, Hachlili & Killebrew 1983.

Rick Jones draws attention to the Roman cemetery at Trentholme Drive, York (A.D. 180–380; fig. 18). Here the sex ratio is 369, and the graves were cut into each other in a chaotic jumble. Jones points out that we find a sex ratio of 251 in the equally crowded and confused fourth-century Bath Gate cemetery at Cirencester (fig. 19). The plot thickens. York was a military base, as Cirencester was in the first century, and perhaps later too. Maybe these cemeteries were for the garrisons. If so, then even in the late empire a major symbolic distinction was being drawn between the army and the locals. This would be interesting, since soldiers' marriages with local women were legalised around 197 and most historians see a merging of the army and civilians in the third century, what MacMullen calls a 'change from an army of camps and forts to one based on walled cities' (1963: 130). However, the 'army cemetery' theory is not convincing. We should be wary of too direct interpretations of symbolism, but the disorganisation of the graves, their age structures and the absence of military-type grave goods all seem incompatible with Roman military traditions; and at Cirencester, only three out of 23 inscribed tombstones were for soldiers, and two of these in fact came from the Silchester Gate cemetery.[15]

Looking further afield, we also find high ratios at Cranborne Chase (258) and Frilford (260), but most interesting of all is the Lankhills cemetery at Winchester. Here 284 skeletons can be sexed, giving a ratio of 158. The imbalance is partly due to the more rapid decay of female bones (fig. 20); but the excavator also identifies changes through time in the sex ratio. In the area west of ditch 12 (fig. 21) there are 71 male, 61 female and 72 child graves. Clarke (1979: 126) suggests that the area was used mainly for men before A.D. 350, then mainly for women in 350–90. East of the ditch (mainly c. 390–410) we find a sex ratio of 410. Clarke argues that 'the cemetery was characterised by relatively short-lived groupings of graves, each appropriate to one or the other sex' (1979: 190).

---

[15] R. F. J. Jones 1987: 824–5. Trentholme Drive, Wenham 1968 (for the civilian nature of the cemetery, see p. 38, but cf. p. 147). Cirencester, McWhirr et al. 1982 (for a military interpretation, C. Wells 1982: 135). On both these sites, see R. F. J. Jones 1984c: 222–3. Herodian (3.8.5) dates the recognition of marriages around 197; by 349 it was taken for granted (*Cod. Th.* 7.1.3). Saller & Shaw (1984: 139–45) show that early imperial tombstones do suggest a strong separation between the army and the local population in Britain and Germany, but Shaw (1984: 472) argues for much greater integration after about 300. See p. 161 below.

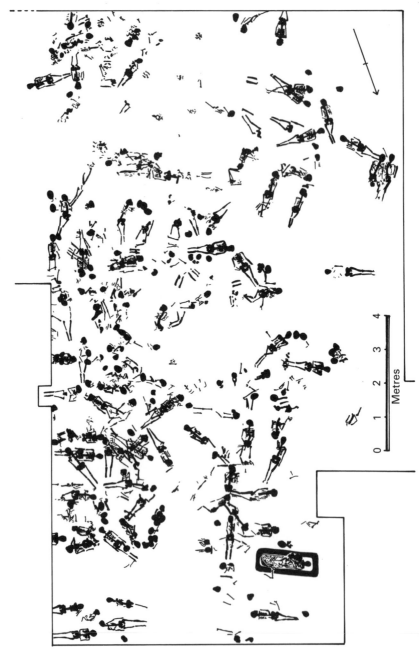

18. The Trentholme Drive cemetery at York (after Wenham 1968)

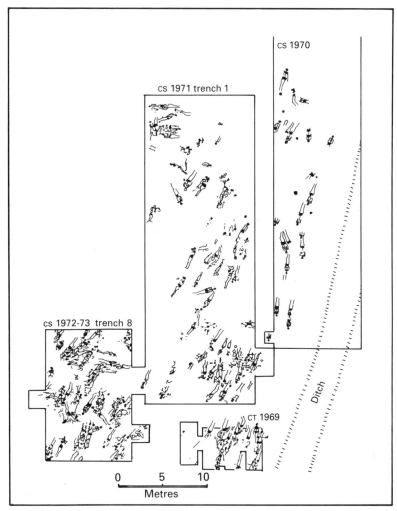

19. Areas CT 1969(b), CS 1970, 1971, 1972–3 trench 8 in the Amphitheatre
cemetery at Cirencester (after McWhirr et al. 1982: fig. 30)

These sex-specific groups later had burials of both sexes dug into
them, and children put around them, thus obscuring the patterns.[16]
Lankhills is less obviously chaotic than Trentholme Drive or

[16] Lankhills sex ratio, Clarke 1979: 123. Decay of bones, Clarke 1979: 137–8. Other cemeteries, Leech 1981: 195–205.

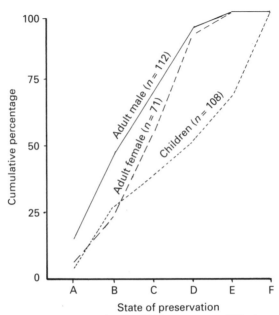

20. Differential bone decay in the Lankhills cemetery, Winchester (data from Clarke 1979: table 9). Categories of preservation: A: almost perfect; B: slight decomposition; C: smaller bones decayed; D: only major bones left; E: only skull and legs left; F: little or nothing left. Note the persistently higher male scores in A–C; the high child score in F (31%) is due to the fact that adults and children can be distinguished even from very scanty remains

Cirencester, but on closer inspection it fits the pattern well. Clarke shows how standards of burial declined in the late fourth century. Graves were shallower; shaft graves were no longer used; the corners of pits were dug more sloppily; wooden covers went out of use; wooden coffins declined in frequency (from 92 per cent of adults west of the ditch to 52 per cent east of it); and fewer bodies were carefully laid out in a supine position. He concludes:

It is difficult to avoid the conclusion that the organisation of burial was breaking down. Whatever had passed in the earlier fourth century for an undertaking business may now have been in rapid decline, so causing disorder and irregularity to permeate the whole cemetery. (Clarke 1979: 144)

We have another disorganised, male-dominated area, at least by 400. Clarke's claim that the cemetery was divided into single-sex

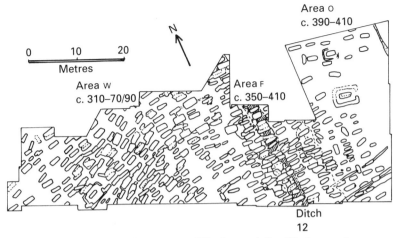

21. The Lankhills cemetery, Winchester (after Clarke 1979)

plots depends on his method of 'stratigraphic scores', and it may be that it is best seen as another part of the general British pattern. The same trend is visible at Poundbury, where the carefully aligned early fourth-century cemetery is disrupted later in the century by shallow pit graves and some cist graves, all without coffins.[17]

Shaw argues from epigraphy that there was a town/country distinction in the treatment of women in death across the western empire. We might identify an urban tradition of careless burial of men and even more careless burial of women versus a rural pattern of more deliberate burial (and higher recovery rates) of both sexes. At one rural site, Bradley Hill in Somerset, we get a more normal sex ratio of 91; but at rural Owslebury we have 13 male inhumations to just 2 female. Collis puts most of these graves in the second century, but as we saw on p. 66 above, they may be much later. He suggests that 'There are two obvious hypotheses: either the women were buried elsewhere, or there was a preponderance of men on the site' (1977b: 29). Putting the site into context, we have to go further and say that women were being buried in another fashion, which makes them hard to find.[18]

Chaotic fourth-century cemeteries also appear in Belgic Gaul at Tournai, Oudenburg and Tongres. Only Tournai has demographic

[17] Stratigraphic scores, Clarke 1979: 121. Poundbury, Green 1977: 50; 1982.
[18] Bradley Hill, Leech 1981. Epigraphy, Shaw 1991.

evidence, and here the sex ratio was just 108. In Brittany and the Rhineland, however, cemeteries are both more organised and have more even sex ratios. So, while disorganisation has some continental parallels, the sex imbalance is peculiarly British and peculiarly fourth-century. Soon after 400 we even find grave pits in what had been the Roman fora at Canterbury, Exeter and Lincoln, but by 450 a new phase was beginning with major changes in the spatial arrangement of settlements and cemeteries, more regular placement of graves (often on a North–South axis) and more balanced sex ratios.[19]

We are faced by new questions, not about demography but about social structure. In some late Roman communities, a mainly male group was buried hastily and informally, while women have largely escaped detection. Are these cemeteries for barbarian war parties? The two-century period of use of Trentholme Drive makes this unlikely, and the identification of 'intrusive' ethnic elements at Lankhills from grave goods and burial customs is not persuasive. The decline-and-fall overtones of this chaotic organisation might also be seen as evidence for ethnic intrusions, but as Esmonde Cleary points out, many of these cemeteries were laid out in the early fourth century as part of a suburban programme which suggests that central authorities were still functioning in the towns. Another catch-all late Roman explanation, the coming of Christianity, is no better. The scarcity of grave goods would then make sense, and the male bias could represent monks. However, the disturbance of earlier burials is difficult to reconcile with the desire to preserve the body for the day of Resurrection, and there is no reason to link random disposition of graves with Christianity; indeed, an East–West alignment of graves is often taken as an indicator of Christian belief. The second-century origin of Trentholme Drive is also too early. At Cirencester, there was a spatial division between the jumbled poor pit graves and cemeteries of stone or lead sarcophagi with rich grave goods. McWhirr suggested that the rich chose sarcophagi, and that these were used in a cemetery near the quarries. It is particularly interesting that there are twice as many women as men in the sarcophagi so far known,

---

[19] Disorderly cemeteries, Brulet & Coulon 1977: 49–50. King (1990: 202–3) gives more orderly examples. Sex ratios, Brulet & Coulon 1977: 4, 125–52; Buchet 1978. Fifth-century burials, Esmonde Cleary 1989: 150–2; Arnold 1984: 136; Hodges 1989: 25–9.

although the sample is very small. Further, none of these theories accounts for the contrast between the scarcity of women on urban sites and their good representation at Bradley Hill.[20]

There are heated debates over social continuity between Roman and Anglo-Saxon Britain. Traditionally, historians have argued that the Saxon invasions in the fifth century created barbarian kingdoms out of a Roman province; while revisionists suggest that a distinct 'sub-Roman' society can be identified fifty years before the first barbarian settlements. The burials have hardly begun to be exploited, but they seem to suggest that significant social changes were underway in Britain in the fourth century, and that by the mid-fifth a very new social structure had emerged.[21]

In recent years there has been an explosion of sophisticated research into literary and iconographic evidence for ancient gender categories, but the archaeological evidence from burial rituals – where roles were defined with particular clarity – has hardly been explored. All too often the way excavators have collected the evidence cuts off promising lines of inquiry. For instance, it has long been known that fifth-century B.C. Athenians used the same vase type, the loutrophoros (water-carrier), in both weddings and funerals; and that this shape was also used in marble in the fourth century for grave markers. The interrelations of the two kinds of rituals could be very important for our understanding of Athenian categories, but the dearth of demographic data makes the whole problem more complex than it needs to be. Kokula suggests that the loutrophoros-amphora was a 'male' shape and the loutrophoros-hydria was 'female', while Moesch uses exactly the same evidence to argue that the funerary meaning of the former was becoming stronger in the fifth century but its 'maleness' declined, while the loutrophoros-hydria became more strongly associated with both weddings and women. Notwithstanding such basic disagreements, Boardman makes the important point that both shapes belong to a tradition of sex-specific grave markers going back to the tenth century, consistently linking men with wine and women with water. The possibility of tracing the changes in such an underlying

---

[20] Lankhills, Clarke 1975; 1979: 377–99; Baldwin 1985. Cirencester, McWhirr 1982: 91. Suburban layout, Esmonde Cleary 1989: 80–1; cf. M. Millett 1990: 142. Anglo-Saxons, Arnold 1984: 131–7. Christianity, Leech 1981: 203–5; Merrifield 1987: 76–9.

[21] E.g. Alcock 1971; S. Haselgrove 1979; Arnold 1984; Brooks 1986; 1988; Esmonde Cleary 1989; M. Millett 1990: 212–30.

assumption across 600 years is fascinating. The relationships between gender and material culture as formed in the burial ritual
could be crucial, but the widespread practice of using grave goods
rather than bones to sex burials reduces such analyses to circularity, and in any case is often simply wrong, as Breitsprecher shows
in exploding the celebrated myth of sex-specific cemeteries in
Roman Germany.[22]

Kinship and race

In 1876, Schliemann breathlessly telegraphed from Mycenae to
Athens that he had gazed upon the face of Agamemnon; just six-
teen years later, a Danish civil servant thought he had found the
skull of Sophocles. In our own day, a brief century after Schliemann, we may be able to reconstruct the faces of Philip of Macedon
and King Midas. With this history of confident attributions, it is no
surprise that classical archaeologists try to use skeletal material as
evidence for racial and familial similarities.[23]

Inscribed grave stones begin in the seventh century B.C. Right
from the start they suggest that kinship was the main principle in
organising cemeteries and the grave plots within them, but by the
second century B.C. occupational groupings were coming into
fashion (see p. 186 below). Osteology could shed light on changing
structures of kinship as expressed in burial rituals. Skeletal pecu-
liarities can be transmitted genetically, and North American prehistorians have tried to reconstruct residential kin groups from
non-metrical cranial variation. Angel believed that he could show a
family likeness between the skeletons in a late eighth-century B.C.
grave plot in Athens, and it has been argued that a pair of late
Roman skeletons in a tomb in Corinth, both with spinal deformities, were brother and sister. A distinctive spinal deformity was also
observed in five out of a group of twelve Roman burials at Cambridge, suggesting close interbreeding. Interesting as these results

[22] Loutrophoroi, Kokula 1984; Moesch 1988; Boardman 1988d. Germany, Breitsprecher
1987; cf. Brush's (1988) and Henderson's (1989) similar conclusions about some Anglo-
Saxon cemeteries. Reece (1982), Baldwin (1985) and Dyson (forthcoming, ch. 7) lament
the poor treatment of Roman skeletal remains, although as Roberts (1986) makes clear,
this is common to all periods.
[23] Agamemnon, Deuel 1977: 228; von Burg 1987: 137. Sophocles, Grmek 1989: 65–7. Philip,
Prag et al. 1984; Prag 1990. Midas, Prag 1989.

are, their small scale raises two problems – first, they inspire little confidence; and second, because they are so small it is difficult for the social historian to do much with them.[24]

At one time identifying ethnic groups from skulls was all the rage, but the racist implications of this *Rassenkunde* have led to its eclipse. It is easy to distinguish major racial groups (e.g. Caucasian, Negroid, Mongoloid), but in classical archaeology that is rarely the issue. The difficulties arise from attempts to identify 'sub-races' to answer questions about the 'origins' of ancient peoples. The sharpest debates were over the Dorian invasion. Thirty years of disputes led to no secure conclusions about 'northern incursions'. Comparing the cranial measurements of specific excavated groups may work better, in spite of problems such as distorted skulls and the inability of different observers to see the same data. The excavators of the late Roman cemetery at Tokod calculated coefficients of similarity between the populations of different cemeteries in the region, showing that those with homogeneous assemblages of typically 'Roman' grave goods are indeed cranially more alike than other cemeteries which have new types or combinations of artefacts. At Frénouville, on the other hand, the bone report suggests that typical 'Saxon' grave goods need not mean a change in the local population.[25]

PALAEOPATHOLOGY

Pathology (even more than demography) quickly degenerates into lists of club-footed pharaohs and giant gallstones, at best illustrating points which are self-evident or already known from literary sources, at worst burying significant patterns in details. For instance, the tone of the fifth-century B.C. Hippocratic treatise *On Fractures* suggests that broken bones were common in Greece. We hardly need evidence to tell us that they occurred. Yet a bits-and-pieces approach to the skeletal evidence can be positively misleading. Warwick uses the frequency of fractures at Trentholme Drive –

[24] Kinship, Humphreys 1980; Fraser 1977: 58–60; Hopkins 1983: 212–27. Skeletal analyses, Angel 1939: 237–41; Gejvall & Henschen 1968; Fell 1956.
[25] Brothwell 1981: 107–8; Droessler 1981; Key 1983; Utermohle & Zagura 1982. Dorian debate, Breitinger 1939; Angel 1945; Charles 1958; 1963. Tokod, Mocsy, ed., 1981. Frénouville, Buchet 1978; Pilet 1980. Teeth are used as evidence for race by Sofaer et al. (1986); similar approaches are reviewed by Hillson 1986: 231–58.

21 out of 342 individuals (6%), all of them male – to argue that the cemetery was military; but Grmek calculates that 10% of all known ancient Greek skeletons have at least one fracture, and four out of every five occur on males. The ancient world was a rough place, and only a broad approach to the evidence can prevent interpretative mistakes.

The negative impact of burial ritual, undermining our confidence in writing a history of disease from biased samples, is as strong as ever. We are unlikely ever to succeed in Grmek's goal of reconstructing what he calls the pathocoenosis, 'the ensemble of pathological states present in a specific population at a given moment in time' (1989: 3), and even McNeill's target – 'a fuller comprehension of humanity's ever-changing place in the balance of nature' (1976: 5) – may be asking too much of this kind of evidence. Using ritual in a more positive way, to examine social structure, is more difficult with disease than with demography. We cannot have such clear expectations of what we should find, which makes it harder to identify patterns of ritual action. In what follows, I describe some of the most common pathologies in the skeletal record and discuss possible uses of our evidence.[26]

PATHOLOGIES OF BONES

1. General infections

The history of tuberculosis is hotly debated. It was common in the ancient East Mediterranean, with the soft tissues of mummies providing the best evidence. Thirty-one cases have been identified in Egypt, dating from 3700 to 1000 B.C. However, there is little trace of it in the western Roman empire. It usually shows up first in the ends of the long bones of the backbone, and can lead to the breakdown of vertebrae and severe twisting of the spine.[27]

The group of diseases caused by the micro-organism *treponema* (including yaws and syphilis) can lead to even worse deformities. Bone changes begin with clustered pits which grow together to

---

[26] Fractures, Warwick 1968: 159; Grmek 1989: 57–9. Generally, see Steinbock 1976; Ortner & Putschar 1981; Brothwell 1981: 127–74; Larsen 1987: 383–6. The best discussion relating modern techniques to classical material is Garnsey 1989, on which I draw heavily in this section. Sallares (1991: 221–93) provides a useful review of much of the recent evidence. For more recent periods, Le Roy Ladurie 1971; Crosby 1986.

[27] Sandison 1980: 31; R. Jackson 1988: 180–2.

form cavities, scars or perforations of the skull. Recent excavations in the Pantanello cemetery near Metapontum (*c.* 580–280 B.C.) reveal that 'a form of syphilis was widely distributed among the population' (Ridgway 1989: 144), but otherwise no traces of treponematoses have been found in the Mediterranean world. Leprosy, which in its advanced stages can ravage the skeleton, is also a largely post-classical phenomenon. Greek doctors perhaps knew it as an eastern disease, and some historians speculate that Alexander's or Pompey's troops brought it to Europe. Angel identified a possible Early Bronze Age leper at Karatas in Lycia, but the lesions are ambiguous. The first definite evidence is four skulls from a second-century B.C. cemetery of thirty-one burials at Dakleh oasis in Egypt. The seclusion of this spot has led to suggestions that it is the world's first attested leper colony. Two possible lepers have been identified in fourth-century A.D. Britain, but both are questionable. There is a sudden jump in frequency in the sixth century, but the disease only became a matter of public concern in the twelfth century. Even this may have more to do with medieval monarchy and the search for enemies within, whether heretics, Jews, lepers or homosexuals, than with actual changes in the biological threat posed by the disease.[28]

2. *Diseases of joints*

Arthritis is older than homo sapiens and can be considered as the most common disease of the ancient world. Unfortunately, many kinds of arthritis can only be identified from the small bones of the hands and feet, which tend to be badly preserved. As with fractures, quantification might help interpretation. It has, for instance, been suggested that the arthritis which afflicted two women whose decapitated skeletons were found in Romano-British cemeteries might have made them bad-tempered, and therefore caused them to be executed as witches. More precise figures on the occurrence of arthritis (and beheading) might allow us to assess the validity of this hypothesis. Similarly, Grmek argues that there was a decline in back problems in Greece during archaic and classical times, which

---

[28] Grmek 1989: 152–76; Manchester 1984; Baker & Armelagos 1988; Angel 1970; Dzierzryk-ray-Rogalski 1980; Møller-Christensen 1966; Reader 1974; Skinsnes 1975; Manchester & Roberts 1989. Medieval leprosy, R. I. Moore 1987. The decline in the late Middle Ages is charted by Lee & Magilton 1989.

he attributes to improvement in the conditions of labour. This could contribute to debates over the growth of citizen autonomy and the role of slavery from 700–300 B.C., but given the paucity of the evidence it remains a speculation. Gout, on the other hand, despite its Greek name (*podagra*) was above all a Roman disease. Seneca (*Letters* 95) thought it the result of moral decay and gluttony, and it too might have important implications for changes in elite lifestyles. Angel found a Middle Bronze Age case from Lerna, but the best examples come from Britain and Egypt in Roman times.[29]

3. Bone changes caused by blood disorders

Many skulls from the ancient Mediterranean have almost symmetrical patterns of rough porous areas on the vault. These are scarred with small holes and sometimes covered by a thin lattice of bone. The outer table of the skull is thinned down and hollowed out. This condition is usually known by Angel's name for it, porotic hyperostosis. This and another strainer-like lesion, cribra orbitalia, were caused by hyperactive bone marrow, but cannot be matched exactly to any known complaint. The closest parallels are thalassemia, a typically Mediterranean anaemia, and sickle-cell anaemia. In a third-century B.C. tomb in Tarquinia containing three burials, two of them (a teenage girl and a child) suffered from porotic hyperostosis, cribra orbitalia and hyperostosis of the spine and long bones. In this case and that of a teenage girl buried at Tiryns in the eighth century B.C., a diagnosis of thalassemia is almost certain, but other examples are less convincing.[30]

Anaemias are caused by iron deficiency, but this has several possible origins. The most important are low intake or poor absorption of iron due to protein-poor diets, and heavy losses caused by haemorrhages or parasites, especially malaria. In one group of twenty-four third-century B.C. skulls from Carthage, it was observed that the skeletons with the lowest iron content also had the strongest signs of cribra orbitalia. Angel argued that malaria

---

[29] Witches, Liversidge 1973: 477. Back problems, Grmek 1989: 81–2. Agricultural slavery, Jameson 1977/8; Wood 1988: 42–80. Larsen (1987: 386–94) discusses the problems of using skeletal evidence to study labour patterns. Gout, Rogers et al. 1987; Waldron 1987a; Angel 1971: 51, 89, 92; Elliot Smith & Wood Jones 1910; C. Wells 1973.

[30] Angel 1964; 1966. More generally, Larsen 1987: 357–62. Tarquinia, Fornaciari & Mallegni 1980. Tiryns, Bräuer & Fricke 1980 (also suffering from spina bifida).

was the main factor in porotic hyperostosis, and used its frequency as an index of fierce malarial outbreaks in Early Neolithic and late medieval Greece. He also suggested that malaria became far worse in the late classical period, lending a new twist to an old and rather simplistic theory that the Greeks could not resist Macedon because they were weakened by malaria.[31]

4. Effects of diet on bone

To some extent, all palaeopathology deals with nutrition, since poor diet helps diseases to spread. Porotic hyperostosis is the most obvious case of overlap: in spite of Angel's insistence on the role of the mosquito in causing low iron levels, there is good evidence that inadequate diet was at least as important. At Herculaneum in A.D. 79 the diet was quite high in protein but low in iron, leading to good general health, but porotic hyperostosis among 41% of women and 28% of men. Bisel could not be certain of the aetiology of the lesions, but a good case can be made for nutritional deficiency.[32]

Other evidence relates to diet more directly. The easiest index is height: protein and calorie shortages inhibit growth. On the whole, ancient adults average about 10 cm shorter than moderns, but there are occasional surprises. The skeletons from Herculaneum and from late Roman cemeteries at Trentholme Drive (York) and Vada in Tuscany are all taller than modern local populations, suggesting better nutrition in Roman times.[33]

Childhood malnutrition leaves traces which can be seen by radiographic analysis, such as 'Harris lines', transverse lines and bands of increased density on the long bones. They are caused by renewed bone growth after periods of arrest, which can be caused by sudden food shortages or by disease. They develop mainly in childhood, and can give information on weaning patterns. However, neither Harris lines nor metacarpal notching (another by-

---

[31] Fornaciari et al. 1981; Angel 1977; 1978. Old theory, W. H. S. Jones 1909: 95–100.

[32] Hengen 1971; Lallo et al. 1977; Bisel 1988: 46, 65. Stuart-Macadam (1985; 1987) has made a similar argument for the importance of childhood nutritional stress in the aetiology of porotic hyperostosis in Roman Britain (cf. O'Sullivan et al. 1989).

[33] Warwick 1968; Mallegni et al. 1980/1; Bisel 1987; 1988. Komlos (1990) uses textual data in a parallel argument. Stature is usually calculated from long bones by Trotter & Gleser's (1958) regression formulae.

product of childhood nutritional stress) have yet been reported on classical material. The cortical thickness of long bones can also provide evidence for arrested growth, as at Hellenistic Jericho.[34]

TEETH

By our standards, ancient teeth wore down quickly, but cavities were rare. The amount of chewing needed for fibrous foods probably explains the abrasion, while the absence of many sugars cut down on decay. Roman writers describe some horrific methods of oral hygiene, but these probably counted for less than changes in diet.[35]

Ptolemaic Egypt is unusual in that both caries and heavy abrasion were common. Earlier Egyptian teeth were healthier, and there may have been big dietary changes after 300 B.C. However, the examined teeth come from a different social group in each period, and caution is necessary. Dental health could vary greatly within a population – access to honey and fruit would accelerate decay, while more meat and less bread would retard it. Sea salt and fish would provide fluorides which strengthen teeth. Powell, in her study of Moundville in Alabama, expected to find that the elite had better teeth than commoners. In fact, she found no real differences; and in the ancient Mediterranean we might expect instead that the wealthy suffered more from decay than the poor.[36]

Childhood illness or malnutrition can also cause enamel hypoplasia, areas of pitted or scored enamel on the labial crown surfaces. These are easy to see and more useful than Harris lines, which can disappear if nutrition improves. No amount of calcium-rich food in later life will obliterate hypoplasia, although heavy abrasion can destroy the enamel. Teeth from Roman sites in Italy, Palestine and Britain all point to relatively good health. Angel

---

[34] Wing & Brown 1979: 81–3; Martin et al. 1985: 253–65; Smith, Bloom & Berkowitz 1984; Larsen 1987: 362–5; Goodman & Armelagos 1989.

[35] E.g. Celsus, *On Medicine* 6.9; Martial, *Ep.* 14.22; Pliny, *NH* 25.105; and above all Catullus 39. Roman oral hygiene, Jackson 1988: 118–21; 1990.

[36] Powell 1985. Larsen (1987: 365–75) discusses more North American evidence. Greece, Angel 1944; 1971: 90; Bisel & Angel 1985; Munz 1970. Grmek (1989: 114–15) claims that Angel's figures for abrasion are misleading. Rome, Warwick 1968: 199–209; C. Wells 1982: 146–51; Bisel 1988; R. Jackson 1988: 118–21. Egypt, Leek 1979. Moundsville, Powell 1988: 179. Smith & Tau (1978: 40) speak of 'an increased caries frequency in Israel as in other regions' under the Roman empire, but the figures are still very low.

studied teeth from 890 Greek skeletons, mainly from Athens. Rather surprisingly, the proportion with hypoplastic lines fell from 37% ($n = 257$) in 1400–300 B.C. to 18% ($n = 124$) in the Hellenistic and Roman periods (table 4 on p. 76), in spite of evidence that food supply crises and temporary shortages became more of a problem in and after the fourth century B.C.[37]

CHEMICAL ANALYSIS

Diet also affects the chemical composition of bones and teeth. There are two main techniques for extracting this information.

1. *Trace element analysis*

Most of the elements taken in with food pass through the body in one way or another, but tiny amounts are incorporated into the bones. There is some variation in 'normal' concentrations of trace elements, but this process can be used as evidence for diet. Plant tissue tends to have more manganese, strontium, cobalt and tungsten than animal, which is richer in zinc, copper, molybdenum and selenium. By obtaining ratios of bone calcium to strontium and zinc, we can get an idea of the balance between vegetables and meat, and the overall richness of the diet.

There are of course problems, since seafood also deposits more strontium than do land animals; and Elias found that the technique failed to distinguish between vegetarians and non-vegetarians in Calcutta. It is crucially important that the same parts of each skeleton are analysed, since different parts of the body may absorb different amounts of strontium; and that bodies of the same age and sex are used. Further, cremation renders the method useless. We must depend on inhumations, but even with these it is vital to analyse post-mortem bone decay before looking at strontium as evidence for diet, and to examine the amounts and types of chemicals absorbed by the bones from the soil after death. Strontium and zinc are little affected by this, but copper, barium and particularly lead levels can be badly distorted. Post-mortem absorption must be circumvented by 'site-corrected' ratios, making allowances for

[37] Larsen 1987: 365–75; Bisel 1988; Smith, Bar-Yosef & Sillen 1984; Smith & Peretz 1986; Warwick 1968: 180; Bisel & Angel 1985: table 4; Garnsey 1988: 150–64; Gallant 1989.

differences in the chemical make-up of the soils the bones were found in. Some archaeologists remain optimistic. Fornaciari and Mallegni read subsistence directly from the ratios (fig. 22), and Sillen and Smith argue that the low level of strontium in human milk means that we can reconstruct weaning patterns. However, Lambert et al. (1984: 111) argue that 'The process whereby strontium is stable in buried bone but calcium clearly leaches out into the soil over time confirms that the use of the strontium:calcium ratio in the analysis of buried bone is entirely inappropriate.' This undermines many reconstructions of ancient diet, and it seems that strontium values alone may have more value than strontium:calcium ratios.[38]

It is also crucial to ensure that all samples are directly comparable. Infants usually have high levels of most essential elements, which decline with age; but zinc levels rise with advancing years. The strontium level of bones is greatest in one- to three-year-olds, but has a second peak for pregnant or lactating women. Lead usually increases until about age sixty, and then declines. Men usually have higher levels of lead and iron than do women; and different elements concentrate in different parts of the skeleton. Great care is needed in interpretation, but both Runia and Waldron suggest that the coming of Rome may have caused a significant increase in the lead content of the diet in the western provinces.[39]

Only a few Greek and Roman skeletons have been analysed, and much more information is needed. The samples are too small to rely on, but do hint at interesting patterns (fig. 22). Snodgrass has claimed that there was a shift towards a pastoral economy in Early Iron Age Greece. Few animal bones have yet been published, but the human bones from Nichoria and Athens suggest a fairly rich, agriculturally based diet. Standards seem to decline in Hellenistic Athens, but the only major divergence comes from a few late Roman sites, where pastoralism may have become more important.

The evidence also allows regional contrasts. If we choose to rely

---

[38] Calcutta, Elias 1980. Decay of inhumations, A. N. Garland 1988; 1989; Garland & Janaway 1989; Garland et al. 1988. Analyses, Fornaciari & Mallegni 1986; Sillen & Smith 1984. Criticisms, Lambert et al. 1984; Pate & Brown 1985; Beck 1985; Mays 1989.

[39] Runia 1987; Waldron 1983; 1987b; 1988; Whittaker & Stack 1984. Rome and lead, Runia 1987: 120; Waldron 1988: 72. Needleman & Needleman (1985) review the literary evidence.

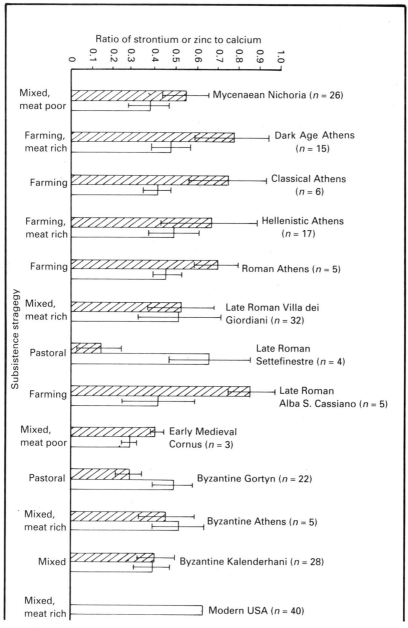

22. Fornaciari and Mallegni's interpretation (1986: fig. 1) of diet, based on site-corrected skeletal mean strontium/calcium and zinc/calcium ratios. The standard deviation and sample size are shown for each

on strontium:calcium ratios, we might interpret Bisel and Angel's observation that Athenian skeletons had a higher score in the Late Bronze Age than those from Nichoria as evidence that the Athenians probably added seafood protein to a largely cereal diet, while the Nichorians relied on scarcer land animals. Gallant has shown that ancient populations could not get all their protein from fish, but access to it could make a critical difference. This may also account for the good health of the skeletons from first-century A.D. Herculaneum.[40]

2. Stable isotope analysis

When we eat plants we absorb carbon from them; and the ratio between the two stable isotopes of carbon in bones may allow us to reconstruct diet. American archaeologists have traced the spread of maize through the continent in this way. Maize was not introduced to the Mediterranean until the seventeenth century, and we can use the ratio between the isotopes to examine the balance between vegetable and marine foods. So far, this technique has not been applied to the ancient Mediterranean, but it has great potential.[41]

In one African case it had been assumed that two groups of skeletons, one near the sea and the other further inland, belonged to a single, mobile population. Chemical analysis disproved this. The coastal group got at most 50% of their nutrients from vegetables, and some of them ate only seafood; while the inlanders ate only terrestrial foods. An even more surprising Danish example from cemeteries within sight of the sea showed that a Mesolithic group had a marine-based diet, while a Neolithic population showed no traces of seafood. Another approach is exemplified by a Norwegian study which linked variations in carbon isotopes to unequal access to seafood resources.[42]

The ratio between the two stable nitrogen isotopes can also tell us about the role of seafood and even of legumes. However, it is not so often measured in radiocarbon laboratories as the carbon ratio, and so far it has been little used in archaeology.[43]

[40] Pastoralism, Snodgrass 1987: 193–209; more generally, Whittaker, ed., 1988. Animal bones, Garnsey & Morris 1989. Fish, Gallant 1985. Human bones, Bisel 1980; 1988; Bisel & Angel 1985; Fornaciari & Mallegni 1986.
[41] Klepinger 1984; Runia 1987: 19–22, 152–60.
[42] Sealy & van der Merwe 1985; Tauber 1981; Johansen et al. 1986.
[43] Schoeninger, de Niro & Tauber 1983.

Cremation destroys the possibility of isotopic analysis, and the cortex of inhumed bones may also absorb carbon and nitrogen from the soil. Some specialists feel that only the collagen provides reliable information, but this requires burning samples of 10 g or more.[44]

CONCLUSION

Classical archaeology generally lags behind prehistory in skeletal analysis. Even today it is not unknown for hundreds of skeletons to vanish after excavations, while associated vases are published in meticulous detail. Many fieldworkers seem unaware of the importance of this material for historians. There are also heavy geographical and chronological biases in what has been done. Although there is little to show so far, the potential of this work is enormous. The combination of textual and skeletal evidence allows us to pursue the history of mortality, disease and diet in individual communities over longer periods.

However, excitement about technical advances must not obscure the fact that the bones are every bit as difficult to interpret as anything else found in graves. This is especially clear in demography, where we have strong expectations of what we will find, from which the skeletal population often diverges. Usually this indicates some special treatment of the dead and a facet of social structure rather than bizarre age or sex patterns within the living group. With pathology, argument from analogy has less force, and we must create the context for our findings from the archaeological record itself. The most obvious approach is to compare the results of trace element and stable isotope analyses with dietary remains from settlement sites, as Runia did in comparing the high lead content of Roman-period skeletons with the lead content of imported pottery. Differences between types of deposit may be very important in terms of divisions within the community. The burial record can also provide its own context. In the New World, Haas and Powell have used skeletons to document differences in diet within communities, and then used these as evidence for unequal access to basic resources. Tainter examined differences in the wear on joints as evidence for leisured groups within society. Wells

---

[44] Schoeninger & de Niro 1982; de Niro et al. 1985.

deployed the same method to document a servile group at Owslebury, and used osteoarthritis at Cirencester to hint at the sexual
division of heavy labour; while Schwidetzky undermined theories
interpreting rich Iron Age graves at Hallein in Austria as 'middle-
class' entrepreneurs grown rich from running the local salt mines
by showing the clear evidence for very hard physical labour and
short lifespan among all types of burials.[45]

Some of these uses of bones for social archaeology are rather
naïve, but they do bring out the fact that even here, where the
ancients intrude most tangibly into our experience, the archaeological record does not provide 'facts' about history. It is there to be
interrogated and interpreted within its context.

[45] Runia 1987: 120; Haas 1981; Powell 1988; Tainter 1980; C. Wells, cited in Collis 1977b:
34; C. Wells 1982: 152–60. Hallein, Schwidetzky 1978.

CHAPTER 4

Taking it with you: grave goods and Athenian democracy

In his endless search for 'the good', Plato has Socrates run into Hippias of Elis. Hippias quickly finds himself boxed into a philosophical corner, and Socrates gets him to define the good as 'to be rich, and healthy, and being honoured by the Greeks to come into old age, and after providing a fine end for his own parents, to be buried well and *megaloprepōs* by his own offspring' (Plato, *Hipp. Maj.* 291D–E).

Like all Socrates' opponents, Hippias soon has to admit that this is muddle-headed, but Plato most likely intended it to be an attitude which many readers would share. Herodotus (1.30) had had Solon express similar sentiments, and it may have been a well-known literary theme. *Megaloprepōs* is usually translated as 'magnificently', as seems to follow from Aristotle's discussion (*EN* 4.1122a 18–23a). Hippias' position would then be one which most archaeologists assume was widespread in the past. One of the commonest guesses we make is that lavish display in grave goods or monuments means a big person, surrounded in life as well as in death by throngs of admirers. But what the word really means is 'what is appropriate for a great man' (Hippias even says that 'the appropriate' (*to prepon*) and 'the good' (*to kalon*) are the same thing [293E]; another blunder, of course, as he works out by 294E). In the next two chapters I concentrate on the Athens of Plato (*c.* 427–347), give or take a generation or two, suggesting that lavish display was not always *prepon* for a *megas*. In this chapter, I draw both negative and positive conclusions about grave goods. First the bad news: once we examine grave goods as part of rituals, many ways of analysing them are open to serious question. But the good news is that we can begin to see how grave goods worked within larger patterns of material culture practices to create social structure in classical Athens. This leads into chapter 5, where I widen the context still further by examining above-ground monuments and by looking at Athens in a panhellenic framework.

WHO PAYS THE FERRYMAN?

Grave goods bring us closer than anything else to the romantic vision of archaeology – Howard Carter prying a block out of the sealed doorway of Tutankhamen's tomb, peering in and seeing everywhere the glint of gold ... But grave goods also offer perfect ammunition for mockery of naïve direct interpretations. Macaulay's *Motel of the Mysteries* indulges this, with Howard Carson excavating the Toot'n'c'mon motel in the belief that it is a necropolis, seeing everything from a television to a toilet seat as ritual paraphernalia accompanying a corpse propped up in bed with his remote control (fig. 23).[1]

It is easy to laugh, but this kind of direct interpretation *is* the way grave goods are usually treated. And up to a point it makes sense. Achilles asks Agamemnon to find for Patroclus 'all that is fitting for the dead man to have when he goes down under the gloom and darkness' (*Il.* 23.50–1). Herodotus (5.92.7) tells a story of how the dead Melissa, the late wife of the Corinthian tyrant Periander, refused to answer messengers sent to the Oracle of the Dead by Periander because she was cold; he had buried fine clothes with her, but had forgotten to burn them, so she could not wear them in Hades. But, as I said, this only works up to a point. It is hard to forget the example of the 'Orphics' (pp. 17–18 above), whose next life was distinctive, but whose grave goods were conventional. According to Lucian, a second-century A.D. satirist, people would say that libations, gifts of clothing and the sacrifice of animals were made to benefit the dead, but everyone knew that they were really only meant to impress other mourners (*On Mourning* 15).

It was Lucian's job to be funny, and such cynicism may have been rare. But Greeks and Romans were not fools, and grave goods must have involved the sort of willing suspension of disbelief which is typical of all ritual discourse. We do not have to doubt that offerings and libations nourished the dead, but we should recognise that they had other functions too. Consider late sixth-century gr. 49 at Rhitsona in Boeotia. What was the person buried here supposed

[1] Carter & Mace 1977: 96; Macaulay 1979.

23. The main 'burial' in the Toot'n'c'mon motel (after Macaulay 1979: 30). Macaulay explains: 'Everything in the Outer Chamber faced the Great Altar (No. 1), including the body of the deceased, which still lay on top of the Ceremonial Platform (No. 5). In its hand was the Sacred Communicator (No. 3) and around its wrist was a flexible golden band (No. 4) bearing an image similar to that on the upper altar. Signs of the ancient burial ritual were everywhere. A variety of garments, including the ceremonial chest plate (No. 2) and shoes designed to hold coins (No. 6), were scattered about the chamber. Various containers (No. 9) which had once held libations and offerings stood on the altar and around the platform. A statue of the deity Watt, who represented eternal companionship and enlightenment, stood faithfully next to the platform. To ensure maximum comfort during eternal life, several pieces of beautifully crafted furniture were placed in the room, along with several garments stacked carefully in a specially designed rectangular pod. Perhaps the single most important article in the chamber was the I C E (No. 14). This container, whose function evolved from the Canopic jars of earliest times, was designed to preserve, at least symbolically, the major internal organs of the deceased for eternity. The Yanks, who revered long and complex descriptions, called the container an Internal Component Enclosure.' (*Motel of the Mysteries* by David Macaulay. Copyright © 1979 by David Macaulay. Reprinted by permission of Houghton Mifflin Company. All rights reserved.)

to do with the 420 pots crammed in on top of the coffin? Not much, if he or she was bound for the same Hades we find in the literary sources.[2]

The most famous grave goods from antiquity must be Charon's obols, small coins buried with the dead to pay the ferryman who

[2] Burrows & Ure 1907/8: 250–6.

Table 5. *Mean numbers of artefacts per intact adult burial and distribution (measured by Gini's coefficient of inequality) at Athens in the Dark Age and the fifth century B.C.*

	Vases		Metal objects	
Period	Mean	*G* score	Mean	*G* score
900–750 B.C.	6.9	0.377	2.8	0.582
500–425 B.C.	2.9	0.537	0.4	0.958

took them across the River Styx into Hades. Lucian (*On Mourning* 10) jokes that the dead might be better off without an obol, because then Charon would not take them and they could come back to life. Had Lucian visited a few more funerals he would have known that most burials did not include a coin for the ferryman. In the fourth century B.C. at Olynthus, only 66 of the 644 graves had a coin in them; and none of the Roman graves in the North Cemetery at Corinth, of roughly the same date as Lucian's satire, were so equipped. The use of coins also went in phases. At Blicquy in Belgic Gaul, for example, coins were six times as common in the second century A.D. as in the first. Strabo (8.6.12) says that the people of Hermione did not need coins for Charon because their town was so close to Hades that they had a short cut past him. But people at Winchester, where coins only became common after A.D. 370, had no such excuse. And some graves had more coins than others. Aristophanes (*Frogs* 140) has Heracles tell Dionysus that he has to pay two obols, one for his servant, before he can enter Hades; but why some people needed a whole drachma (six obols) or more is not apparent. In spite of Lucian, those without coins – a good 95% of our burials – were probably not sent home. Coins may have paid the ferryman, but this was not all that they did. There can be no one-to-one correlation between grave goods and eschatology.[3]

But it is equally naïve to treat grave goods as a simple index of wealth. Table 5 shows that at Athens from 900–750 B.C. grave goods for adults were more lavish than in 500–425, and that in the first period they were more evenly spread around than in the second. I quantify the evenness of their distribution with a statistic

[3] Olynthus, Robinson 1942: 205. Corinth, Palmer 1964: 294–300. Blicquy, de Laet et al. 1972. Winchester, Clarke 1979: 166.

called Gini's coefficient of inequality. This allows us to range distributions along a scale: from 0, complete equality, where every burial has exactly the same grave goods as every other burial, to 1, complete inequality, where all the grave goods known come from a single burial. These scores show that grave goods were both more common and more evenly spread in the ninth century than in the fifth, but concluding that Athens was richer and more egalitarian in the earlier than in the later period would be odd indeed. This is a problem of interpretation; but even attempting to interpret grave goods is sometimes a mistake. In the Trentholme Drive cemetery at York, for example, something of the rites for early third-century A.D. cremation gr. 32 could be reconstructed. The body had been burned in a coffin on a bier, on a pyre of coal and wood. Parting gifts, including a domestic fowl, three pots and a glass vessel were thrown into the flames; then, after the pyre died down, some of the bones, ashes and fragments of offerings were shovelled into an urn and the burial shaft. A rather random selection of what happened in the funeral was excavated. Some burials have most of their offerings still with them; some have none. Detailed analysis of these objects would probably be futile. However, this is not a blanket condemnation of the study of grave goods. Usually we cannot know whether a specific study will repay the effort put into it until we have tried it. Ninth-century B.C. Athenian cremations are rather like those at Trentholme Drive, with burned bones and some of the pyre refuse placed in an urn, and more debris piled over it; but the objects found with these burials are strikingly homogeneous over the whole of Athens and show distinct chronological patterns, clearly indicating that in this case we *are* dealing with deliberate deposition. For each cemetery we examine, we must take care that we are comparing like with like and that we have understood the formation processes of the archaeological record.[4]

In some cases grave goods were important, but were displayed and then removed (as ordered in the fifth-century B.C. law from Ioulis on Kea) or were given away as prizes in funeral games or the like. Such 'archaeologically invisible' actions complicate our task, but again, do not make it impossible. If grave wealth is kept among the living, this is qualitatively different from the destruction of

[4] Athenian grave goods, Morris 1987: 140–51; Whitley 1991. Trentholme Drive, Wenham 1968: 31.

wealth, in the sense of removing it from circulation, involved with 'proper' grave goods or with votives in sanctuaries. Of course it would be better if we had records of what was displayed or given away; but even without them, we can still learn much from the alternation of periods of destruction and preservation of wealth (see p. 28 above).[5]

Grave goods are part of the total burial assemblage; taken away from it, they mean nothing. What we find is determined by the actors in ancient rituals, who put objects into graves because it seemed like a good idea at the time. The artefacts can tell us about these rituals. Questions about trade, wealth, aesthetics or technology, important as they are, cannot be answered until we have understood the logic of the ceremonies which created the archaeological record.

It is easier to be negative about grave goods than to make positive contributions. Ucko[6] lists plenty of ethnographic nightmares, and there is no point in my repeating the exercise here. Instead, I try to show that although proper attention to ritual context makes it difficult – even impossible – to solve some problems, it also allows us to ask new questions about social structure, which can be even more interesting.

GRAVE GOODS IN CLASSICAL ATHENS

The jewel in the crown of classical archaeology is Sir John Beazley's monumental work cataloguing tens of thousands of Athenian vases and attributing them to painters, schools, manners, etc. But recently Michael Vickers has challenged the Beazleyan paradigm, precisely by pointing out that the bulk of its subject matter consists of grave goods. He attacks specialists for seeing all changes as internal, artistic processes. Vickers argues that the history of vase painting is merely a shadow of the history of vessels in precious metals, which Athenians did not use as grave goods and which have therefore rarely survived. A few silver vessels with figured decoration in gold leaf ended up in graves in southern Russia and Bulgaria, drawing attention to the gaps in the evidence from Athens itself. 'Many puzzling features of Attic pottery', he says, 'can be

---

[5] Ioulis, Sokolowski 1969: no. 97.
[6] Ucko 1969: 265–7.

explained if we think of it as a cheap down-market surrogate for vases being made in silver for a wealthy élite' (Vickers 1984: 89).[7]

He claims that Athenian pots aped not just the designs but also the colour schemes of metal. Drawing on a newly found fragment of Thrasyalces, saying 'silver is black', he argues that the Greeks liked their silver tarnished. The black paint on pots therefore evokes silver, and the orange-red slip reminded people of gold; added details in purple paint stand for copper, and in white for ivory. The black-figure – red-figure transition was not a struggle to realise artistic potential, but an imitation of a shift from using silver figures against a background of gold leaf to using gold figures directly on a silver vessel, thus economising on the amount of gold which had to be used. The end of the Athenian red-figure style, around 320 B.C., is explained by the flood of Persian gold into Greece after Alexander; the rich went over to solid gold vessels (although Vickers suggests that at Athens, where 'black-glaze' pottery continues, poorer nobles had to struggle on with solid silver). In a linked argument, Vickers would move the beginning of the 'gold-figure'/ red-figure style down from the conventional date around 530 B.C. to about 470, explaining it as the Athenians' use of booty captured after the Persian Wars.[8]

Vickers sees two reasons for our errors. One is methodological naïveté. 'The sheer volume of the extant material', he explains, 'has clearly contributed to the current view that pottery was of such major importance in ancient Greece' (1984: 88). Out of sight, out of mind; precious metals not used as grave goods have simply been forgotten about. The second is Beazley's intellectual background, and, by implication, the failure of classicists to challenge authorities. Vickers sees William Morris and John Ruskin as formative influences on Beazley, and accuses him of creating an idealised arts-and-crafts Athens where pottery and honest craftsmanship

[7] Beazley, Ashmole 1970; Kurtz, ed., 1985. *Contra*, Vickers 1984; 1985; 1986; 1987; Gill 1986; 1988a. Bulgarian graves, Filow 1934: 106–11. Panagurishte treasure, Kondoleon 1962; D. M. Lewis (1986: 76–7) argues for an Attic origin. South Russia, Lordkipanidze 1971; Gill 1987a.

[8] Thrasyalces, Hughes & Parsons 1984: no. 3659.5–8. Chronology, Francis & Vickers 1981; 1983; 1988; Gill 1988b; Gill & Vickers 1989. *Contra*, Boardman 1984; 1988a; Amandry 1988. The debate continues with Gill & Vickers 1990. R. M. Cook (1989) gives a full bibliography and serious critique of the revisionist dating. Responses to Boardman are listed in Francis & Vickers 1988: 167, n. 157. Hurwit (1989) also points out problems with the supposed 'fixed points' of Athenian dating.

were more esteemed than showy treasure. For Beazley, Athens was a mirror to hold up to the horrors of industrialism and the kind of social structure I talked about in chapter 2. In a discipline not given to introspection, the claim that the idol rather literally had feet of clay has provoked fierce responses.[9]

Some of Vickers' claims have been sternly rebuffed, and the aesthetic status quo will probably survive; but Vickersism has enormous implications, which can be taken in two directions. The first, pressed hardest by Vickers himself, is art-historical. He argues that we have distorted vase painting by not looking at the context of the finds: we have to rethink 'the supposed dependence of one fabric of pottery on another, the supposed influence of a single pot painting on the design tradition, or the supposedly major importance of the "pottery trade"' (1984: 90). The idea that painted pottery was cheap stuff exported only to fill in the corners of more valuable cargoes has set off a third row, again with art-historical implications: most of the finest pots come from Etruscan graves, and first had to get to Etruria in the holds of ships.[10] In what follows, I challenge one of Vickers' specific suggestions about the interpretation of the vases which we find in Athenian graves, but only in order to develop another line of argument from his insights.

This second approach concerns the role of material culture in Athenian social structure. For this, we must concentrate on the functions of pottery in burial rituals, which Vickers has not so far explored in detail. He describes the use of pottery rather than metal grave goods merely as 'the very sensible Athenian practice' (1984: 89). He does make one venture into interpreting the rituals, however, suggesting that cremation was reserved for the rich, who would have thrown onto the pyre metal vessels and ivory lekythoi filled with oil, going through the ashes to recover the fragments before the actual burial. White-ground lekythoi are seen as imitations of ivory vessels, cheap enough to leave in the grave. Cremation and white-

---

[9] Especially Vickers 1985: 122–6; 1987: 100; Gill & Vickers 1989: 300–1. Bernal (1987: 204–11) and Turner (1989: 70–80) have useful comments on the 'small-is-beautiful' theme of Romantic Hellenism, beginning in the eighteenth century. Responses, M. Robertson 1985: 20–6; Boardman 1987: 295.

[10] Colours, Boardman 1987; R. M. Cook 1987; response in Gill & Vickers 1989. Trade, Gill 1987b; 1987c; 1988a; Boardman 1988b; 1988c; McGrail 1989. This debate will also continue with Gill 1991.

ground lekythoi both declined in popularity around 400 (all dates here on the traditional chronology); and Vickers suggests that 'the demise of the white ground *lekythos* may well ... represent a "change in funerary practice" rather than simply a "change in fashion"' (1984: 95). He is not saying that white-ground lekythoi were used solely in cremations and therefore stopped being made when cremation lost favour; but he is saying that there is some relationship between the rite of cremation and the use of these vases.[11]

The best way to examine this important suggestion, and to open up discussion of the functions of Athenian pottery in burial rituals, is through statistical analysis. Most white-ground lekythoi do indeed date 425–400, just the time when cremation was the main burial custom at Athens (see fig. 32 on p. 140 below). But is this correlation meaningful? That is, is there any *causal* link between the two variables? Quantification can clarify the discussion and make a decision easier.

If Vickers is right, then there ought to be some difference between how white-ground lekythoi were used in cremations as compared to inhumations. Maybe white-ground pots were used alongside ivory flasks, and so most lekythoi should come from cremations; or maybe rich, ivory-using, cremating Athenians scorned cheap imitations, most of which will then be found in inhumations. Either way, there should be a pattern. Statistical analysis is only possible at a few Athenian cemeteries, so I concentrate on two well-known cases, the Kerameikos and Charitonides' dig in Syndagma Square (see figs. 28–30 on pp. 133–7 below). The Kerameikos was in use continuously from about 1100 to 200 B.C., and then again in Roman times; Syndagma Square is a small part of the much larger Diocharian Gate cemetery, in use from at least 750 to 300, and possibly much longer still. The Syndagma graves all date *c.* 425–390, roughly the time of the greatest popularity of white-ground lekythoi, and I will be comparing them with the Kerameikos graves of the same period. Fig. 24 shows that in both cemeteries white-ground lekythoi are found more often in cremations than in inhumations, but fig. 25 shows some variation between the cemeteries. White-ground lekythoi tend to occur together

---

[11] White-ground lekythoi, Vickers 1984: 95, partly followed by Gill 1988a: 737–8. Herbert Hoffmann (1988: 152) makes a similar argument, seeing Athenian vases as 'tokens and symbols ... substitutes for *realia*'. White-ground lekythoi, brief account in Boardman 1989: 129–43; more fully in Kurtz 1975.

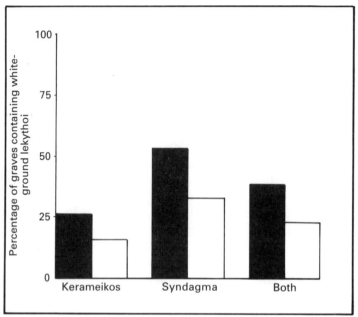

24. Percentage of graves containing white-ground lekythoi

in larger numbers in cremations than in inhumations in the Kera-meikos; at Syndagma, the reverse is true. Taking the mean number of white-ground lekythoi in all graves, the Kerameikos cremations are again better provided than the inhumations, but in Syndagma there is no difference.[12]

This is interesting. Perhaps these two groups of people meant different things when they put white-ground lekythoi in graves; or maybe they shared a system of meaning, but wanted to mark themselves as different from each other. But before flying off to the realm of meaning, we have to answer a more basic question: is there a case to answer? Is the pattern *real*, in the sense of being produced by purposive human action? Take fig. 25a, based on just forty-six graves. This pattern could be caused by accidents of exca-vation and reporting or the variability which we always find in rituals. We must begin by proposing a 'null hypothesis', that there is really no pattern at all. The variations in figs. 24 and 25 would

---

[12] Kerameikos, Schlörb-Vierneisel 1964; 1966; Kübler 1976. General account, Knigge 1988. Felten (1976) catalogues the numerous fragments of white-ground lekythoi from de-stroyed burials. Syndagma Square, Charitonides 1958.

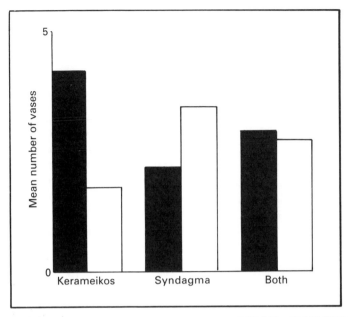

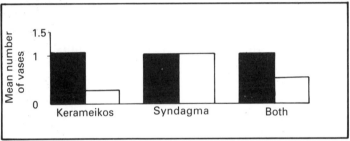

25. (a) Mean numbers of white-ground lekythoi per grave, counting only those graves which contain at least one white-ground lekythos. (b) Mean numbers of white-ground lekythoi per grave, counting all intact graves

then be the insignificant results of random factors. Next, we test this null hypothesis against what has actually been found, to establish the likelihood of its being correct. The simplest method is called the χ^2 test. We compare the number of graves which actually contain white-ground lekythoi with the number which would contain them if their distribution were entirely random. The more the observed data deviate from this hypothetical ('expected') random distribution, the higher the χ^2 score will be. Once we have calculated this score, we consult a standard table of χ^2 values. We decide whether to accept or reject the null hypothesis by setting a 'significant level'. Any distribution of finds could be entirely fortuitous; a significance level is simply the point at which we feel that an explanation purely in terms of accidental factors is so unlikely that we can ignore it. There is no universal law which says just how statistically significant a correlation has to be before we say it is important, but archaeologists generally set a level of 0.05, meaning that unless the probability that the observed data were generated purely by chance is 5% or less, we accept the null hypothesis, rule that there is no case to answer, and look for something more interesting to do. Calculating χ^2 is described in all basic statistics books,[13] so I will not go into details. The score here is 4.83, which is higher than the 3.84 required at the 0.05 level of significance, so we should reject the null hypothesis and assume that there is an important relationship somewhere in these data.

As it is helpful, I will use χ^2 again in chapter 7, but it can also mislead us badly. It is no more than a comment on the size of the samples: if we have enough graves, we will get a statistically significant χ^2 score for just about any pair of variables. It only tells us how likely it is that some relationship exists, not what its strength is nor how the variables are related. If we have chosen to compare the wrong variables in the first place, we may get a statistically significant score even though the proposed relationship is in fact spurious.

We can clarify matters with a measure of association called Yule's Q, looking at what happens to the burial rite/white-ground lekythos link when we introduce a third set of variables. This goes beyond χ^2 by giving us scores ranging from $+1$, total covariation, that is, the two sets of data we are comparing are identical, to -1, 'negative covariation', where the two sets are each other's mirror image. A high positive score means that the data sets are very like each other; a high negative score, that they are diametrically opposed; and a score around zero, that there is no very strong relationship here at all. By doing a series of tests using different pairs of variables, we discover which features of the burials are linked.[14]

[13] For excellent explanations illustrated by archaeological examples, see D. H. Thomas 1978; S. J. Shennan 1988: 65–76.
[14] For Q and more complex log-linear modelling, see S. J. Shennan 1988: 79–100.

Table 6. *Yule's Q coefficients for use of white-ground lekythoi in fifth-century Athens*

	Kerameikos	Syndagma Square	Both cemeteries
White-ground lekythoi and choice of rite	0.31	0.38	0.38
Control for choice of cemetery	—	—	0.34
Control for use of metal	0.31	0.36	0.38
Control for use of 3+ vases	−0.01	0.11	0.11
White-ground lekythoi and 3+ vases	0.79	0.89	0.89

The first line in table 6 shows the correlation between the use of white-ground lekythoi and choice of rite in each of our two cemeteries, and then for both of them combined. The scores are quite respectable, telling us that there is a mild positive correlation here. But now we can bring in a third variable, to see whether the initial correlation which we observed was in fact masking something more significant. If, when we bring in another factor, Q is closer to zero than it was when we only had two variables, then it is this third element which in fact accounts for the relationship between the first two. This is called 'controlling for' the third variable. We proceed by trial and error, trying out different variables. In this case, most made little difference. For example, the third line in table 6 shows what happens when we ask if it is really the presence of metal grave goods rather than the choice of rite which explains the variations in the use of white-ground lekythoi. The scores are a little lower, but not much. The only variable of those I looked at which makes a real difference is the number of pots in each grave. When we divide the graves into two groups, those having three or more pots and those having two or less, Q is close to zero. This result is confirmed when we correlate the presence of white-ground lekythoi with these two groups, ignoring the choice of rite: we get extremely strong positive correlations, from 0.79 to 0.89.

The correlation between choice of rite and use of white-ground lekythoi was spurious, masking the real observation that the presence of these vases is a function of whether a grave falls into the 'three-or-more-pots' group. This raises new questions. We will want to know why three vases, rather than two or four, is the dividing line; whether white-ground lekythoi covary with any other shape or motif; or whether they were put in the graves randomly above the 3+ line but not used much at all below it. The test shows that we have asked the wrong question and that we need to think about new ones. The fact that no grave in either cemetery has yielded any traces of melted metal plate or burned ivory seems to reinforce the case. It can be hard for the non-expert to tell burned ivory from bone, but both these sites were meticulously excavated, and the objects put into graves, as opposed to surface pyres, were rarely burned. The pyres could include many pots – 83, including five red-figure, in fourth-century Sacred Way deposit HS 374 – but again, no traces of melted metal or ivory fragments have been found.[15]

It is hard to know what would show that cremations were 'richer than' (as opposed to 'different from') other burials. On average, fifth- and fourth-century cremations had more pottery but less metal than inhumations. All seven gold objects from fifth-century graves, 34 of the 36 alabaster vessels and the only silver object came from inhumations. The two fourth-century warrior burials are both inhumations. The only precious metal from a cremation is a group of ten gilt clay rosettes from Kerameikos gr. HS 196.[16]

The uses of cremation, inhumation and grave goods seem to vary from place to place around Athens (fig. 26), and no single, direct interpretation will cover them. Some cemeteries are very cremation-oriented; in the fifth century, 34 of the 63 adult graves excavated in Syndagma Square and 15 of the 17 on Sapphous St were cremations. The Syndagma graves were pottery-rich (both inhumations and cremations averaged 6.3 vases per grave, compared to the overall means of 2.5 and 3.6 respectively), but not especially distinguished in other ways. The nearby cremation-oriented cemetery excavated at Panepistimiou St no. 17 (21 of the 39 adult burials being cremations), on the other hand, scored well below

---

[15] HS 374, Schlörb-Vierneisel 1966: 72–5.
[16] Gold, Kerameikos grs. HS. 24, HS 35 (Schlörb-Vierneisel 1966: 99, 92–3); C261 (Kübler 1976: 81–2); Veikou St. gr. 3 (Alexandri 1970: 44); V. Benaki St. gr. 9 (Alexandri 1968: 46). Silver, Dipylon gr. 33 (Brückner & Pernice 1893: 167–70). Fourth-century warrior graves, Madytou St. (Alexandri 1972: 68–70); G. Olymbiou St. gr. 2 (Alexandri 1973/4: 134). Kerameikos gr. HS 196, Schlörb-Vierneisel 1966: 85. This was clearly a very special grave, cut into the mound of Eukoline.

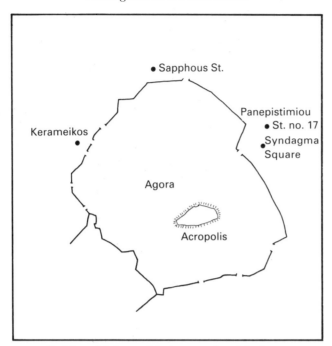

26. Map of Athens with sites mentioned in the text

average for all classes of grave goods, with just 2.3 pots per cremation and 1.4 per inhumation.[17]

Red-figure pots are the only type of even vaguely 'prestigious' grave goods with which white-ground lekythoi regularly occur. In the Kerameikos cremations, gr. c443 held 1 white-ground lekythos and 12 red-figure vases, but white-ground pottery was never found with metal. Turning to the inhumations, 3 of the 22 containing bronze also had white-ground lekythoi. Some of the late fifth-century child graves with very striking monuments (e.g. Kerameikos gr. hs 193 with the Lissos stele and hs 202 with the Eupheros stele) did hold white-ground vases; others, such as the important Kerameikos series grs. c246–64, and above all c261, the only fifth-century grave with gold and ivory, did not. In Syndagma Square, 7 of the 18 cremations and 7 of the 10 inhumations with white-ground lekythoi also contained red-figure vases, but only

[17] Syndagma, Charitonides 1958. Sapphous St., Alexandri 1968: 89–92; 1977: 26–8. Panepistimiou St., Alexandri 1970: 84–7.

inhumation gr. 20 held a bronze object (a mirror). Only one of the six graves with enclosure walls (inhumation gr. 44) held white-ground lekythoi, although it did have 11, along with 23 other vases, 4 of them red-figure. Gr. 2, a cremation with a stele bearing an epitaph, held 5 white-ground lekythoi and a further 22 vases (1 red-figure).[18]

These details could mean many things. Perhaps white-ground vases were not needed in Kerameikos gr. c261 because it had an actual ivory figurine; but overall, I think, the position that cremations are 'rich' and associated either positively or negatively with white-ground lekythoi is untenable. Grave goods did not covary strongly with other features of the assemblage. We might question whether much thought went into the selection of most of them, were it not for the coherence which has been identified in the iconography of some fifth-century grave vases.[19] But one thing is clear. The grave goods may say different things in different parts of the city, but they are all talking the same language: that of restraint. So far I have been challenging Vickers' arguments, but I am completely persuaded by his main point, that when the Athenians put pottery in their graves it was not because they valued it more highly than silver or gold. It is not just that precious metals are virtually absent from burials; pottery too was used sparingly. In the well-published graves, even red-figure vases by the best painters are rare. I would suggest that we should not see pots as symbolic substitutes for more valuable materials, but on the contrary should take the buriers' parsimony as having a positive message about abstention from display. As usual, to examine this idea we need to put the grave goods into a broader context.

WEALTH IN OTHER CONTEXTS

Thucydides (6.27–9, 60–1; cf. Andoc. 1.36–53) tells us that in 415 B.C., as the Athenians were about to attack Syracuse, some people went round the city one night and vandalised nearly all the statues called herms. The Athenians took this very seriously.

---

[18] Kerameikos grs. c246–64, 443, Kübler 1976: 73–83, 132. Lissos and Eupheros graves, Schlörb-Vierneisel 1964.
[19] H. Hoffmann 1977; 1986; 1988.

Informers and counter-informers soon appeared. The blame was thrown on young aristocrats and above all on the flamboyant Alcibiades. Many of the noble youth were soon languishing in jail. Alcibiades offered to stand trial, but his enemies put this off from fear that his support among the people would get him acquitted. He sailed off to Sicily, only to be indicted in his absence. He then fled to Sparta with dire consequences for all involved. Executions followed.

I repeat this story because parts of inscriptions recording the sale of property confiscated from the fifty or so condemned men survive (*I G* I³ 421–30), dating between summer 415 and spring 413. Some of the items may be those of Alcibiades himself. The text mentions a silver object and silver coins (*I G* I³ 427.93; 422.182), but no other precious metals. Tools, often made of bronze and iron, were abundant but expensive. Pots abound, but never with references to their decoration, except for a group of 102 Panathenaic amphoras (422.21, 41–60), pots given filled with oil as prizes for victories in the Panathenaic games, but sold off as empties. These fetched 17 to 26 times as much per pot as did unpainted amphoras.[20]

The evidence is not easy to use. As David Lewis points out, we should not be surprised that silver and gold are virtually absent: after all, the inscription only records property sold by auction. Precious metals would be sold by weight and would not appear in our text. Even the apparent references to silver and coins may mean something else completely.[21] Further, an endangered noble could have buried his loot or sold it and fled. Thucydides (6.60) and Andocides (1.52) do say that some escaped. Pritchett's conclusion (1956: 210) that 'Our record of the sale of confiscated furniture seems to show that there was little sense of personal luxury in Athens in the last quarter of the fifth century, even among men of wealth' is not the only one possible. Aristophanes has the slave Carion describe Chremylus' household after the god Wealth has visited it:

---

[20] Text and commentary, Pritchett 1953; 1956; 1961; Amyx 1958. Parts are translated in Fornara 1983: no. 147. On the standing of the accused men, see Ostwald 1986: 537–50. Date, Pritchett 1953: 232–4; D. M. Lewis 1966. Silver object, Pritchett 1956: 308–9; D. M. Lewis 1966: 190, n. 37. Tools (30 types are mentioned), Pritchett 1956: 287–306. Panathenaic amphoras and prices, Amyx 1958: 174, 178–86. There is a heated debate over the price of painted vases, with Boardman (1988b; 1988c) favouring high prices and Gill (1988c) low. The evidence is summarised in A. W. Johnston 1979.
[21] D. M. Lewis 1966: 183.

Every pot in the house is crammed with silver and gold – you'd be amazed
… Every bowl, every plate and vinegar cruet, has turned to bronze, and
all our rotting old fish dishes are solid silver. Even our lamps suddenly
turned into ivory. (*Wealth* 808–15, performed 388 B.C.)

Which picture of the 'typical' rich home should we prefer? Earlier
in the play (*Wealth* 535–47) Chremylus evokes the Athenians'
grinding poverty before he brought the god to them. We might
expect exaggeration of both extremes for comic effect, and neither
the play nor the inscriptions inspire much confidence.

The same sort of problems surround the excavated evidence for
riches in domestic contexts. No precious metal has been found, and
doubtless departing houseowners took their best things with them.
What was left would swiftly be removed by looters, as several
sources confirm. In one house near Vari the roof tiles had been
taken away in antiquity; and an Attic rental lease of 306/5 B.C.
requires the tenant to provide his own doors and tiles. Our evidence comes mainly from rubbish-pits, dumps from the levelling of
buildings, or objects incorporated into beaten earth floors. The
difficulties of interpreting such redeposited items are acute.[22]

Some houses had plenty of base metals. The floors of one in the
Agora at Athens included scores of iron nails. The excavator interpreted these as hobnails and combined them with a cup base
inscribed 'Simonos' to claim (rather optimistically) that this was
the house of Simon the shoemaker, mentioned much later as a place
where Socrates went to talk. The rubbish dumps of the 'Priest's
House' at Zostir included 89 fourth-century bronze coins, 48
bronze nails, 56 bronze fish-hooks, 19 bronze ornaments and many
lead fragments; and two cisterns filled with debris from the house of
Mikion and Menon in the Agora yielded 94 bronze coins.[23] Most
excavation reports, though, do not mention metal finds. Some
people are more careful than others, but can we really believe that

---

[22] J. E. Jones (1975) provides an excellent summary of the excavated houses. More recent
volumes of *AD* have very brief reports on finds at Ano Voula. Looters, Thuc. 2.14, 17;
Lys. 19.31; *Hell. Ox.* 17 (12).4–5. Vari roof tiles, J. E. Jones et al. 1973: 361. Lease of 306/
5, *IG* II² 2499.11–14, 30–7; cf. *IG* XII 5.872.52, 53, 63, 94 from Tenos. Sometimes (e.g. *IG*
II² 2493.21–4 from Amorgos; *SIG*³ 25–6 from Amorgos; *SIG*³ 964A 11–14 from Kea) the
roof came with the house. See R. G. Osborne 1985b. Problems of redeposition are treated
well by Schiffer (1987) and Binford (1981).
[23] House of Simon, D L 2.13.122; Burr Thompson 1960. Zostir, Stavropoullos 1938. House
of Mikion and Menon, Burr Thompson 1954: 88; Shear 1969: 383–92.

Table 7. *Contents of Athenian houses*

House	Red-figure	Black-glaze	Coarse	Combed ware
Dema House, c. 425–400 B.C. (R. E. Jones et al. 1962: 89–100)[1]	2 kraters 1 lebes	1 amphora 9 skyphoi 10 cups 4 tea-cups 16 other shapes	19 amphoras 5 mortars 7 casseroles 6 lids 1 hydria 1 bowl	—
Vari House, c. 325–275 B.C. (R. E. Jones et al. 1973: 374–94)	2 krater sherds 1 Corinthian sherd	2 shoes 4 olpai 3 cups 3 bolsals 8 kantharoi 3 tea-cups 12 bowls 5 plates 2 lekythoi 1 mini-plate 2 lamps	4 amphoras 1 wide jar 20 lekanai 1 hydria (?) 10 jugs 2 water pitchers 2 handles 4 closed vessels 10 mortars 7 chytrai 10 casseroles 5 lids 11 storage amphoras 2 large pithoi	23 kalathoi 12 rings 8 lids

[1] Plus 1 (?) Boeotian black-figure sherd, 7 banded lekanai and 2 banded lids; dating c. 350 B.C., 6 bowls, 1 bolsal, 2 kantharoi

there were houses where for centuries no one lost a coin? There may be something special about these three houses, but varying standards of excavation and publication provide a more prosaic explanation. Probably most abandoned houses included a certain amount of the base metals, but virtually no silver or gold.

The pottery is no simpler to interpret. It has been fully published from only two sites, shown in table 7. In both cases, black-glaze pottery was common, but red-figure was almost absent. The less precise evidence from other sites seems to support this, since when excavators tell us in brief reports about coarse-ware pottery, they will probably describe red-figure pots in at least as much detail. The most interesting exception to the pattern is Agora well U13:1, which yielded a little red-figure and 'thousands of black-glazed fragments' (Shear 1975: 361), but this is apparently debris from shops. Another layer in the well included vast quantities of cooking ware, probably from a taverna.[24]

If we take it at face value, this means that figured pottery was virtually absent from most homes. But breakage patterns vary. Kitchen wares in constant use will break and be thrown away more often than red-figure only brought out on special occasions; and the best pots might be mended if dropped. Two of the three pieces of lead found in the Vari house were probably used for this purpose. Yet the scarcity of fine painted pottery is striking, and my feeling is that it was used as sparingly in everyday life as in death rituals.[25]

Sanctuaries present a third pattern, although retrieval is once again a problem. Inscriptions suggest that *pinakes* (probably painted wooden panels) were common votives, but few have survived. What we can say is that huge numbers of pots began to be dedicated in the eighth and seventh centuries, with some metal votives from about 700 onwards. Theophrastus (*Peri euseb.* fr. 7.52– 4, Pötscher) says that 'The gods like what is cheap', but apparently not everyone shared his views. In the sixth century, cheap offerings decline, while the number of precious objects – especially in the big sanctuaries – may have increased.[26]

Gold and silver votives are rare. Looting sanctuaries to finance wars was a possibility in the fifth century and a reality in the fourth; and Hellenistic crises and Roman conquerors often finished the job. However, the textual record is full of riches. Our best source is the inventories of the Parthenon at Athens from 433 to about 300 B.C. The sanctuary was enormously rich, although nearly all its fifth-century wealth was apparently melted down by 404 to pay for the Peloponnesian War. By the 330s the lists are again full of amazing

[24] Fully published pottery, J. E. Jones et al. 1962; 1973. The same general impression comes from houses at Athens (R. S. Young 1951a: 187–252), Draphi (Daux 1958: 681) and Thorikos (Spitaels 1978). Agora deposit P21:4, a destruction dump in a cistern, is heavily dominated by fine wares, but dates *c.* 225–150 B.C. (Shear 1973: 146–56).

[25] Vari pot mends, J. E. Jones et al. 1973: 373. The evidence for pottery production is fully presented by Arafat & Morgan (1989).

[26] *Pinakes*, van Straten 1981: 78–80. Other votives, Wachsmuth 1975; Brommer 1985. Rouse (1902) is outdated but still useful. Tomlinson (1976: 23) is one of the only explicit discussions of changes through time. Eighth/seventh century, Snodgrass 1980: 51–65 (Olympia is an exception; see C. Morgan 1990: 28–30, 52–5, 243–7). Cheap archaic votives, Kyrieleis 1988.

things, but they end around 300 with the ominous words 'these [things] we did not hand over to our successors'.[27]

Animal sacrifices were another form of deliberate consumption of wealth in both sanctuaries and funerals, and could involve great expense. The animal bones from graves are rarely published, but those from altars are better known. The excavated evidence consists mainly of sheep and goats, except for the sanctuary of Demeter at Knossos where pigs were the rule. The texts again fill out the picture. According to [Xenophon] (*Ath. Pol.* 2.9), state spending on cattle for sacrifices allowed the poor to eat beef just like the rich. In 410/409, at the height of the Peloponnesian War, 5,114 drachmas were spent on cattle to sacrifice at the Great Panathenaea; and in 334/3 a single group of officials was responsible for selling off the hides of about 1,500 sacrificed cattle. Theophrastus (*Char.* 21.7) mocks the 'Man of Petty Pride' who would nail up the skull of any ox he sacrificed so everyone could see it. He would put the skull by the entrance to his house (which may account for some of the scarcity of cattle bones from sanctuaries!), but sacrificial calendars from Marathon, Thorikos and Erchia and a *genos* inscription from Salamis make it clear that when state funding was not available, cattle were rarely killed. There is nothing from Athens to compare with two fourth- or third-century inscriptions from Cyrene recording Hermesandros' sacrifices of 120 cattle. Athenian rituals combined private restraint with state lavishness, a pattern I will say more about in chapter 5.[28]

The evidence for contexts other than burial is varied and bitty, but I think that there is enough to suggest a crude typology of the uses of wealth. In funerals, it was hardly appropriate to use precious metals at all in the fifth century; bronze is also rare, although it occurs more often in the fourth century, along with some gold. Even pottery was used frugally. In settlements, coarse-ware pottery was abundant and black-glazed was quite common, but black-

[27] Parthenon inventories, D. M. Lewis 1986. End of the lists, Koumanoudes & Miller 1971. Robbing of votives, Thuc. 1.143; 4.97; DS 16.30.1. Vickers 1985: 115–17; 1987: 138–40. There are also good inventories from the Athenian Asklepieion, dating *c.* 350–100 B.C. (Aleshire 1989: 103–369). Linders (1988) summarises the evidence from Greece as a whole.

[28] Archaeological remains, Jameson 1988a: 90–3, with references; Reese 1989. Athenian sacrifices, *IG* i³ 375.7; ii² 1496 = *SIG*³ 1029. Sacrifices in 334/3, Jameson 1988a: 96. Deme and Salamis lists, Jameson 1988a, with references. Cyrene, Carratelli 1961/2: nos. 161, 162. General account, Jameson 1988b.

figured and red-figured vases were rather rare, and white-ground still more so. Bronze and iron were probably used quite widely for tools and utensils. Just what the best vases were for, other than export to Etruria and burial there, is equally obscure. In sanctuaries, though, wealth was much more visible. The humble gifts of the eighth and seventh centuries became less acceptable, and David Lewis even suggests that the pottery water jugs carried by girls in the Panathenaic processions were replaced in the fourth century with silver jugs weighing 4 kgs each.[29] Let no one say the Athenians were getting soft.

If this typology is crude, the distinction I would make on the basis of it between family-oriented (grave/household) and state-oriented (sanctuary) display must be cruder still, and I will go some way towards breaking it down in the next chapter. But it gives new importance to the grave goods, and lets us go beyond arguments against art historians. Vickers is right to imply that artefacts are too important to be left to archaeologists and to try to combine the literary and excavated records, but I do not agree with his results. He argues from the written sources that 'Athenian aristocrats clearly lived high on the hog' (1986: 140) in the fifth and fourth centuries. He correctly throws out extreme claims like Strong's (1966: 74) that 'for most of the fifth century no plate was manufactured for private domestic use in Greece', but then goes to what I see as the opposite extreme, arguing that silver and gold were regularly used by the rich and must have been imitated in more plebeian media. He draws an analogy with Madame de Pompadour setting the tone in eighteenth-century France to show how 'Taste in most societies is created by a wealthy élite, and as often as not by a small group or even an individual within that élite' (1985: 113). But the analogy is misleading.[30]

---

[29] D. M. Lewis 1986: 75.

[30] The most important texts are Hdt. 9.81; Thuc. 6.32.1; 6.46 (for Segesta, but relevant); Plato, *Symp.* 223c; Pind. *Ol.* 9.90 (Marathonian games); Ath. 1.28b–c (quoting Critias); Plut. *Alc.* 4; *Cim.* 13.2; D.S. 11.67.5 (Syracuse); 13.3.2. Vickers does not mention Dem. 22.75, which reveals complex attitudes (see Ober 1989b: 243). Arafat & Morgan (1989: 335–6) make a similar argument for elite control of symbolism. At this point discussion is required on chronology. Vickers is most interested in the period of the finest black- and red-figure vases, on the traditional chronology roughly 560–480 B.C. However, his down-dating of Athenian art moves this period to *c.* 480–400 B.C. (see n. 19). Putting the evidence in context therefore becomes very complicated. If we move the pottery it takes all other archaeological evidence with it, so that is not a problem; but the events described in texts are dated on independent criteria. I am not comfortable with the lower dates (see R. M. Cook 1989), and to treat Vickers' case on its own terms I should therefore put the

Being rich was complicated in Athens. Wealth was very unevenly distributed, but having it was not always something to shout about. In Thucydides' account (2.37) of the funeral oration delivered by Pericles in 431/0 B.C., we are told simply that no one should be ashamed of being poor; but Demosthenes repeatedly reminded juries that wealth bred *hubris*, an arrogance which poisoned social relations. Nothing was such good evidence of the presence of *hubris* as deliberate displays of wealth. The rich might feel less loyalty to the *polis* than the poor did and might betray it, preferring to side with the wealthy in other cities against their own poor. Wealth was something which should be used for the common good, and being able to help out poorer kin or demesmen, or to fulfil the obligations of the rich towards the state, was agreed to be a good thing. But even this could be dangerous, as help shaded off into patronage, a decidedly undemocratic relationship. Grave goods should be seen in this context. In theory, they would be put into the grave by near kin. Where this was not possible – as, perhaps, in the case of Aristophanes' comic characters who were too poor to carry out a funeral (*Ecc.* 592; *Wealth* 555) – a good man might step in to cover the cost, like Nicophemus, the father of one of Lysias' clients (Lys. 19.59). Failure to provide the adequate amount would probably have incurred the same kind of disapproval as being stingy with the dowry of a dependent kinswoman; ˎinappropriate lavishness would, equally probably, have been seen as a kind of social climbing.[31]

grave goods in the context of the literary sources for sixth-century Athens. These sources are very poor. Hdt. 6.125 has the fortunes of the Alcmaeonid line founded in the 590s in gold, but the anecdote is hardly credible; [Ar.] *AP* 15.2 and Hdt. 1.64 have Pisistratus enrich himself in Thrace, almost certainly from gold and/or silver mines (see P. J. Rhodes 1981: 207). Ar. *Pol.* 5.1314b5 puts Pisistratus in the class of 'half-wicked' tyrants, who do not lavish other people's money on 'courtesans and aliens and craftsmen', which might be (over?)interpreted as meaning that he set an example of frugality; and *Pol.* 5.1313b24 could be read as meaning that he so drained the rich for funds for his temple of Olympian Zeus that they had nothing left for silver and gold. The first big strike of silver within Attica seems to have been in 483 (Hdt. 7.144; [Ar.] *AP* 22.7; Plut. *Them.* 4 and many later sources). However, since Vickers takes his arguments for the relationship of metal and pottery down until 320 B.C., rather than agonise over the archaic sources, I will concentrate (as he does) on the fifth and fourth centuries, leaving aside the important question of the origins of the practices under discussion. ·This does not do justice to Vickers' position, but my concern here is more with what we can get out of the patterns of grave goods for the analysis of Athenian social structure.

[31] Ober (1989b: 192–247) provides a masterly discussion of the ambiguities of wealth. Distribution and scale, J. K. Davies 1971; 1981, although Davies' distribution graph is criticised by Ober (1989b: 28, n. 64). Wealth and *hubris*, Dem. 18.320; 21.133, 158; 36.45; 38.27; 40.50–1; 42.24; etc. Rich men's 'treason', Herman 1987. 'Good' wealth, Thuc. 6.16;

Certainly poverty was nothing to revel in, and Thucydides says that those who take no steps to avoid it incur real shame (2.40). The horribly rich Apollodorus' main point in making a spectacle of himself by claiming abject poverty ([Dem.] 45.73) was probably mainly to make the opponent who had supposedly ruined him look even more evil. It was far more common to find rich men boasting in court of how they used their plenty in the service of the state. When fourth-century speech writers complain about wealth, it is not the fact that some are richer than others which bothers them so much as a feeling that there has been a moral decline from the good old days, whether set in Solon's time or in the fifth century, when the rich lived simply and spent their wealth for the good of the city, private display was minimal, and the poor were content. Ober argues that the real strength of Athenian democracy lay not in its constitutional forms but in the ability of the mass of citizens to define the terms of social and political discourse. It was this which made wealth problematic, and in such a context the assumption that elite gold and silver plate must have determined the forms of vulgar pottery is unsafe. As with the spread of inhumation in second-century A.D. Rome, we cannot take for granted a top-to-bottom diffusion of symbolism.[32]

The elite had their own symbols to set themselves off from the poor, but these were very tame. Thucydides (1.6) tells us that by 400 B.C. old-fashioned luxuries like men's use of golden cicadas to tie up their long hair had gone out of style, being replaced, apparently, by a more democratic austerity (see further chapter 5). But the long hair stayed. In the 390s Mantitheus had to beg a jury not to be biased against him because of it, and to remind them that many soberly dressed men were bad for the city (Lys. 16.18–19). The lavish display was gone. In 422, when Aristophanes had Bdelycleon convert his father Philocleon into a symposium-going aristocrat (*Wasps* 1129–537), there was a ready-made aristocratic

---

Xen. *Oec.* 11.9; Lys. 16.14; 19.59; 21.1–10; 31.15; Andoc. 1.147; Dem. 18.311; 57.25; [Dem.] 59.72; Plut. *Nic.* 3; Ath. 12.532f–33c (quoting Theophrastus) with [Ar.] *AP* 27.3; Plut. *Cim.* 10; J. K. Davies 1971: no. 8429. Generosity within the deme, Whitehead 1986: 234–52. Patronage, P. Millett 1989. Responsibility to perform funeral rites, Humphreys 1980; Whitehead 1986: 137–9.

[32] Boasting, see n. 27 and Whitehead 1983; on motives, cf. Ober 1989b: 196, 212–13, 221–6. Good old days, Dem. 3.26; 23.206–7; Isoc. 7.31–5 (see Johnstone 1989: 162–9); cf. [Dem.] 45.77–8. Political discourse, Ober 1989b: 35, 332–9; 1989c. *Contra*, Hansen 1989a; 1989b: 103–6; 1989c. Rome, see ch. 2 above.

pattern of dress, conversation and behaviour, well enough known to get laughs. But neither Philocleon nor Theophrastus' 'Oligarchic Man' (*Char.* 26.4, *c.* 330 B.C.) exactly flaunted wealth, and those whose sympathies lay with Sparta (Philocleon's definitely did not) might affect an even simpler style of dress by putting on rough Spartan cloaks. A very rich man like Meidias could behave outrageously and get away with it (if we can believe Aeschines (3.52)), but it was a decidedly risky business. While aristocratic clubs perhaps provided contexts where the rich could eat off gold plates, sing Theognis and plot against the democracy, it is far from certain that the diners paraded luxury in other situations, or that this kind of metal use was emulated further down the social ladder. Mme de Pompadour would not have liked Athens.[33]

TENTATIVE CONCLUSIONS

By taking Vickers' insights on the gap between excavated grave goods and the circulation of art in Athens and putting them into a wider context of Athenian practices, an interesting picture has started to emerge. So far it is fuzzy, but we can make out a ritual system where wealth could not be used up in grave goods, although it could be put out of circulation almost as permanently in the more communal context of the sanctuary. We have seen the ideological problems of wealth in democratic Athens, and that this pattern of behaviour would work very well within such a structure of thought. But to explore the evidence further, and to see if it can contribute to our understanding of Athenian society rather than merely illustrating themes drawn out of the literary sources, it needs to spill out of the confines of a single chapter. So, I now turn to look at the ways Athenians marked their tombs, and how this fitted into their strategies of display and restraint.

[33] Aristophanes (*Knights* 580) also has long-haired aristocratic youths beg indulgence; cf. Aristoph., *Knights* 1121; *Wasps* 474–6, 1068–70; *Birds* 1281–2. See Ostwald 1986: 235, n. 140. This section of the *Wasps* is penetratingly analysed by Konstan (1985) and Johnstone (1989: 153–62). Aristocratic clubs, Connor 1971: 18–22; J. K. Davies 1981: 96–9, 114–20.

CHAPTER 5

Monuments to the dead: display and wealth in classical Greece

> Whether you are a townsman or a stranger coming from elsewhere,
> Take pity as you go by on Tetichos, a good man.
> Falling in war, he lost his fresh youth.
> Mourn for these things, and go on to good fortune.
> (*IG* i³ 1194 bis (*CEG* 13), Attica, mid-sixth century B.C.)

Eight hundred years later, Ulpian ruled that a funerary monument was by law 'something which exists to preserve memory' (*D* 11.7.2.6). The continuity is striking, but so too are the changes in the functions of monuments. I use most of this chapter to continue the story of display in classical Athens, concentrating on cycles of lavishness and restraint. Grave goods and grave markers are very different kinds of display, the first seen mainly by those taking part in the funeral, the second by those who come later. A Thasian inscription of about 500 B.C. makes this explicit, saying 'Whoever was not present when they carried me out in death, let him now lament me; the memorial of Telephanes' (*CEG* 159]. However, both forms of display are (with a few exceptions) created by the buriers in the ritual process of disposing of the dead, and can only be understood in terms of each other. I argue that they offer a framework around which to organise a history of social structure.

GRAVE MARKERS AND DEMOCRACY, AND BEYOND

Sixth-century Athenian grave markers are impressive: massive, blocked-out *kouroi*, fetching millions on the art market, even when their authenticity is suspect; slender stelai topped with sphinxes; or huge mounds like that for Cimon, probably murdered by the tyrant family in 528/7 B.C. (Hdt. 6.103.3). In fact, we have found almost as many sixth-century funerary sculptures as graves. But around

500 B.C. all this ends, and monumental tombs disappear from Athens until about 425. Big tombs then return, getting bigger still until banned by Demetrius of Phaleron, probably in 317 (fig. 27). Cicero (*Laws* 2.64–5) refers to a law 'somewhat later' than Solon, which decreed that ' "no one shall make a tomb requiring more work than ten men can do in three days" '. Many historians believe that Cleisthenes, who passed reforms in 508/7, or Themistocles, most active in the 480s, promulgated this law, and that it explains fifth-century restraint. Clairmont even suggests that 'a decree … may have been seriously envisaged by the former, but enforced only by the more radical latter statesman' (1970: 11).[1]

The end of restraint, *c.* 425 B.C., is usually seen in similarly contingent terms. Some suggest that the sculptors who rushed to Athens in the 440s to work on the Parthenon later turned to knocking out gravestones. Johansen, for instance, described funerary sculptures 'almost as a by-product' of the number of artists in Athens (1951: 146–7). Others stress the plague which hit Athens in 430. After all, Thucydides (2.52.3–4) does say that it made people neglect traditional burial customs. Clairmont again gets both in: 'While it is essential to keep in mind the external causes – the war and the plague – that led to the rebirth of classical gravestones, the sculpture of the Parthenon, in the very broadest sense, is the preliminary *per se* for the creation of grave reliefs' (1970: 43).[2]

My criticisms of these theories should be predictable by now: they take the monuments out of their ritual setting and can only account for a small part of a large set of interrelated data. We learn more by drawing on other evidence and in particular by following up Nicole Loraux's work, which puts restraint into the context of state funeral orations for the war dead.

Only a minority of Athenians died in battle, but the state funerals were a crucial part of democratic ideology. They are best known from Thucydides' description:

In that winter [431/0 B.C.] the Athenians, following the ancestral custom,

---

[1] Grave sculptures, Richter 1961; 1968; 1970. I thank Anna Maria D'Onofrio for pointing out to me the relative numbers of sculptures and graves. The chance incorporation of statues into the city wall of 479 B.C. has much to do with this, but the contrast with the later pattern remains valid. On the 'post aliquanto' law, as it is called, see Eckstein 1958; Richter 1961: 38–9; Kurtz & Boardman 1971: 89–90; Stupperich 1977: 71–85; R. Garland 1989: 5–7.

[2] Sculptors, M. Robertson 1975: 363–4. Plague, Stupperich 1977: 243–4.

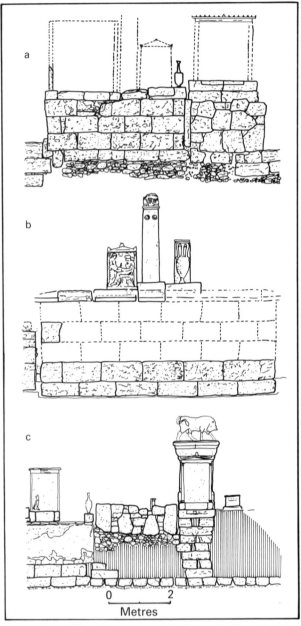

27. Reconstructions of fourth-century peribolos tombs from the Kerameikos: tombs of (a) Makareus, (b) Dionysios of Kollytos and (c) Koroibos (after Knigge 1988: figs. 109, 120, 127)

held a public funeral for those who had been the first to die in the war. On the third day before the ceremony, the bones of the dead are displayed in a tent, and whoever wishes to can make offerings to his dead; then they are carried out in a procession, with wagons carrying coffins of cypress wood, one for each tribe; and each holds the bones of that tribe. One empty coffin is decorated and carried along, for those whose bodies could not be found and recovered. Whoever among the citizens and aliens wishes to do so can join in, and the women who are related to the dead make their laments at the tomb. Then they place them in the *Demosion Sema* [public cemetery], which is in the most beautiful part of the city outside the walls, and where they always bury those killed in war, except for those at Marathon; because of their surpassing virtue, they were buried on the battlefield itself. When they have been covered with earth, a man chosen by the whole *polis* for his wisdom and vision and moral worth speaks an appropriate eulogy for them; after this the people leave. This is how they bury them. (Thuc. 2.34)

The war graves had altar-like dressed stone monuments topped with statues and ten inscribed stone casualty lists, and, at least in 394 B.C., a sculpted frieze. In Homer's eighth-century epics, the monumental tomb helped to create the deathless glory of the individual hero; in fifth-century Athens this was turned on its head, with households refraining from elaborate markers, while the *polis* used the tomb to create a communal ideal.[3]

Half a dozen orations or imitations survive in whole or in part, dating *c.* 430–320. The same general themes appear in them all: the valour of the citizens killed in battle perpetuates the virtue and timelessness of Athens as a community of warrior equals, and the Athenians, the only Greeks born from the soil, are citizens of the greatest and truest of all *poleis*. Loraux sums up this 'Athenian history of Athens': 'In burying its war dead, then, the Athenian community appropriated them forever, and at the Demosion Sema all distinctions, individual or familial, economic or social, that might divide the Athenians even in their graves were abolished'

[3] Athenian war casualties, Strauss 1986: 70–86, 179–83; S. Todd 1987: 41–2; Hansen 1988: 14–28. The origins of the state funeral are disputed, but it probably grew up gradually from around 500 B.C. on (Jacoby 1944; Loraux 1986: 28–30; R. Thomas 1989: 207–8). The earliest casualty list known is for the Drabescus campaign of 464, although some fragments may be earlier (Bradeen 1969: 154). Pausanias (1.29.24) says that the Drabescus tomb was 'the first', but it is not clear whether he means first in date or the first to be seen on leaving the city. No actual war grave has been found, but Clairmont's reconstruction (1983: 60–73; cf. Brückner 1910: 183–200) is persuasive. Possible *polyandrion*, Clairmont 1981. Contrast with 'heroic' tombs, Loraux 1982. General details on war burial, Pritchett 1985b: 94–259.

(Loraux 1986: 23). The power of the monument and the glory of the war dead were taken over by the *polis* from the individuals within it, but Loraux is quick to point out the ambiguities. The casualty lists, an integral part of the monument, included the names of non-Athenians, subverting the orators' message of a unified citizen state. The hoplite of the orations was also at odds with the real base of Athenian strength, the poorer citizens who rowed in the fleet.[4]

Moving beyond the texts, the contradictions are even sharper. There are a few monumental tombs dating 500–425, and at least two *sequences* of monuments – not just a handful of eccentrics setting up tasteless tombs (after all, Athens had plenty, and rejoiced in them), but families who for three generations consistently ignored restraint. The most important is in the Kerameikos, within sight of the *Demosion Sema* where the state funerals took place. The gigantic mound G of 560 B.C. was followed over the next fifty years by eleven shaft graves and, on its west edge, two smaller mounds. At this point, monumental burials stopped elsewhere in Athens, but in the 490s, gr. C246 was dug into mound K, and the kidney-shaped mound L was heaped over it. This was covered by tomb d and mound M in the 460s, and by the large mound N in the 440s. In the 420s the remarkable gr. C264 was dug: a cremation of an adult male with his ashes in an ornate bronze urn, wrapped in purple cloth and placed in a wooden box inside a huge sarcophagus. It was marked by tomb e and mound O. The series culminated with the huge tomb f shortly before 400 (fig. 28).[5]

---

[4] Orations, Thuc. 2.35–46; Lys. 2; Pl. *Men.*; [Dem.] 60; Hyp. 6; Gorgias fr. DK 82 B 5a–6. Textual problems, Ziolkowski 1981; Loraux 1986: 8–14; R. Thomas 1989: 209–11; Coventry 1989. Ambiguities, Loraux 1986: 32–7. *Xenoi*, Gauthier 1971. Josiah Ober (personal communication) suggests the possibility that most of the orations were not about hoplites and did in fact glorify the rowers (cf. Ober 1989b: 290).

[5] Mound G burials, Kübler 1973; 1976: 5–21, 65–90. Clairmont (1983: 36, with references) points out that the postholes under the road through the Kerameikos, less than 100 metres from mound G, may be from the wooden platform for the orations. The other sequence of mounds is on Peiraios St., where tumulus A is the last stage of a series of smaller fifth-century mounds. The mudbrick wall enclosing a mound 10–12 m in diameter is late fifth- or fourth-century, as is tumulus B with walls FF and KK (Brückner & Pernice 1893: 86–100). The Lenormant St. mound (diameter 9 m) probably dates 475–450 (Schilardi 1968: 44–8). The radial arrangement of graves at Panepistimiou St. no. 11 (Alexandri 1970: fig. 33) probably indicates an early fifth-century mound here. The only other monumental tombs which may be of this period are from the Kerameikos – mudbrick tomb hs a, *c.* 450, on the south side of the Sacred Way (Vierneisel 1964a) and the sequence γ (510/500), ζ (500/490), δ, ε, η (500–480), θ (*c.* 450) and ι (*c.* 420, built of stone) on the north side

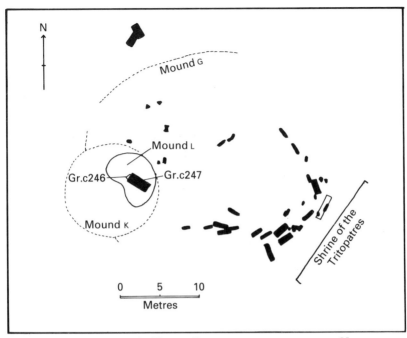

28(a). Mound G area in the Kerameikos cemetery, *c*. 500–475 B.C. New graves are shown in solid black; earlier graves in dotted outline (for the sixth-century burials in this area, see Morris 1987: fig. 45).

Fig. 29 shows how these graves were superimposed, and we have to see it as a family line disregarding the general practice. These buriers linked themselves unambiguously with the past. Not only did they tap into the associations of the massive mound G, but gr.

(Vierneisel 1963; 1964b). However, Clairmont (1983: 263, n. 42) casts doubt on Vierneisel's dates. The small mound T (Kübler 1976: 148–50) dates to the early fifth century, but should probably be seen as the very end of the sixth-century tradition. Kübler's dating (on stylistic grounds) is flatly contradicted by the stratigraphy of the site, and I generally follow Stupperich's suggestions (1977: 82–4), with a few revisions of my own. Petrakos (1976: 11–15) dates a round stone tomb at Rhamnous *c*. 450, but R. Garland (1982: 127) puts it in the fourth century (note that this is M6 in Garland's catalogue; the references to M5 on his p. 127 are misprints). The 'mound' over Tavros gr. VI (440s; Schilardi 1975: 81–95) was just a mudbrick platform 20 cm high.

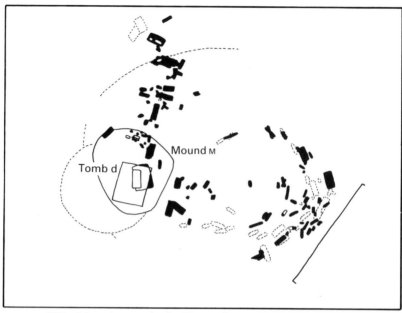

28(b). Mound G area in the Kerameikos cemetery, *c.* 475–450 B.C.

c264 was surely a self-consciously 'Homeric' cremation. The war-
riors at Troy continued to furnish aristocratic role models, and
mounds with stelai must have evoked the heroic noble to many
fifth-century viewers. White-ground lekythoi betray hankerings for
this form of elitism, representing tombs by a stele on or in front of
an egg-shaped mound; but one group of Athenians was, for reasons
now lost, able to deploy ostentatiously undemocratic symbols.[6]

In chapter 1 I described Loraux's approach as being too static.
The archaeological evidence shows that there were major changes
around 425 B.C. Suddenly, there are monuments everywhere. In
Garland's catalogue of 140 peribolos tombs (groups of graves surrounded by an enclosure wall, often with sculpture and inscrip-

---

[6] Homeric burial, Andronikos 1968; Petropoulou 1988. Homeric role models, Donlan 1980:
1–2, 155–80; Herman 1987: 156–61. Clairmont (1983: 62) suggests that the vase paintings
represent visits to the *polyandria*, but as Lissarrague (1988: 100) stresses, only one vase can
possibly be seen in this light. In any case, Clairmont's own reconstruction of the *polyandria*
shows that they were not marked with mounds; and the stelai shown are not like those used
for listing the war dead. See also Bazant 1986; Baldassarre 1988.

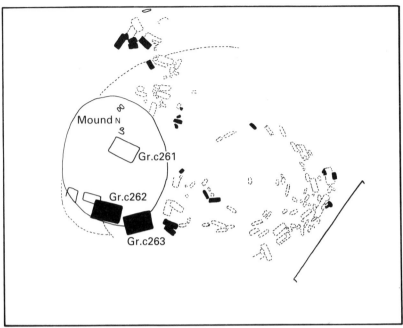

28(c). Mound G area in the Kerameikos cemetery, *c.* 450–425 B.C.

tions), only two or three might predate 425; and only 1.5% of the funerary sculptures in Veddar's catalogue date to 500–425. The massive reshaping of the Kerameikos into the series of walled tombs known as the 'Terrassenanlage' probably began shortly before 420. Less than 5% of Athenian graves dated 500–425 can be related to monuments, and the real figure may be under 1%. It is difficult to be precise about the proportion of graves within fourth-century monumental tombs, since so many of the periboloi are only partially excavated or poorly published, but the figure is clearly also fairly low. Most of the fourth-century periboloi held just three or four graves, although one at Ano Voula had thirty-one. Access to monuments was wider in the fourth century than the fifth, but still only open to a relatively small group, which, at a guess, I would put around 10% of the population. In the late fifth-century Syndagma cemetery, just six adult graves out of a total of sixty-nine have periboloi (fig. 30). But several thousand epitaphs have been found, usually out of context, and it may be that in the fourth century most

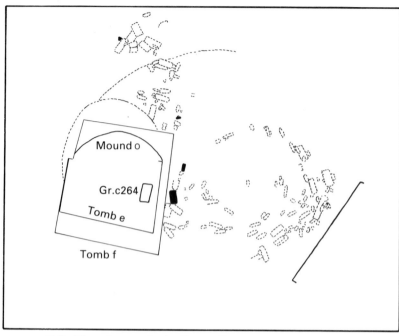

28(d). Mound G area in the Kerameikos cemetery, *c.* 425–400 B.C.

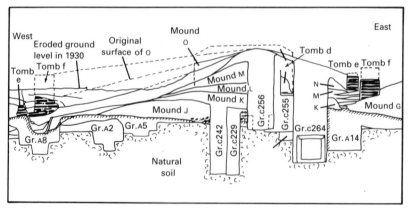

29. Section through the Mound G area of the Kerameikos cemetery (after Kübler 1976: Beil. 36.1)

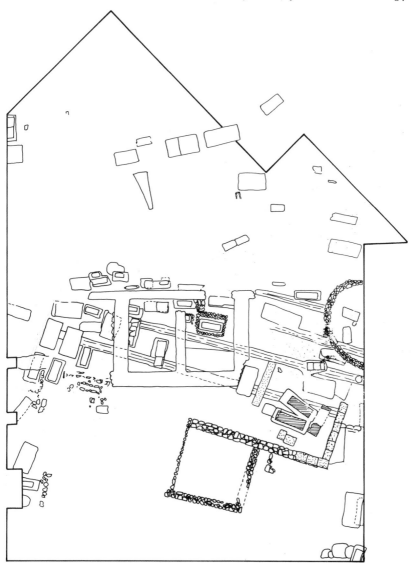

30. The Syndagma Square cemetery (after Charitonides 1958: pl. 1)

Athenian graves had a simple inscribed stele, while a much smaller group was also buried in periboloi.[7]

Literary sources give some prices. In 409 one Diogeiton was asked to spend 5,000 drachmas (probably enough to feed a family of four at subsistence level for five to seven years) on his brother Diodotos' tomb. Apparently he only spent half this and kept the rest (Lys. 32.21). There is no suggestion that 5,000 drachmas was considered an excessive amount. By 349 [Demosthenes] (45.79) was telling a jury that Stephanos spent over two talents (12,000 drachmas) on a tomb for another man's wife after he had debauched her. The web of moral outrage here is complex, and the price is no doubt exaggerated, but this general scale must have seemed credible. In 326/5 Harpalus stole 700 talents from Alexander's treasury at Babylon and fled to Athens, where he built such a huge tomb for his mistress Pythionice that it earned a place in Diodorus of Sicily's chronicle (17.108.5) three centuries later. It is not just a matter of literary genre that we have no such stories from before 425: this sort of spending would not have been acceptable.

This was a major change in the *form* of markers. As in chapter 2, the next question is how far it was also a change in the *structure* of the rituals; and the answer must be that to some extent it was, but not on anything like the scale of the eighth-century example discussed on pp. 25–7 above. I begin by returning to grave goods. Table 8 shows their distribution, as measured by Gini's coefficient of inequality (explained on pp. 106–7 above). The fifth century is divided into four quarters, but the shortage of closely dated fourth-century graves means that I have to treat them as a single group to get a decent sample. Since the issue here is the changes around 425,

---

[7] R. Garland 1982; Vedder 1985. 'Terrassenanlage', Freytag 1976: 37, correcting Brückner's date (1909: 35–42); and now Kovacsovics 1990: 6. The fifth-century figure depends on whether we accept a mound at Panepistimiou St. no. 11 (see p. 132, n. 5 above). Tombs have been published at a startling rate since Garland's catalogue appeared, particularly from Ano Voula. In addition to reports in *AD* since vol. 30.2 (1975), see Petrakos 1977a; 1978; 1979: 1–2, 16–22; 1982: 154–8 (Rhamnous); Steinhauer 1982 (Spata); Zachariadou et al. 1985; Catling 1989: 12–15 (Athens). Large Ano Voula tomb, Petrakos 1977b: 42. Humphreys (1980: 114–21) discusses the size of groups using periboloi. There are more than 8,000 epitaphs in *IG* ii², with 260 more in *SIA* 1 and 310 from the agora in Bradeen (1974). Bradeen left unpublished a further 900, which were too fragmentary to be of any use. The hundreds listed in *SEG* are only a small proportion of those published from 1940–1969 and again since 1976; M. J. Osborne (1988) collects a further 340 to fill the gap between the two series of *SEG*. Grave stones can be identified after repeated reuses, so they are certainly over-represented in our evidence, and caution is needed with statistics. Social distribution of tombstones, Nielsen et al. 1989.

Table 8. *Distribution of artefacts (as measured by Gini's coefficient of inequality) between intact burials in classical Athens*

Dates	Vases	Adults Metal objects	n	Vases	Children Metal objects	n
500–475	0.547	0.927	122	0.530	0.969	97
475–450	0.601	0.965	191	0.521	0.986	206
450–425	0.601	0.920	156	0.514	0.968	132
425–400	0.625	0.883	137	0.654	0.945	71
400–300	0.587	0.805	253	0.621	0.952	37

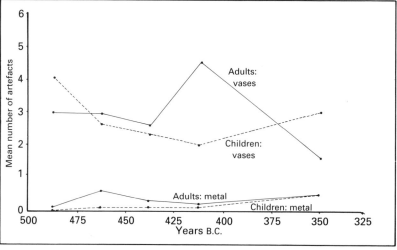

31. Mean numbers of pottery and metal grave goods in Athenian burials, 500–300 B.C.

this should not be a problem. During the fifth century the distribution of pottery grew less equal and that of metalwork more equal, but the changes are minor. Fig. 31 shows an increase in the mean numbers of metal objects in graves after 400, but little change before, other than a temporary leap in pottery in adult burials in 425–400. This is caused by the unusual Syndagma Square cemetery. Without this group, the mean score is 2.8, in line with the steady decline from 500 to 300 B.C. The richness of the Syndagma

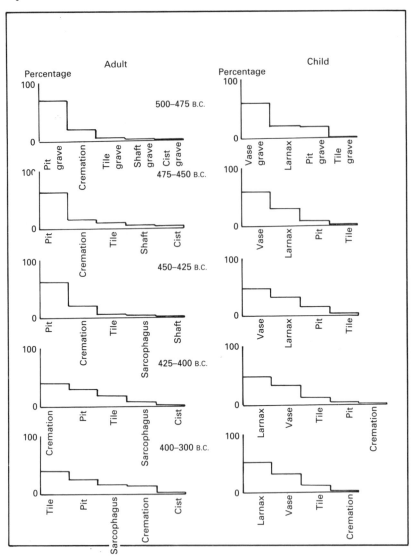

32. Use of different burial types at Athens, 500–300 B.C.

graves deserves attention in its own right, but it is not evidence for a major shake-up in the use of grave goods during the Peloponnesian War.

Fig. 32 shows the proportions of graves accounted for by the five main disposal types in each period. The most interesting changes here come in the late fifth century. Starting with adults, sarcophagi became more popular from *c.*450 on; but there is also a more fundamental change. From 500 to 425, there is a clearly dominant burial type, inhumation in a simple pit, accounting for between 62 and 69% of the burials. From 425–300, there is no such orthodoxy. Cremation is briefly popular at the end of the fifth century, and tile graves dominate in the fourth. The rapid changes in symbols are interesting enough, but more important still is the fact that after 425 the dominant type only accounts for about 40% of the graves. The ritual system was opening up, allowing a wider range of choices and the expression of more gradations of adult status.

There is a change in the child graves around 425, with burial in a clay chest (*larnax*) becoming more popular than vase burial; but the dominant type always accounts for 50–60% of the graves. Vase burial was apparently used for the youngest children, and the increase in the use of *larnakes* may represent a lowering of the age of graduation from the status of infant to that of child. However, there are few demographic data, and this cannot be explored. The child: adult ratio (making a crude distinction around 15 years) declines consistently from 1:1.3 in 500–475 B.C. to 1:2 in 425–400 and 1:7.3 in the fourth century; and just about the time that children become rare, so do pit graves, with tile graves becoming proportionately better represented. Possibly many child burials after 425 were in simple pits with few or no grave goods, making them hard to identify; if so, then we would see a pattern like that among the adults, with rapid changes in symbols and a loosening of the constraints in the late fifth century.[8]

So far, I have been working with a simple opposition, with public/state burial on one side and private/household burial on the other. This has its value, but it may obscure more than it reveals. State monuments were also bigger after 425. We know little about the war graves, but the simple markers put up by the *polis* over the graves of Pythagoras of Selymbria (*c.*450 B.C.) and the Corcyrean envoys of 432/1 compare poorly with the impressive tomb for the Spartan officers killed at Athens in 403 or the tomb at Horos 3

---

[8] A weakness in this idea, though, is the fact that the average number of grave goods in the child burials which we have identified does not decline from the fifth century to the fourth, nor does its distribution change much. The idea that in the fourth century children were cremated in informal surface pyres (R. S. Young 1951b: 110–14) has been disproved, and the pyres are probably connected with animal sacrifices (Shear 1973: 151, n. 66).

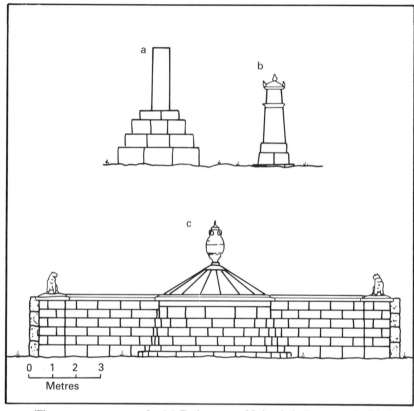

33. The state monuments for (a) Pythagoras of Selymbria (*c.* 450 B.C.), (b) the
Corcyrean ambassadors (433/2 B.C.) and (c) the tomb at Horos 3 (*c.* 350 B.C.) in
the Kerameikos cemetery, Athens. Compare the size of the Roman monuments
shown in fig. 5 on p. 43 above

(*c.* 350; fig. 33), thought by some to be for the famous general
Chabrias. There was a *general* increase in scale, and we are not
dealing with the collapse of a putative public/private distinction.
Something altogether more complex was going on.[9]

[9] Pythagoras, the Corcyreans and Silenos (died 433/2), Knigge 1972; Hoepfner 1973; Willemsen 1977. Tomb of Lacedaemonians and Horos 3, Ohly 1965: 314–27; Willemsen 1977;
Mallwitz 1980. Knigge tentatively identifies the tomb of Anthemokritos (1980: 70–5),
probably dating to 431 (P. J. Rhodes 1985: 17–18), which (along with the tomb of the
Corcyreans) was renewed with more lavish monuments in the fourth century; and (Knigge
1988: 159) a possible state grave of *c.* 480, consisting of a simple poros block enclosing a
cremation in a bronze urn. Kaempf-Dimitriadou (1986) suggests that the tomb for the
battle of Chaeronea in 338 has also been found. Generally, see Clairmont 1983: 29–45.
There were of course special reasons to give the Spartans an imposing tomb in 403, but
these do not change the overall pattern of growth.

34. The monument of Dexileos, *c.* 394 B.C. (after Knigge 1988: fig. 107)

Households began to reappropriate from the *polis* some of the honour and glory of their war dead. The famous precinct of Dexileos (killed in the Corinthian War, in 394 B.C.) is a good example (fig. 34). His family set up a cenotaph in the Kerameikos, showing him on horseback trampling down his enemies. His name is preserved on a monument set up for the noble 'knights' killed that year, and it was no doubt inscribed again in the casualty lists over the mass grave in which he was buried. The iconography of Dexileos' monument is very similar to that of a relief of the early 420s now in the Villa Albani, which probably comes from a state war grave. We see a change in the external referents of the monuments of the wealthy by 400. Instead of the heroic tumulus or a mudbrick tomb recalling sixth-century monuments, the new trend was to take over the symbols by which the *polis* channelled the glory of the war dead towards communal ends. We can trace this process back as

far as the 410s, when a relief with the same iconography was set up
at Chalandri, a few miles north of Athens, with an inscription
proclaiming '...and my country (knows) how many enemies I
have destroyed ... [bear] witness how many trophies of my
prowess in battle I set up' (*IG* II² 7716). The cost of Diodotos' tomb
in Lysias' speech (32.21) takes on an extra dimension when we note
that he was killed in battle at Ephesus in 409. Not only did his
family take over what had been the state's right to commemorate
him, but his sons even prosecuted their uncle Diogeiton for his
failure to do it grandly enough; and all this at a time when Athens
was having great difficulty paying for the war against Sparta.[10]

   Humphreys proposes that 'the state funerals for the war dead ...
first brought the honours of heroic burial within the range of every
citizen' (1980: 123), but I see these strands of evidence leading in
the opposite direction: in the fifth century, the state funerals took
away the right of heroic burial, even from its richest citizens. We
have already seen that before 425 there was a tension between the
communal ideal of Athens and some individuals' desire for a more
elevated status than that of citizen, with the restraint broken in a
few cases. In the 420s far more of the wealthy set up their own
monuments, some even taking over the very symbols of the state.
The archaeological evidence allows us to see how the social construction of meaning changed through time. The last quarter of the
fifth century is the crucial period, as the rich take over what had
been communal symbols, and the overall structure of burial rituals
begins to loosen; and at the same time there is a general increase in
the level of spending, by the *polis* as well as by its individual
citizens.

---

[10] 'Knights' inscription, *IG* II² 5222, with Clairmont 1983: 209–14. Dexileos' own inscription is *IG* II² 6217. Villa Albani and Chalandri reliefs, Clairmont 1983: 67–8. Knigge
(1980) points out that the round stone tombs of the fourth century continue to evoke
tumuli (like Augustus' mausoleum). Bugh (1982: 28–9; 1988: 137–9) and Strauss (1986:
124) cite an unpublished paper by Colin Edmonson suggesting that *IG* II² 6217 included
Dexileos' birthdate to show that he was not associated with the Thirty Tyrants of 403 B.C.,
and that '*IG* II² 5222 and *IG* II² 6217 represent an effort to refurbish the image of the
Athenian cavalry' (Bugh 1988: 139). Mike Jameson (personal communication) suggests
that Dexileos' family was not so much trying to appropriate the *polis'* images for political
ends as to assimilate their son to it, freeing him of the taint of involvement with the
tyrants. The two aims seem perfectly compatible to me; and any personal factors created
by Dexileos' relationship (or lack of it) to the Thirty cannot be read back to explain
developments in the 410s or earlier. Dexileos' monument is fully discussed by Ensoli
(1987).

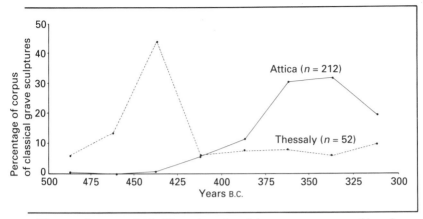

35. The use of grave stelai in Thessaly and at Athens, *c.* 500–300 B.C. (data from Biesantz 1965; Vedder 1985)

THE BIG PICTURE

In chapter 2, I showed how the geographical scale at which we study a pattern affects our understanding of it. The same is true here. Similar processes of restraint and display occur all over the Aegean. Around 500, display declined everywhere, even in rather marginal areas: the great tumuli at Vergina and Trebenishte stop, and the Lycian series of rock-cut tombs breaks off, although a few podium tombs in the Persian tradition continue. There are very few monuments within the Hellenic world proper. A handful of chamber tombs on Aegina date around 450, and several relief stelai and small block gravestones have turned up around the Aegean and in Boeotia. The only good series of stelai is from Thessaly, which flourishes just as Athenian stelai become rare (fig. 35). There are some large chamber tombs of the first half of the fifth century at Pharsalos and Krannon, but these are far less imposing than the sixth-century burials with their huge tumuli.[11]

Restraint ends everywhere by 400. On the fringes, the Lycian

[11] Sixth-century monuments, Schmaltz 1983: 149–89; Morris 1987: 128–37, 152–4, 183–9. Sixth-/fifth-century tombs in Macedon, Hammond and Griffith 1979: 91–7, 141–5. Lycian rock-cut tombs, Bruns-Özgan 1987. Podium tombs, Kjeldsen & Zahle 1976. Links with Persian tombs, Jacobs 1987; Cahill 1988. Aegina, e.g. Welter 1938: 57; Lazarides 1966: 100–3; Kranioti & Rozaki 1979: 69. Aegean relief tombstones, Akurgal 1955: 26–8; Hiller 1975: 48–88; M. Robertson 1975: 197–208; Karouzos 1951; Politi 1953/4. Boeotia, stelai, Schild-Xenidou 1972; block gravestones, Keramopoullos 1934/5; Plassart 1958. Thessalian reliefs, Biesantz 1965. Pharsalos, Verdelis 1955. Krannon, Theochares 1960; Milojcic (1960: 176–7) suggests slightly later dates.

monuments begin again with the astonishing Nereid tomb and
escalate steadily until Roman times; to the North, the vaulted
'Macedonian' tomb type begins in the fourth century. The only
monumental tomb at Olynthus, gr. 598, is early fourth-century,
and the free-standing funerary monument by the city gate dates
after 400. The only large-scale classical tomb known at Corinth is
late fifth- or fourth-century. Thessalian tombs become impressive
again after 400, and begin to include even richer grave goods than
they did in the sixth century. I could go on piling up examples, but
the point is clear. Restraint from 500 to 425 and rapidly increasing
display thereafter are genuinely panhellinic phenomena, the only
exceptions being disturbing places like Sparta where burials elude
us altogether.[12]

Seeing private restraint as the mirror image of state war graves
does not work outside Athens. Other *poleis* normally buried their
war dead on the battlefield. As with cremation and inhumation in
the Roman empire, we must move back and forth between general
and local readings. We could make laws and/or a Periclean ethos
followed by the Parthenon sculptures and/or the plague responsible
for Athenian developments, and argue that Athenian cultural
hegemony was so strong that the rest of Greece followed suit. The
later fifth-century funerary laws from Ioulis and Delphi do not limit
monuments, but they could be deliberate emulation of Athens. But
quite apart from the question of whether this is plausible in
425 B.C., let alone 500, it does not get us any further with appreciat-
ing how restraint worked outside Athens. In Athens, the Lorauxian
approach provides valuable insights; but what about in a (before
378) strikingly non-democratic city like Thebes?[13]

[12] Nereid tomb, Coupel & Demargne 1969; Martin 1971; Bommelaer 1986. Lycian tombs,
Waywell 1980; Waelkens 1982; Cormack 1989: 36–8. Macedonian tombs, Rhomaios
1951; S. G. Miller 1982; Andronikos 1984; Borza 1990: 256–76, with Andronikos 1987 on
chronology. Olynthus, D. M. Robinson 1942: 133–7. Corinth, Carpenter & Bon 1936:
297–301; H. S. Robinson 1962: 133, n. 125. Thessaly, Verdelis 1951; S. G. Miller 1979;
1986, with references. Schmaltz (1983: 190, n. 462) lists more examples. Laconia, site list
in Cartledge 1979: 325–34. Truly monumental tombs only appear at Sparta after 200 B.C.
(Cartledge & Spawforth 1989: 72, 132–3).
[13] War graves, Pritchett 1985b: 125–39, 249–51; N. Robertson 1983. Athenian cultural
hegemony, Schuller 1974: 122–4. Delphi and Ioulis, texts in Sokolowski 1969: nos. 77, 97.
Discussed by R. Garland (1985: 21–6, 40–5; 1989: 8–9, 11–13). Theban burial, Symeonoglou 1985: 146–7. For nearby Tanagra, see Andreiomenou 1985. Theban gravestones,
Schild-Xenidou 1972; Demand 1982: 106–16; Fraser & Rönne 1957. On the character of
Theban government, the (somewhat defensive) *locus classicus* is Thuc. 3.62; on the brief
democracy of the 450s, Ar. *Pol.* 5.1302b29.

When our sources say why funerary laws were passed the reasons are always religious rather than political, and one response to the problems of transferring the Athenian model to other states would be to seek panhellenic intellectualist explanations. However, there is no evidence for a massive shift in ideas of the afterlife which would have 'caused' the changes in burial, except in the weak sense that since tombs are part of the rituals which incorporate the soul into the next world, then restraint in them means *a priori* that lavishness was considered inappropriate for the dead. That is not very helpful.[14] But in an important paper, Aubrey Cannon offers a more interesting approach, proposing a law of what he calls 'expressive redundancy' to explain long-term cycles in display. He notes that when the general level of funerary expenditure is high, it is among the wealthiest that display declines first, and that modest funerals become a symbol of 'good taste', only gradually spreading down the social ladder. This pattern, he says, has relatively little to do with democratic or aristocratic tendencies; rather, any style of mortuary symbolism has a point beyond which continued elaboration fails to impress anyone, and the only strategy left to someone wishing to make a point is to reduce the scale of display. It is *difference*, not the form it takes, which counts when symbols are being used to create hierarchy. In a suitably post-modern flourish, he suggests that we need to leave more room for life to imitate art: 'if expressive restraint is seen as part of the same trajectory as expressive elaboration, then such ideological change as does occur must be considered as much the consequence as the cause of shifts in mortuary symbolism' (Cannon 1989: 447).

Cannon's theory raises two big issues. The first is the perennial sociological question of how we draw lines between cultural systems. Seeing a nobleman buried simply at Pharsalos and seeing the same in Athens may have meant very different things, even if the observers at both knew that restrained rituals were a 'Greek' custom. The Thessalian aristocracy had its own traditions of symbolism, and a history of the use of wealth very different from that in Athens. Can we really expect to find an explanation which holds true for both cases? But on the other hand, can any account of

---

[14] Religion and laws, Toher 1986; R. Garland 1989. Fifth-century ideas of afterworld, Rohde 1966 [1890]: 411–62; Bremmer 1983; R. Garland 1985. The problems of explanations in these terms, Morris 1989a: 297–9.

Athens be adequate if it does not also cover the very similar developments in Thessaly?[15]

The second issue is the social control of symbolism. In chapter 4, I sketched a model of Athens where the mass of citizens defined the evaluation of material culture. Cannon's general theory proposes a symbolic version of Michels' Iron Law of Oligarchy, that the few always control the many, no matter how democratic appearances may be. This would have the rich cutting back on display to distance themselves from the poor, like Aristotle's 'Magnanimous Man' (*EN* 4.1124b), who would never dream of sinking so low as actually to compete for honour against the riff-raff. Following Cannon's model, the lower orders would continue for a while to indulge in what had been redefined as 'vulgar' theatricality, before dropping into line. Loraux suggests a similar view, that democratic ideals were 'undermined from the inside by aristocratic values and representations' (1986: 217).[16]

We could combine the two models, seeing a tendency among the rich to restrict display beginning all over Greece around 500, gradually being appropriated in Athens by growing popular power, as part of a symbolic system focused on the state monuments. Such democratisation may have been less important elsewhere. It is widely and naïvely assumed that restrained rites must have been imposed by a law, which must have been democratic in intent. Neither need be true. Just as I argued that the Athenian aristocracy took over *polis* symbols in the 420s, so too the people may have taken over elite restraint by the 480s, giving a radical twist to a panhellenic custom.[17]

The return of monuments around 425 could fit into Cannon's cyclical model, but even accepting expressive redundancy, we have to ask 'Why then?' Why did the symbolic capital of restraint not burn up sooner, or last longer? The model reduces burials to part of the unending respiration of an autonomous artistic world, forever

---

[15] Wealth and its uses in Thessaly (mainly as perceived by Athenians), Pind. *Pyth.* 10; Critias, frr. 8, 31 Diels; Pl. *Meno* 70a; Isoc. 8.117; Xen. *Hell.* 6.1.3.

[16] Michels 1915: 50–1, 61–77, 85–128, 333–71; cf. Finley 1985: 3–12; Ober 1989b: 15–16, 334–5. Ober (1989b: 262, 290) replies to Loraux (1986: 180–202, 217–220, 334–5); cf. also R. Thomas 1989: 213–21.

[17] The only literary evidence is ambiguous. Thuc. 1.89–91 describes the building of the city wall in 479, which incorporated many grave markers. This might show lack of aristocratic interest, or it might show elite powerlessness in the face of the people.

oscillating between poles of display and restraint. We need a more particularist approach.

GROUPS AND INDIVIDUALS

Another archaeological approach to cycles of display can help here. Renfrew makes a distinction between 'group-oriented' social structures, where unpretentious graves are accompanied by 'public' display, and 'individualising' structures, where lavish tombs complement modest communal facilities. It has been developed by Bradley as a way to analyse the whole course of British prehistory, with outstanding success. It is also a good way to organise the Greek data. Basically, we move from an individualising Dark Age to a group-oriented late eighth century. After very varied patterns in the Archaic period, the group is dominant through most of the fifth century, with a move towards the individual in the fourth. The advantage of this perspective is that it focuses attention on long-term patterns.[18]

In the Dark Age, from about 1100 to 750, we find almost nothing we could call a communal monument. For that matter we do not find much in the way of lavish graves either, but the marker vases of the Kerameikos and the Lefkandi Toumba cemeteries are more imposing than any other monuments. One house at Nichoria and the controversial apsidal building in the Toumba cemetery at Lefkandi (fig. 36) are larger than normal, and we may see individualising use of settlement space. However, so few Dark Age villages have been explored that the point should not be pressed.[19]

There were rapid shifts towards the group ethos in some places in the late eighth century. In many areas grave goods and grave markers briefly became more impressive before declining again, and by 700 both were generally quite restrained. At the same time,

---

[18] Renfrew 1974; Bradley 1984, esp. pp. 68–93, 157–67. The approach is criticised in Shanks & Tilley 1987: 22–4.

[19] Religious buildings, Mazarakis Ainian 1985. Early hero cults, Calligas 1988; Lambrinoudakis 1988. Grave markers, Morris 1987: 151; Boardman 1988d (Kerameikos); Popham et al. 1982; 1989 (Lefkandi). Dark Age and eighth-century settlements, Drerup 1969. Fagerström's (1988a) catalogue is more up-to-date, but there are some omissions. Mazarakis Ainian (1988) describes the various 'rulers' houses'. The Lefkandi building is not fully published; see Calligas 1988; Mazarakis Ainian 1985: 8–9. Nichoria Unit IV–1 has been published in commendable detail (McDonald et al. 1983: 19–48), and Fagerström's (1988b) attack on the excavators' interpretation is not persuasive.

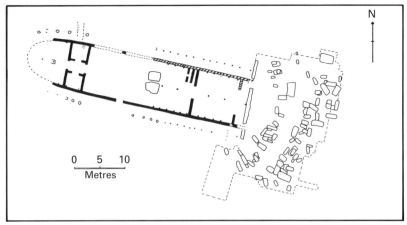

36. The apsidal building and the Toumba cemetery at Lefkandi (after Popham et al. 1989: fig. 28)

there was an explosion in sanctuary activity. Votive offerings to the gods increased a hundredfold; suddenly every little village had its own temple, often quite substantial, and dozens of major sanctuaries were built. There is evidence for competition over whether certain classes of rituals, such as hero cults, would be group- or individual-oriented; but, generalising broadly, we end up around 700 with two patterns, the *polis* states which were group-oriented and the *ethnos* states which were more individualising. The evidence for houses is still poor. They increase in complexity, growing from single- to multi-room dwellings, often built around a courtyard. However, few houses stand out as especially lavish and there is no evidence for palaces in early Greece, even under the tyrants.[20]

But this was by no means the beginning of a steady march towards a fifth-century peak in group-orientation. The intervening period was one of intense social conflict, and the patterns blur. There is a great regional variety, and in some places the late eighth-century move towards the group was stopped or even reversed.

[20] Morris 1987: 183–96. Sanctuaries, Mallwitz 1981; de Polignac 1984; C. Morgan 1990. Hero cults, Morris 1988; Snodgrass 1988; Whitley 1988; Antonaccio 1992. I am very grateful to Carla Antonaccio for letting me read her paper in advance of publication. Settlements, see n. 19. Tyrants and buildings, e.g. Shear 1978; Salmon 1984: 201–2; Shipley 1988: 72–3, 75–80 (with Hdt. 3.60; Ar. *Pol.* 5.1313b24); Shapiro 1989: 5–8, 21–4.

Extremely 'communal' monumental stone temples appear in the seventh century, especially in the north-east Peloponnese, but few panhellenic processes can be identified. In Thessaly, both tombs and temples are imposing; in Sparta, Euboea and to some extent Argos, we have good sanctuaries but almost no graves at all. In *Burial and Ancient Society* I argued that communal developments were reversed at Athens after 700. Tombs were well marked, but sanctuaries were extremely poor; nor is there evidence for Athenians making large dedications in sanctuaries in other parts of Greece. Hoplite warfare can be seen as another ritual expression of *polis* identity, and the absence of positive evidence for Athenian involvement before 506 should perhaps be understood as one more aspect of the decline of the communal structure. In sixth-century Crete, we can only find inscriptions; cemeteries, settlements and sanctuaries all enter an archaeological black hole. Some regions, like Samos and Boeotia, become increasingly group-oriented in the later sixth century; in Corinth and Argos, as I mentioned on p. 145, there is a drift back towards individualising behaviour, with some lavish monuments appearing after 550.[21]

Traces of houses are scantier than in the eighth century, but our first literary evidence for personal display in clothing appears. Xenophanes (fr. 3, West) mentions the luxurious habits of Colophonian aristocrats, and in a famous passage already mentioned on p. 126 above Thucydides (1.6.3) tells us that the Athenians were the first to stop carrying weapons and take up 'a way of life which was more relaxed and more luxurious'. He goes on: 'In fact the elder men of the rich families who had these luxurious tastes only recently gave up wearing linen undergarments and tying their hair behind their heads in a knot fastened with a clasp of golden cicadas'. Aristophanes (*Knights* 1321–34; *Clouds* 984–6) associates this kind of display with the generation of Marathon (i.e. 490s–

[21] Social conflict, Lintott 1982: 13–81; Stahl 1987. Stone temples, Mallwitz 1981; Snodgrass 1986; R. Rhodes 1987; C. Morgan 1990: 130–4; Antonaccio 1992. Sparta, Cartledge 1979: 119–23, 356–61. Euboea, Mazarakis Ainian 1987; Morris 1987: 165–6. Argos, ibid.: 183–5; Foley 1988. Athens, Morris 1987: 205–10. Hoplite warfare, Cartledge 1977; Frost 1984; Connor 1988b. Peter Callaghan kindly informs me that in 1989 he was able to identify sixth-century black-glazed pottery at Knossos, and that the archaeological gap may yet be filled. There are no good regional surveys of Crete or Thessaly in this period. Athens, Morris 1987: 128–37, 152–4; de Polignac 1984: 83–6. Samos, Morris 1987: 148. Boeotia, ibid.: 188. Corinth and Argos, see n. 11.

470s), and Gomme, helped by Beazley, argued from vase paintings that the fashion died out after this.[22]

This brings us into the fifth century and the swing to group-oriented display, abrupt in Athens, more gradual in most other places. I have already described the restraint in burials, and the fifth century saw some of the most impressive public architecture. In chapter 4, I suggested that Athenian houses were furnished on a modest scale, and the same is true of private house design all over Greece. There were differences between houses, but overall they were simple structures (see n. 25 below). Around 430 B.C. [Xenophon] (*Ath. Pol.* 2.10) talks of some of the rich having private 'gymnasia and baths and changing rooms', but goes on to say that 'the people' have built even more of these for themselves, presumably out of state funds. In spite of its polemical purposes, there is much to be said for Demosthenes' description:

> if any of you know the sort of house that Themistocles or Militiades [early fifth century] or any of those distinguished men of old lived in, you may observe that it is no grander than the common run of houses. On the other hand, both the structure and the equipment of their public buildings were on such a scale and of such quality that no opportunity of surpassing them was left to coming generations. (Dem. 23.207)

Thucydides' account of Greek dress goes on to 'the modern taste', pioneered by the Spartans, 'who first used moderation in dress ... with the better sort as much as possible living on an equal footing (*isodiaitoi*) with the many' (1.6.4). The wording is important. Thucydides clearly thought that the control of display was working from the bottom up, unlike the Cannonian model; and not just in Athens. The implication is that 'the modern taste' was a general Greek fashion. I see no reason to think that he is misleading us, and I propose a tentative hypothesis, that the fifth century *was* a time when display was muted all over Greece as part of a strong communal ideal, not as a manifestation of subtle elite control of the

---

[22] Xenophanes' comments are preserved in Ath. 12.526a, which also cites Phylarchus (*FGrH* 81 F 66) on this theme. Gomme 1945: 101–3. Cf. Asios (fr. 13, Kinkel = Ath. 12.525f) quoted in Douris, *FGrH* 76 F 60, on Samos, probably in the fifth century (Bowra 1957). Thucydides was perhaps mistaken in thinking that Athenian luxury was copied by the Ionians, rather than the reverse, but there is really no way to know.

masses. A 'communal ideal' would have meant very different things in Sparta, Athens, Thessaly and Corcyra, but in all cases we are dealing with rituals creating social structures which were more egalitarian and solidary than those of the sixth and probably the fourth centuries.[23]

Its disappearance was a complex process, which is best understood as a loosening of the communal bonds of the *polis*, rather than the abrupt end of an historical cycle of group-oriented display. The changes in grave markers did not coincide with a decline in temple building or rich votives, nor do private houses suddenly become spectacular, in spite of the way Demosthenes continues the passage which I quoted above:

today [352 B.C.] every man who takes part in public life enjoys such superfluity of wealth that some of them have built private dwelling houses more magnificent than many public buildings ... while as for the public buildings which you put up and whitewash, I am ashamed to say how mean and shabby they are. (Dem. 23.208; cf. 3.25–6; 13.20)

Demosthenes knew plenty of things we do not, and some of the rich in Athens may have ignored restraint in housing; but there is no archaeological trace of it, suggesting that it was not very common. The only good evidence for huge Greek houses comes from Hellenistic and Roman times. There are distinctions among the fourth-century houses at Olynthus, but compared to later periods they are very minor. In fact, town planning often took on an aggressively egalitarian ethos in the fourth century. Those who could afford to doubtless struggled against this, but the sharpest division in

[23] Public building, Lawrence & Tomlinson 1983: 174–238. Herbert Hoffmann (1988: 152) also draws attention to the rich votives/poor grave goods connection. Hdt. (1.82.7) tells a story that Argive women stopped wearing gold and Argive men gave up long hair after the Battle of the Champions, probably in the 540s. Whatever we make of his aetiology, fifth-century Argive dress must have been restrained for the story to make sense (cf. Hdt. 5.88 for a sixth-century change in Athenian women's dress). The relevance of [Xen.] *Ath. Pol.* 1.10 on Athenian clothing is less clear. Houston (1947: 33–82) gives a general account of dress; Geddes (1987), though briefer, is far more penetrating. Sealey (1967), Ruschenbusch (1978; 1979) and Pope (1988) argue in various ways that constitutional distinctions between democracy and oligarchy were not significant in Greek society before the 420s. The 'constitution debate' (Hdt. 3.80–4) may well be borrowed from Protagoras (Waters 1985: 78–9).

domestic space in fourth-century Greece was between male and female, not rich and poor.[24]

Looking at these cycles of display focuses attention on the long term. As early as the eleventh century we can distinguish between two broad types of social structure in Greece, and in the eighth century a further development takes place, with the very 'communal' rituals of the *polis* appearing in the Aegean region, while the larger, looser *ethnos* states typical of northern and western Greece continued with more old-fashioned ceremonial systems. The ideological distance set up between the two types of state had begun to be eroded by the fifth century, as the restrained rituals of the *poleis* began to influence *ethnē* like Thessaly and Macedon. Welskopf suggests that in the fifth century the economic and military institutions which had given the *poleis* their strength were also absorbed at the fringes of the Greek world. In both cases, *polis* activities were reconstituted within more autocratic systems. Armed with new ideas and skills and enormous resources, but in a framework which allowed them to wield far greater power than any central authority could do in a *polis*, a series of Thessalian, Phocian and then Macedonian rulers attempted to dominate the city-states from the 360s on. Had the battles of Chaeronea (338 B.C.) or Krannon (322) gone the other way, Macedon might not have succeeded; but more challengers would have come along, and in responding to the increasing scale of economic and military forces in the fourth century, the *poleis* were in any case gradually turning themselves into looser states more like the *ethnē*.[25]

We might see the loosening of *polis* bonds through changes in

[24] I owe the phrase 'loosening of the bonds of the *polis*' to Paul Millett's Cambridge lectures on 'Demosthenes and Athens', which I was fortunate enough to attend in 1986. Fourth-century public building, Lawrence & Tomlinson 1983: 239–59. Athenian houses, Rider 1964: 210–38; J. E. Jones 1975; and especially Jameson 1990a; 1990b. Isoc. 7.52 (cf. Thuc. 2.65.2) speaks of the best Athenian houses being in the countryside, and since excavation has concentrated on urban sites, our sample may be skewed. Olynthus, Robinson & Graham 1938. Hellenistic and Roman houses in Greece, Rider 1964: 239–67; Bruneau et al. 1970; Reber 1988. Wallace-Hadrill (1988: 47, 51) makes good comparisons. Egalitarianism, Hoepfner & Schwandner 1986. Gender distinctions, Vitr. 6.7.2–4; G. Morgan 1982 (with Jameson 1990a: 185–6, n. 20); S. Walker 1983; Jameson 1990a: 170, 181–90. Pesando (1987) has argued for sharp class divisons in Greek housing, but he is not persuasive; see Jameson 1989; 1990b.
[25] Eleventh-century pattern, Morris 1989b; eighth-century, Morris 1987; fourth-century, Welskopf 1974. Thessalian tyrants, Xen. *Hell.* 2.3.4; 6.4.20–37. Macedonian social structure, N. G. L. Hammond 1990: 49–70, 89–99, 152–87.

ritual as part of this process. The literary sources from Athens can be read to reveal what Ostwald calls a 'polarization of the 420s' – new forms of politics, aristocratic reaction, inter-generational conflict, an intellectual crisis – and these must form a part of any interpretation of the burials; but our explanations must also account for changes at a panhellenic level. Perhaps the most important contribution that the burials can make is to show that the social changes documented at Athens during the Peloponnesian War were part of a wider pattern that can only be understood by much broader approaches than have so far been customary. The scale of the Greek world was expanding, and the narrow confines of the group-oriented *polis* could not cope with the levels of economic and military power which it had itself created. Consequently, by 425 the elites of the Greek cities were beginning to envisage a social structure in which they had much greater prominence. In such a world, the city state might not be the most practical form of organisation, and McKechnie has documented the fourth-century tendency for more and more people to look outside their own *polis* both for fulfilment and for the means of life. This does not add up to a swing back to 'individualising' display, nor to the beginning of a 'fourth-century crisis' and the collapse of the democratic city. But the last quarter of the fifth century is revealed as a crucial period of change around the whole of Greece, and any social history must take the burials into account.[26]

We are now far from the graves themselves, but it is only when integrated into a much larger kind of social history, including war and finance as well as dress and art, that their potential emerges.

[26] McKechnie 1989. Whitehead (1975) and Ober (1991) help explain the paradox that the greatest justification of the *polis*, Aristotle's *Politics*, was written by a metic who had tutored Alexander the Great. 'Polarization', Ostwald 1986: 199–290; cf. Connor 1971: 87–136; P. J. Rhodes 1986. The 'fourth-century crisis' was forcefully propagated by Rostovtzeff (1953: 90–125) and developed by Mossé (1962). It is surveyed in massive detail in Welskopf, ed., 1974. Survival of democratic institutions, Gauthier 1985; Bernhardt 1985.

CHAPTER 6

Famous last words: the inscribed tombstone

'[A]lmost an embarrassment of riches', says Rick Jones (1977: 21), in describing a cemetery of 150 Roman graves at Lattes, where thirty-four inscribed tombstones were found *in situ*. If these few are embarrassing, what of the other 180,000 epitaphs from the western Roman empire, or the 10,000 from classical Attica alone? Inscribed tombstones combine the second and fourth levels of the hierarchy of sources which I set out on p. 10, and sometimes the third as well. By examining ancient decisions to inscribe or not to inscribe a monument and then what to say on it, we should be able to enlarge substantially our understanding of the symbolic construction of society that took place in funeral rituals. But on the whole, this has proved extremely difficult to do. Tombstones are only rarely found in direct association with the burials for which they were set up; most have turned up reused as building blocks or in the diggings of antiquarians, who did not bother about recording contextual details. Consequently, there are major problems in treating them as part of the rites which separated the living from the dead, or in assessing their visual impact in the landscape of later generations. Their standard presentation, as serried ranks of repetitive entries in yellowing tomes known to initiates by obscure acronyms like *ICUR* or *IG* II/III², makes the imaginative leap still greater.[1]

In this chapter I examine several recent attempts to use funerary inscriptions in social history. I adopt a more 'cautionary-tale' tone than I did in the other chapters. In spite of the success of some of these approaches, still greater attention needs to be paid to the way ritual processes controlled the formation of the archaeological

---

[1] Numbers of tombstones: Rome, Saller & Shaw 1984: 124, n. 1. Attica, see ch. 5, n. 7, on p. 138 above. Lattes, R. F. J. Jones 1977: 21; Demougeot 1972. Millar (1983) provides an excellent introduction to epigraphical skills and sources.

record. Of course, for most of the tens of thousands of tombstones known it is too late: they have already been torn from their original setting. But new inscriptions continue to be found, and it is depressing to see how often the burials themselves are dismissed in epigraphic accounts with throwaway remarks. But even when looking at evidence collected long ago, it is still possible to embed inscriptions in the rituals for which they were created, as Day shows in his recent study of archaic Greek epigrams, elucidating the poems by seeing them as an extension of the burial ceremony. However, like most of the literary sources for rituals which I discussed in chapter 1, the rarity of such elaborate inscriptions limits their value.[2]

Most of our huge corpus of Roman tombstones record no more than the name of the deceased, the identity of the commemorator and the age at death; and often not even that much. Athenian inscriptions are still briefer, with little beyond a name, the father's name and the demotic (the administrative area of Attica which the deceased belonged to). This is less exciting than the epigrams, but the same problems (and opportunities) of ritual and context remain. For instance, Gomme found that in the fourth and third centuries B.C. tombstones from the coasts and plains of Attica tended to belong to citizens who were buried in the deme where their ancestors had lived 200 years earlier, while tombstones from Athens itself included more citizens from the coasts and plains than from the town itself. Gomme drew the obvious conclusion, that from 500 B.C. onwards there was significant migration from the country to the town, while those who did not move to Athens tended to stay in the same place for generations. But this evidence is open to many interpretations, depending on how the rituals worked. Possibly many Athenians moved from one area of the countryside to another, but continued to identify strongly with their ancestral deme and wished to be taken back for burial, as happens in modern China; while those who moved to the city did not. Or perhaps the rich tended to be buried at Athens in lavish periboloi, even if they had not lived there, while the poor would be taken back to their ancestral home. More detailed study of the archaeological context, identifying whether certain demotics

---

[2] Day 1989; cf. Svenbro 1988; G. Hoffmann 1988. Thematic collections, Lattimore (1942); Vérhilhac (1978).

tended to occur with certain types of burial or monument, will narrow down the range of options; but in the absence of such a study, moving directly from demotics to residence patterns is as misguided as moving from grave goods to wealth.[3]

TOMBSTONES AND DEMOGRAPHY

I commented on p. 72 that, although Roman inscriptions provide our richest source for ages at death, their demographic value is limited. Szilágyi collected the evidence in six articles, offered as a population history of the western provinces. There are some obvious minor problems: in a world where record-keeping was the exception rather than the rule, age-rounding was very common; and wherever age confers authority, we might expect exaggeration of longevity. But in a brilliant piece of debunking, Hopkins shows that the problems go much deeper than this. The distribution of ages at death cannot be fitted to any plausible life table. Szilágyi's approach can only be made to work if we overlook the fact that inscribing a tombstone was a ritual action. Not everyone received an epitaph; what the evidence is actually telling us about is who, in different parts of the empire, was felt or felt themselves to deserve such a form of commemoration in their death rituals. Within certain limits we learn what their ages at death were, but these may not be the same as those of the people who did not get tombstones. Hopkins shows that we cannot generalise from our sample to the wider population from which it is drawn.[4]

TOMBSTONES AND THE FAMILY

When looking at palaeodemography, I argued that for the historian of social structure the bones are at their most useful when their age and sex patterns make least sense, and the same is true with epitaphs. Hopkins has demolished naïve arguments and shown the implausibility of the age structure of the inscriptions, but he did not try to explain *why* the observed data deviated so far from what he

---

[3] S. Walker (1985) and Dyson (forthcoming: ch. 7) offer introductions to the Roman material. Attic residence, Gomme 1933: 44–5, with comments on a much larger sample in Hansen 1983: 234–5; Damsgaard-Madsen 1988. China, Whyte 1988: 291–4.

[4] Szilágyi 1961; 1962; 1963; 1965; 1966; 1967. Age-rounding, Duncan-Jones 1990: 79–92. Hopkins 1966; 1987, with comments in Shaw 1982a: 24–9 (cf. Clauss 1973).

expected to find. The reason for this deviation should be clear by now: the funerary inscriptions were created to satisfy the needs of ritual performers, and they do not tell us as much about brute demographic 'realities' as about what Roman buriers thought *ought* to be said in such a context. The evidence produced by the buriers' ritual behaviour may sometimes be a direct representation of what historians want to know about births, deaths and marriages; but equally well (as Hopkins proves in this case) it may not, and moving straight from inscriptions to vital statistics involves an unacceptable leap of faith.

The most rigorous application of these principles has been Saller and Shaw's work on Latin epitaphs from the first century B.C. to the third A.D., extended in another paper by Shaw to 600. Both studies aim to find traces of 'real' family relationships, starting from two statements by Ulpian that in the third century A.D. it was widely (if incorrectly) believed that heirs were under legal obligation to commemorate with funerary monuments those from whom they inherited. Saller and Shaw argue from this that we can assume that our epitaphs were produced by heirs, and the family relationships that they reveal are likely to reflect inheritance patterns and therefore family organisation. Their case is strong, and the family relationship which the buriers chose to celebrate may well normally have been that between the deceased and his or her heir; but we cannot be certain of this, unless we want to generalise Ulpian's remarks across seven centuries and half a continent. But what we can be sure of is that the epitaphs were produced in ritual action. Whether or not commemorators put up tombstones because they had inherited from the deceased, we can still say that the relationships expressed in the epitaphs are those which the buriers felt were appropriate in the context of a funeral.[5]

However, looking at epitaphs in this way encourages a retreat to the 'Nuer paradox' approach to ritual (see pp. 7–8 above), saying that the tombstones are evidence for 'ideal' family relationships, which are rigidly separated from 'real' patterns of marriage and inheritance. I argued in chapter 1 that this is not a very productive starting point; but if our only sources for marriage patterns are a few anecdotes and the epitaphs themselves, what else is there to do?

---

[5] Saller & Shaw 1984; Shaw 1984. Heirship, Saller & Shaw 1984: 126–7; E. Meyer 1990; Ulpian in *D* 11.7.4; 11.7.14.8.

The difficulty, I think, disappears if we return to a point I have been making throughout this book: we cannot analyse any feature of the burial ritual in isolation. The tombstones are indeed problematic if we expect that just because they have writing on them they will unlock the secrets of the empire; but in context – as one element of the burial, to be looked at alongside disposal methods, grave goods, spatial patterning, etc. – they are a formidable addition to our evidence.

Further, for many questions these theoretical problems can simply be bypassed. For example, Saller and Shaw challenge Veyne's claim that Augustus' cultural renewal tamed a competitive aristocracy and triggered a shift in family form during the first two centuries A.D., from an extended group to an affectionate nucleus (see p. 61 above). Saller and Shaw show that as early as the first century B.C. 75–90% of the commemorations on non-military tombstones were made by members of the deceased's nuclear family. Whether we are looking for the structuration of society, a ritual contradiction between theory and practice, or for actual marriage patterns, we must share their conclusion that 'there is in fact little change to explain ... the family, like most other basic institutions, underwent no radical changes during the transformation from the Republic to the Principate' (1984: 135–6).[6]

In other cases, though, there are greater problems. Saller and Shaw point out that in most of the empire, husband-to-wife commemorations are more common than wife-to-husband, but that the reverse holds in Spain, where mothers are also unusually common as dedicators. Strabo (3.4.18) perhaps hints at matrilineal inheritance in Spain, and they suggest that this might explain the epitaphs. Daughter-to-mother epitaphs also outnumbered daughter-to-father, whereas in the rest of the empire the proportions are more equal. The samples involved are very large – 723 epitaphs from Spain alone – and there is no doubting the statistical validity of the Spanish anomaly; but there is simply no way to know whether it was caused by matrilineal descent or by equally interesting matrifocal death rituals within a patrilineal system.[7]

The difficulties are still more acute with servile inscriptions. Saller and Shaw note the paucity of commemorations by or for

[6] Veyne 1978; cf. P. Brown 1987. Saller & Shaw 1984: 134–7.
[7] Saller & Shaw 1984: 138–9.

slaves outside Italy, and suggest that it indicates the relative unimportance of slavery in the provinces. But the only thing it tells us for sure is that slaves did not put up or receive tombstones very often in the western provinces; going beyond this statement runs the risk of committing the Szilágyi fallacy, cutting out the ritual decision-making process and moving directly to demography.[8]

Saller and Shaw have been challenged most forcefully on their interpretation of military tombstones, but the critics have shared their 'behavioural' approach. Saller and Shaw show that before A.D. 250, only 40% of soldiers in Britain were commemorated by nuclear family members, and these were often brothers who might well also have been serving in the army. Forty-nine per cent of the dead were honoured by 'friends' or non-kin heirs. Similarly, in Germany, the figures were 34% and 60% respectively. But elsewhere military commemorations were much more like civilian. In Spain and the Danube provinces 70% of military commemorations were within the nuclear family; at Lambaesis in North Africa, 80%. That the funerary rituals of these areas differed is indisputable, but Saller and Shaw make a bolder claim, that Britain and Germany were garrisoned mainly by soldiers brought in from overseas, who had no close kin to take care of their funerals, while the other provinces recruited locally. Mann has disputed this, claiming that Britain simply did not adopt the epigraphic habit from Rome. He sees just a few outsiders stationed in Britain, but having higher epigraphic visibility than the natives. However, graffiti on potsherds reveal that Britons in a wide range of settlement types were able to write, and Britons in the army of the Rhine commemorated themselves visibly enough. In a similar vein, Cherry suggests that what distinguishes Britain and Germany from the rest of the empire is stronger enforcement of the ban on soldiers' marriages in the first two areas, because they were active military regions. But what if we return to the basic fact that the inscriptions were created for funeral rituals, and are really telling us about ritual structures, which may not be the same as inheritance patterns? Then the evidence relates to quite different questions – not about local recruiting, but about MacMullen's concept of 'the legion as a society', and the ways soldiers related to the community around

---

[8] Saller & Shaw 1984: 139. MacMullen (1987) makes a similar case in more detail, but is challenged by Samson (1989).

them. In short, the evidence falls into the same category as that which I briefly discussed on pp. 83–9 above for the relationships between men and women in late Roman cemeteries in Britain.[9]

Shaw extends the study of the later empire. According to Eusebius (*Vit. Const.* 1.3), Christians did not need monuments, since only God could give immortal memorials. Appropriately, numbers of inscribed tombstones decline after 300, and their messages are briefer. These processes make the evidence harder to use, but are themselves highly revealing. Shaw notes greater emphasis on the nuclear family, rising from 80% of the commemorations in the first three centuries A.D. to a mean of 97% in the next three. The shift affects all groups, including the army, with an overall rise from 56% before 300 to 82% after – roughly the same as the highest military score, from Lambaesis, in the early empire. This seems to point to the idea of the army as a distinct society being eroded in fourth-century Britain, although one interpretation of the evidence reviewed in chapter 3 would suggest precisely the opposite (see p. 83 above). The epigraphic material cries out for integration into a wider archaeological framework.[10]

Shaw also identifies shifts in the wording of dedications within the nuclear family. The most striking change is the decline in naming the commemorator, which severely restricts the types of analysis possible. Before 300, 28% of these commemorations were from parents to children, what Shaw calls the 'descending nuclear family' type, and 23% were from children to parents, or 'ascending' type. In the small number of post-300 inscriptions which give names, 42% are descending and just 11% ascending (fig. 37). However, age at death continued to be recorded, and in an ingenious argument, he shows that in the tombstones where descending commemoration occurs, the under tens and under twenties are far more heavily represented than in the tombstones where we do not find this pattern: we can therefore infer from the age structure of the inscriptions that the same descending pattern was extremely common all over the empire, even when relationships are not stated.

Shaw sees the new pattern, dominated by descending commem-

---

[9] Military statistics, Saller & Shaw 1984: 139–44; Mann 1985; Cherry 1989; Evans 1987; cf. R. F. J. Jones 1984c: 219–20. Britons on the Rhine, Saller & Shaw 1984: 142. Legion as a society, MacMullen 1984b.
[10] Shaw 1984.

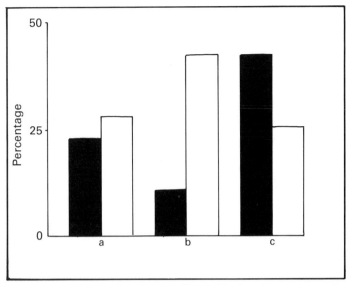

37. Ascending (black bars) and descending (white bars) commemorations in
Latin funerary inscriptions, (a) A.D. 0–300; (b) A.D. 300–600; (c) Altava in North
Africa, A.D. 300–600

oration, as part of the move to a Christian social structure. By no
means all fourth-century gravestones are Christian, and by the fifth
century not having a memorial at all may have been the most
Christian form of burial, but his argument is persuasive. He notes
that the group of pre-300, 'pagan' epitaphs which most closely
parallels this Christian pattern is the urban poor. He suggests that

A peculiar *type* of social life was forged by them [the urban lower classes]
in the milieu of the Roman town and city that was taken to be *their*
practice and was, moreover, apparently hypostatized as an ideal of behaviour in the centuries after A.D. 300. (Shaw 1984: 474)[11]

Along with the switch from ascending to descending patterns,
Shaw notes that the word *heres*, probably to be understood in pagan
inscriptions as meaning non-kin heir, disappears as a description
for commemorators, but starts being used to describe the deceased
as *heres Dei*, the heir of God. Similarly, servile commemorations

[11] MacMulfen (1986a) offers a wider review of the impact of Christianity. For a similar
argument on the urban context of Christianity, see Meeks 1983. Wiedemann (1989) also
argues for changes in the perceptions of children in the third century, but *contra*, see
Golden 1990b. Comments on Shaw, E. Meyer 1988: 188.

disappear altogether, but the deceased can be 'the servant of God'. He concludes that we see

the impact of an ideology which no longer oriented personal relationships at death horizontally, to converge in writing on the tombstone upon commemoration of the deceased, but which oriented both the dead and the survivors related to them 'vertically', *ad caelestem*. (Shaw 1984: 481)

With the triumph of Christianity we see new power structures emerging, as control of these vertical links became a crucial factor.

The only area where ascending commemoration continues to be very common after 300 is North Africa. At the rural site of Altava, descending inscriptions account for only 25% of the nuclear family dedications, and ascending for 42% (fig. 37); and all African village sites have extremely low representation of the under twenties, ranging from 4% of the total (Castellum Celtianum) to 23% (Altava itself). The urban sites of Carthage and Sufetula both scored 38%, but the mean Christian score from the whole western empire was 50%. Several interpretations are possible. If descending relationships are a Christian phenomenon, perhaps what we see here is rural Africa converting more slowly than the rest of the empire. The earliest definite example of a Christian tombstone from Altava only dates to 398, and it may be that Castellum Celtianum was slower still. But Shaw proposes two more 'sociological' arguments, which, like those for twentieth-century burial discussed in chapter 2, are by no means incompatible with a 'religious' approach. He suggests firstly that North Africa had an unusually hierarchical and patriarchal social structure, and even though Christianity did undermine it, 'elders' were always more important here than in other parts of the empire. He is also able to produce literary evidence to support this. The second idea is even more interesting: there was a major city/country distinction in ideologies of the family. This is something I will come back to in a very different setting in chapter 7.[12]

TOMBSTONES AND WEALTH

Saller and Shaw point out that, overall, about 40% of the civilian commemorations before A.D. 300 are between husbands and wives. However, among imperial senators the figure is only 22%, while

[12] African data from Shaw 1984: tables E, F, G, 12. Altava, Marcillet-Jaubert 1968: 228. Conversion theory, E. Meyer 1988: 185. Elders, Shaw 1982b; 1984; 1987b.

among the lower orders in the city of Rome it is 66%. They suggest that class differences in family structure explain this, with the idea of the family as a property-transmitting group being important in upper-class thought, with children assuming great responsibility for commemoration; where there was less property to transmit at death, the spouse was the normal dedicator.[13]

This, like their other arguments, could be treated as evidence for actual inheritance patterns or for the social structure of family relations; but either way, one of the most important points is that here we may have textual sources produced by and for Romans who were outside any conceivable 'elite'. Saller and Shaw acknowledge that 'the Roman leisured classes are no doubt over-represented in our samples', but still suggest that 'while not all Romans were commemorated after death, memorial stones were within the means of modest men' (1984: 128). At Lambaesis, an officer was seven times as likely to have an inscribed tombstone as a regular *miles*; but all the same, plenty of *milites* did have epitaphs.[14]

Shaw has subsequently argued that the simple and crude carving of the grave stones of the fourth century onwards is evidence that they belong mainly to the free poor, and that the pre-300 elite bias disappears. This direct interpretation – sloppy engraving = poor burial – is not persuasive. When humility and anonymity within the community of God became the organising principles of social structure, as Shaw himself argues about the reorientation of ties *ad caelestem*, we cannot link display and secular standing in any straightforward way. As we shall see later in this chapter, the decline in standards of epigraphy is part of a larger set of processes in late Roman burial.[15]

The only way to assess the class distribution of tombstones is through quantification of cemeteries like Lattes, but even there the evidence is too poor. The epitaphs proclaim the dead as wealthy people, but none of them were magistrates. Lattes must have had other cemeteries, and we are unable to talk about the use of tombstones among either the poor or the *decuriones*. The fact that only 20% of the graves had inscribed tombstones does not mean very much until we know their relationships to other cemeteries. Eck has

[13] Saller & Shaw 1984: 138.
[14] Lambaesis, Saller & Shaw 1984: 140, n. 63. Nielsen et al. (1989) make a similar argument for classical Attica.
[15] Shaw 1987b: 42: *contra*, E. Meyer 1988: 188, n. 375.

made the most serious attempt to tackle the problem in a series of studies of the inscriptions from Ostia and the Vatican cemetery. Eck points out that the ratio of inscriptions to burial places is always low, and that it varies strikingly from tomb to tomb, especially in the Vatican. From this he suggests that only the rich appear in our evidence, and that the samples are hopelessly biased. The consequence would be that Saller and Shaw's use of the inscriptions does not provide as good an alternative to the anecdotal literary tradition as they think. However, Eck exaggerates the problems by neglecting the details of post-depositional disturbance. The Vatican cemetery only survives because Constantine had St Peter's church built on top of it. The tombs were enclosed by a terrace wall and filled with earth. The builders took care not to destroy the tombs, since that would have been sacrilegious; instead a level platform was created by removing the upper parts of most of the tombs, along with the majority of the inscriptions. At Ostia, where later damage was less extreme, the epitaphs are relatively more numerous and more evenly distributed.[16]

Eck's approach will produce important results if deployed on sites which are better preserved, but at the moment we still have no good evidence for how far down the social ladder the use of epitaphs went. Obviously some Romans will have been simply too poor to pay for a tombstone; but the patterning that Saller and Shaw identify makes it clear that within at least part of the population ritual selection rather than economic compulsion was the main process determining the formation of the archaeological record. The best example is the massive over-representation of freedmen in the inscriptions and monuments from Rome in the first centuries B.C. and A.D. There must have been plenty of rich freedmen for them to have become such a well-established theme in Roman literature, but they were not the only Romans who could afford epitaphs. It was especially important for the descendants of those whose status had changed to proclaim this fact in their funerary rituals; perceptions of position within the social structure, not simply wealth, were at work here.[17]

[16] Lattes, R. F. J. Jones 1977: 21. Eck 1988: 133–5; 1989, with a full collection of the texts in Eck 1986. Toynbee & Ward-Perkins 1956: 12–13. Eck's argument about the burial of slaves in family tombs (1988: 137–9) would, if correct, reinforce Saller and Shaw's arguments, reviewed on pp. 159–64; but see the comments at p. 44 above.
[17] Freedmen, L. R. Taylor 1961; Kleiner 1977; 1987; Eck 1988: 135–6, with consequences discussed in Shaw 1987b: 40–1.

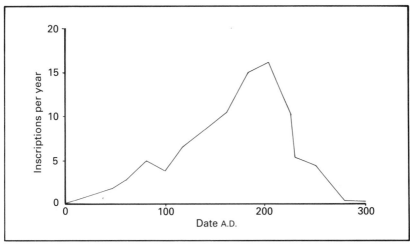

38. The 'Mrozek curve' showing the distribution of Latin inscriptions through time (after MacMullen 1988: fig. 2)

TOMBSTONES AND TIME: THE MROZEK CURVE

Many accepted wisdoms about the Roman empire depend on the frequency of attestations of institutions or offices in funerary inscriptions, but few historians treat this evidence with the kind of critical awareness which they bring to Tacitus or the *Historia Augusta*. The main exception has been MacMullen, who draws attention to what he calls the 'Mrozek curve', the chronological clustering of Latin inscriptions in the period *c.* 175–225 (fig. 38). The traditional approach, he says, 'assumes ... that the body of all inscriptions against which attestation is measured does not itself rise or fall – a false assumption. So administrative, economic, social and religious history need to be rewritten' (1982: 244). Strong stuff! He shows by a comparison with Egyptian papyri and ostraka that the number of inscriptions is not simply a function of literary production generally. He hints that the decline in inscribing in the third century may be due to a change in the idea of the community, 'what we can only call the sense of audience', but merely comments that 'I cannot see in the evidence anything less than the sign of some very broad psychological shift' (1982: 246).[18]

The effect of MacMullen's argument is broadly comparable with

[18] MacMullen 1982; Mrozek 1973; 1988; extended to Lydia in MacMullen 1986b.

Hopkins' for demography: it undermines much previous work and provides a launching point for the investigation of social structure. Elizabeth Meyer has taken up where MacMullen left off. Like Saller and Shaw, she emphasises the link between tombstones and inheritance, and goes on to build up a sophisticated argument about the perception of Roman citizenship. She suggests that we can treat Roman-style deceased-commemorator tombstones as evidence that the dead person had the right to make a will valid under Roman law, and was therefore a Roman citizen. Possession of citizenship was a necessary condition for erecting these tombstones; but paradoxically, it is immediately after Caracalla extended citizenship to the whole empire in 212 that the numbers of tombstones decline. Drawing on Cannon's arguments about competitive display (see pp. 147–9 above), she suggests that for a brief period in the late second century, Roman citizenship was an extremely important part of the social structure expressed in commemoration. The spread of grants of citizenship in the West is not a sufficient explanation of this, particularly since we see a similar increase in numbers of tombstones in some areas of the East, where block grants of citizen status were less common. But after 212, when everyone had citizenship, there was less to be gained by displaying this status, and the frequency of this style of tombstone declined rapidly. By this time it was more important to be an *honestior* than a *civis* (see p. 65 above), which may account for the Cannonesque shift from display to restraint. This not only explains the patterning in the evidence but also opens up a whole new set of questions about competition for status in the provinces.[19]

Like Saller and Shaw's arguments, this has the potential to be taken further by more detailed use of archaeological evidence. As we saw in chapter 2, there is an apparent interruption of many cemeteries in the western empire around 250, which may need to be taken into account. Since tombstones are rarely found *in situ*, we should not assume that graves are being dated by inscriptions and that a decline in epigraphic production has made mid-third-century burials archaeologically less visible; but the two processes may nevertheless be linked. The Romanising function of tombstones also needs to be seen against the background of the slow spread of inhumation, which comes to most parts of the empire just as the use

[19] E. Meyer 1990.

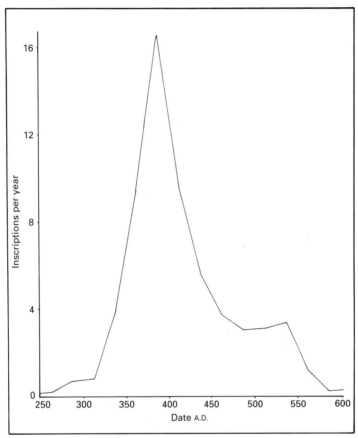

39. The 'Meyer curve' for Christian epitaphs at Rome (after E. Meyer 1988: fig. 17)

of tombstones reaches its low point. This could be built into a model like Cannon's, with anonymous inhumation replacing cremation with a monument in the third century, perhaps beginning as elite imitation of Roman practices, and later being reinterpreted as a Christian practice, as Jastrzebowska (1981: 67–8) has shown happened with feasts of the dead in third-century Rome.

The massive decline in numbers of Christian epitaphs in the fifth century (fig. 39) also needs to be seen in context, as one part of a larger set of ritual changes. While this development was certainly a matter of 'religion', narrowly defined, to treat it as this alone would be to impoverish crucial evidence for changing social structure. In the fourth century a resident of Rome wishing to make a tomb stand out tended to do so by giving it an elaborate, and often inscribed, marker; by the end of the fifth century the only acceptable way to mark a tomb out as special was through space – that is, use of privileged location. Beginning around 280, a few burials in the Roman catacombs (by then the main cemeteries) were singled out by placing the sarcophagi in cubicles with lavish painted decoration, and by 300 some of the cubicles were much larger, occasionally with offering tables and platforms. But when around 325 Constantine built a mausoleum and basilica to hold his mother Helena's remains, display was redefined. About a dozen richly decorated sarcophagus burials were made in the annexes of the basilica, and a much larger number of burials took place under its floor. At the same time, the catacombs changed radically. Virtually no cubicles were painted after 325, but the use of platforms and tables, previously limited to a few burials, was extended; even burials in the passages of the catacombs, as opposed to those with their own cubicles, might have these features. For about twenty-five years there seems to have been a battle of symbols. Those who were buried in the basilica had prestige from their proximity to Helena, while those who used the catacombs could only escalate older forms of display. Cannon's model makes good sense here. By 350 the battle was over; space had won out over scale. Those who used the basilica stopped decorating their tombs with frescoes, and the catacombs were being taken over by unadorned burials. One catacomb was actually lengthened so that its tunnels reached under Constantine's monuments, in a rather sad attempt to muscle in on the new spatial symbolism.[20]

The change from monuments to space provides the background to the decline of inscribed tombstones, but we also need to know *why* space was the best form of symbolism in the fourth and fifth centuries (cf. pp. 83–9 above). The most potent force was a religious idea, that proximity to the bones of the holy – whether Helena or a saint – offered safety and the possibility of intercession by this protector to ease access to Heaven. By the late fourth century, burial *ad sanctos* had become the surest sign of high status: as one burial inscription said, it was something that 'many desire and few obtain' (*ILCV* 2148). The best example comes from Milan,

---

[20] Guyon 1983; 1986.

where the relics of saints Gervasius and Prostasius were rediscovered in 385. Just two days later, Ambrose, bishop of the city, moved them from the cemetery and reburied them under the altar of the basilica he had just built, where his own sarcophagus was to be placed. He argued (*Ep* 22.9–10) that a few graves should 'begin to stand out' as being 'of use to all' by their location in his basilica; everyone could draw on their power when at prayer, and the privileged few could – as they did – bury their dead around them. As Shaw argued (see p. 164 above), we see a reorientation of lines of power *ad caelestem*. Christian ideology militated against lavish personal display in the funeral, but burial near saints – or even personal possession of their bones – involved no such tastelessness. Augustine's writings (e.g. *Ep*. 22; *de cura ger.* 18) show how he was caught between his ideal of the unity of the Catholic social structure and the desire of its elite to recreate in death rituals their prominence, which cannot be separated into 'social' and 'religious' categories. By the middle of the fifth century burial in a basilica, preferably one with important relics, was by far the most important status symbol in funerals in North Africa and Italy. The situation is less clear in Britain and Gaul, where warrior burials reappear in the fifth and sixth centuries, perhaps as a result of the barbarian invasions and the retreat of Christian social structures. However, as noted in chapter 3, most British cemeteries of the late fourth to sixth centuries are noticeably simpler and more uniform than those of earlier periods, which may form part of the same move away from monuments towards space seen in the western Mediterranean lands.[21]

The end of epitaphs at Rome comes in the sixth century, and coincides with a second stage of spatial change, the movement of cemeteries inside towns. Various explanations have been put forward for this. Some stress urban depopulation. Large areas of Rome, Milan and Carthage were abandoned, and burials within these spaces may not have been thought of as being among the living. Others object that it is hardly likely that a thousand-year-old ban on burial within the city walls would be forgotten so easily. In a classic paper, Dyggve argued that burials moved into the cities

---

[21] P. Brown 1981: 23–49. Background, Février 1978. North Africa and Italy, Y. Duval 1986; N. Duval 1982; Février 1986; Guyon 1986. Gaul, B. Young 1984; 1986; Dierkens 1986; Reynauld & Jannet-Vallet 1986. Britain, Esmonde Cleary 1989: 184–5, 201.

because of the 'translation' of the relics of martyrs from basilicas like Ambrose's to urban churches. People still wanted the intercession of the saints, so they buried their dead in the churchyards. But things were not this simple. At Rome, the catacombs were already declining as burial places in the late fifth century, and the latest known grave dates to 535. Some surface burials continued outside the city until at least 567, but an epitaph dated to the same year shows that graves were being dug within the city walls. The same picture emerges at Carthage, with several intramural cemeteries in use by 600. But the translation of relics from the cemeteries of Rome to its churches is not documented until the reign of pope Paul I in 757–67 (*Lib. Pont.* 1.464–5), and it probably began still later in most areas. This marks a third stage. In the seventh or eighth century the first large churchyard cemeteries begin; by the eleventh century they were normal in western towns and villages.[22]

The most popular explanation, that sixth-century wars against barbarians made it unsafe to use extramural cemeteries at Rome, is no more convincing. These wars did not influence the pattern of settlement or even fortification significantly, and we should beware of assuming that they would have profound effects on something as important to Christians as burial. The movement of cemeteries was part of a new use of space that had begun as early as the third century. Christian basilicas made the old cemeteries into assembly places, and by the sixth century new towns of the living were growing up around them. The process extended far beyond Rome: medieval Bonn, for example, developed around a church on the site of a seventh-century basilica, which in turn stood above a late third-century shrine to saints Cassius and Florentinus, in the cemetery outside the Roman walls. Traditionalists were scandalised by such developments, but Jerome rejoiced that 'the city has changed address' (*Ep.* 107.1). Church authorities seized on the new opportunities that the cemetery gave them for public building and shows of display which were not in direct competition with the pagan past. Christianity was working with a new spatial structure which undermined the certitudes of classical antiquity and posed fundamental questions about the nature of community: as Brown points out, the

---

[22] Dyggve 1953; J. Osborne 1984; 1985. However, the dates for burials come from epitaphs, and since very few are known after *c.* 550, there is a danger of circularity in this argument. *Disabitato* at Rome, Krautheimer 1980: 237–59. Carthage, Ellis & Humphrey 1988. Milan, Krautheimer 1983. Churchyards, Ariès 1981: 29–42; 1985: 12–17.

new space included women, the poor and country-dwellers in entirely novel ways.[23]

Competing nobles in sixth-century towns could focus their power either on an intramural church built on the site of the old Roman civic centre or on a basilica in a cemetery, and the great cathedrals of the Middle Ages tend to appear in one or the other of these locations, depending on which group won. The possession of relics of saints was both a symbol of a faction's success and a means to attract further support. At Arras in 540, when the time came to take the body of Bishop (soon to be saint) Vaast to the cemetery, the corpse was found to be too heavy to move. The archpriest realised that there had been a miracle, and ordered Vaast's body to be buried by the cathedral altar; and the body became light again. By the eighth century intramural churches had generally won and the translation of relics from basilicas to cathedrals began, but long before this urban churches were already offering powerful attractions. The disappearance of funerary epigraphy in the fifth and sixth centuries may or may not be evidence for Christianisation or declining literacy, but we cannot assess its relevance to these problems until we have located it within the changing ritual practices of the period and the power struggles of early medieval society.[24]

The implications of excavated cemeteries like these need to be addressed by the same kinds of historians who are undertaking massive statistical analyses of inscriptions. The scholarly division of labour between text-based historians and classical archaeologists is the real problem here. So far, at least, the twain have not met; and the ritual context of burial monuments has fallen down the gap between them.

[23] Whitehouse 1985; cf. Christie 1989: 263–82. P. Brown 1981: 42–6. Bonn, Ralegh Radford 1968: 31, 34. The processes are less clear in Britain, Esmonde Cleary 1989: 124–7.

[24] Vaast, Ariès 1981: 36.

CHAPTER 7

At the bottom of the graves: an example of analysis

A realist, he has always said
'It is Utopian to be dead
For only on the Other Side
Are Absolutes all satisfied
Where, at the bottom of the graves
Low Probability behaves.'
W. H. Auden, *New Year Letter*

This is a poem that archaeologists are fond of quoting; my excuse
for using it is that it is peculiarly relevant to the problems discussed
in this chapter. So far, I have looked at grand themes: how burials,
in context, help us understand the rise of the *polis*, democratic
Athens, the fall of Rome. I have tried to show that burials are worth
study. Now I will give an example of how study can proceed at a
much more detailed level. I end not with a bang but with a
whimper: no all-embracing model of antiquity in ten pages, but a
blow-by-blow analysis of Vroulia, a small site at the southern tip of
Rhodes (fig. 40).

Vroulia may seem an odd choice for a closing example. It was
excavated in 1907–8 and the site report, published in 1914, is not
easy to find. The demographic data are scanty and the textual
sources available from Rhodes in the period the site was occupied,
c. 625–575 B.C., are worse. Further, the site report itself is in many
ways 'pre-modern', lacking the conventions which nowadays define
authoritative archaeological discourse. But some of these failings
are actually advantages for my purposes. Much of the archaeologist's energy goes into interpreting the silences and contradictions
of site reports, a complex genre which has to be read as closely as
any ancient text. *Fouilles de Vroulia* typifies the kinds of problems to
be faced. It has other advantages too. As well as the cemetery,
Kinch excavated some houses and two small sanctuaries, which

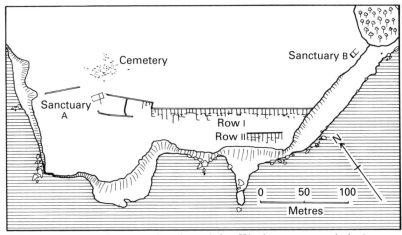

40. Vroulia: the site and environs (after Kinch 1914: general plan)

provide a context; but there is not so much detail that a thorough analysis would burst the bounds of this book. Archaic Rhodian society is poorly understood, but, so far as I know, the burials from Vroulia have never been analysed in detail; and finally, it is full of strong patterns. Many ancient cemeteries are frankly rather boring, but here there is a lot going on.[1]

This chapter proceeds more or less as my study of the site did. I reduced the descriptions of the graves to tabular form, summarising those aspects of the evidence provided by Kinch which I assumed to be important. There is no universally applicable 'best' way to classify archaeological evidence, and table 9 actually

[1] I want to thank Alexandra Coucouzeli for discussing the site with me, but without implying that she shares my interpretation of it. Dating, Kinch 1914: 89. The earliest datable vases are Corinthian piriform aryballoi (Kinch 1914: 66, 69, 69–80), but these probably come after the transition from Protocorinthian to Early Corinthian. Even Payne, who took the replacement of this shape by the pointed aryballos as the transition to Ripe Corinthian, treated the similar vase from gr. p as overlapping with Early Corinthian (1931: 56, 290 no. 579). Rhodian imitations of piriform aryballoi (Kinch 1914: 75) are probably much later than their Corinthian prototypes (Johansen 1923: 163, n. 2, 175; cf. Archondidou-Argyri 1983). Neeft (1987: fig. 186) dates his ovoid aryballos list CVI, to which he assigns a pot from gr. p (Kinch 1914: 43 no. 1), to the 650s, but puts gr. p itself in the last quarter of the seventh century (ibid.: fig. 188). The dating of the different classes of pottery is discussed in Rumpf 1933: 72, 79; R. M. Cook 1934: 58, n. 3, 88; Hopper 1949: 172–4, esp. nn. 43, 48; Schiering 1957: 1–12, with R. M. Cook 1958. Gates (1983: 22, 32) would compress the cemetery into his period I, of 625–600 B.C. On Corinthian chronology, see now Neeft 1987: 361–80; Amyx 1988.II: 397–434. The site report as a genre, Shanks & Tilley 1987: 12–18; Tilley 1989; Hodder 1989.

Table 9. *The burials at Vroulia*

Pot burial	Group	Pot type	Height	Grave goods
a	I	Cooking pot	?	—
b	I	Cooking pot	?	—
c	I	Jug	?	—
d	II	Amphora	0.77 m	—
e	I	SOS amphora	?	—
f	II	Amphora	0.68 m	3 pots
g	II	Jug	?	—
h	II	Jug	?	—
i	IV	Jug	?	—
j	V	SOS amphora	?	—
k	V	Jug	?	—
l	V	Cooking pot	?	—
m[1]	V	Amphora	0.66 m	1 pot
n	V	?	?	?
o	V	Hydria	0.46 m	—
p[2]	V	Amphora	?	4 pots, 2 sea shells
q	III	Cooking pot	?	—
r	III	SOS amphora	?	—
s	III	Amphora	1.00 m	10 pots, 2 clay scarabs, 2 bronze fibulas, 2 sea shells
t	III	Cooking pot	?	—
u	IV	Hydria	0.45 m+	—
v	IV	Cooking pot	?	—
x	IV	Hydria	0.43 m	—
y	IV	Hydria	0.45 m+	—
z	IV	SOS amphora	0.60 m	—
aa	IV	Cooking pot	0.38 m	—
bb	IV	Amphora	0.51 m	4 pots
cc	IV	Cooking pot	0.39 m	—
dd	IV	Hydria	0.45 m+	—
ee	IV	Hydria	0.45 m+	—
ff	IV	Jug	0.30 m	? 2 pots
gg	IV	?	?	?
hh	IV	Cooking pot	?	—
jj	IV	Cooking pot	0.36 m	—
kk	IV	Cooking pot	?	—
ll	II	Cooking pot	?	—
mm	I	Hydria	0.45 m+	—
nn	I	?	?	?
oo	I	?	?	?
pp	V	Cooking pot	?	—
qq[2]	V	Amphora	0.54 m	1 pot

Table 9 (*cont.*). *Cremation burials at Vroulia*

Burial	Group	Length × width × depth (in metres)	Number of cremations	Grave goods
1	I	2.1 × 0.75 × 0.8	2	6 pots, 1 pierced sherd disc
2	I	2 × 1 × 0.94	8–9	33 pots, 2 loom-weights, 3 conical feet, 5 pierced sherd discs, various sherds, 1 bronze fibula, 1 bronze ring
3	I	1.15 × 0.65 × 0.25	1[3]	2 pots
4	II	1.8 × 1 × 0.75	2–3	3 pots, 1 pierced sherd disc
5	III	1.94 × 0.9 × 0.75	3	—
6	III	2.43 × 1.2 × 0.9	9	9 pots, 3 pierced sherd discs, 3 bronze fibulas, 1 faience vase
7	III	1.85 × 0.9 × 0.3	2	2 pots
8	V	1.75 × 0.75 × 0.5	1–2	2 pots
9	V	1.8 × 0.9 × 0.64	3	2 pots
10[4]	V	1.85 × 0.78 × 0.7	2–3	1 pot
11	V	1.88 × 0.75 × 0.65	2–3	13 pots, 1 faience bead
12[4]	V	2.15 × 0.96 × 1.1	2–3	10 pots
13	V	2.18 × 0.97 × 1	1–2	4 pots
14	VI	Very shallow	1	—
15	VI	Eroded	?	3 pots, 4 bronze fibulas
16	V	1.75 × 0.8 × 0.61	2–3	1 pot, 2 pierced sherd discs
17	V	1.85 × 1.05 × 0.43	?1	8 pots
19	III	2.02 × 0.92 × 0.87	5–6	4 pots, 1 pierced sherd disc, 1 faience alabastron
20	III	2.08 × 0.9 × 0.87	4	11 pots, 1 pierced sherd disc, 1 clay bead, 1 silver ring, 2 bronze fibulas
21	IV	1.72 × 0.84 × 0.6	4	4 pots, 1 pierced sherd disc
22	IV	1.88 × 0.73 × 0.27	2	7 pots, 4 pierced sherd discs, 2 bronze fibulas
23	IV	1.9 × 1.06 × 0.48	1	3 pots, 2 pierced sherd discs
24	IV	2 × 0.9 × 0.25	2	6 pots
25	IV	2 × 0.9 × 0.18	1	2 pots
26	IV	1.85 × 0.9 × 0.5	1	7 pots, 3 bronze fibulas, 1 iron brooch

At the bottom of the graves

Table 9 (*cont.*). *Cremation burials at Vroulia*

Burial	Group	Length × width × depth (in metres)	Number of cremations	Grave goods
27	IV	1.9 × 0.85 × 0.29	1	7 pots, 1 pierced sherd disc, 1 bronze fibula
28	?	1.95 × 0.85 × 0.25	1	1 pot
29	VII	2.7 × 1.3 × 0.33	1[5]	1 plate, closing 1 jug
31	II	1.66 × 0.74 × 0.42	1	5 pots, 1 pierced sherd disc, 3 bronze fibulas
32	II	1.87 × 0.88 × 0.6	2–3	4 pots, 1 iron brooch
33	III	1.68 × 0.7 × 0.6	1[6]	—

[1] Child, aged 1–2 years
[2] A hole had been cut in the body, probably meaning that the child's skeleton was too large to fit in through the mouth of the pot
[3] Child cremation
[4] Gravestone
[5] Cremation of a child with ashes in a jug
[6] Adolescent, aged 14–16 years

represents the final stage of the work. Making a table of this kind is usually the first step in recognising possible patterns, but on further reflection, some of the categories used will turn out to be unimportant, while some which were not used – in this case, the dimensions of the graves – will be essential. Classification should be an aid to thinking, not a straitjacket on it.

A historian studying a site should always begin with a specific question. For example, Gallant (1982) has argued that in eighth-century Attica an expansion of settlement led to the consolidation of aristocratic power over the peasantry; we might ask whether a similar theory is valid for Rhodes. We could even begin with a specific answer in mind, drawn from literary sources, other sites or comparative reading. There is no point in pretending to be the mythical empiricist approaching 'The Data' with a completely open mind. Such a vacant analyst would have nowhere to begin. Once we start searching for order in the evidence, though, we may have to abandon the starting point altogether; but the patterns we find will often be more interesting than those we began with. That was certainly my experience with Vroulia. I first read about the site seven years ago, looking for evidence for population growth in the late seventh century. Instead I found a rural world which the literary sources rarely reach.

In practice a lot of time is wasted pursuing ideas which turn out to be red herrings. I discuss one or two of these, but reading about other people's mistakes is not very interesting, so I consign most of the dead ends to a well-deserved oblivion and move fairly smoothly, and misleadingly, towards an interpretation of Vroulian social structure. I have broken up the analysis into subsections based on the axes of analysis defined in chapter 1, but, as with chapters 2–6, no class of evidence will stay neatly in its box. The argument is cumulative, and material discussed early on constantly resurfaces.

TYPOLOGY

There are three main grave types (see table 9): 43 child inhumations in vases (grs. a–qq); 2 inhumation graves, one of a young man (gr. 30) and the other of four adults, probably all men (gr. 18); and 30 cremation graves, all except gr. 29 being primary cremations (i.e. the body was burned in the grave cutting). Some graves were used only once; others were reused, holding up to nine cremations. On average, each cremation produced an ash layer 10 cm thick. These were usually separated by distinct layers of earth, with only occasional exceptions (e.g. gr. 24).[2]

There are no clearly chronological developments in the graves, nor is their alignment particularly informative: they run along the contours of the hill, following the course of the wall. Our starting point must be the seven spatial groups identified by Kinch. These seem sensible enough from the plan (fig. 41). We might quibble over grs. 17 and 28, but Kinch was in a better position to judge the visual impact of the groupings than we are, so I follow his division.[3]

Throughout this book I have tried to find *patterns*. Any cemetery has a few unusual graves, 'outliers' as I like to call them. These can be important, but we must not become obsessed with them. The

---

[2] 10 cm rule, Kinch 1914: 55, 89. Relevance to other sites, Gates 1983: 32–3. Time span of vases, Payne 1931: 26, n. 1; Hopper 1949: 174, n. 48. Gr. 24, Kinch 1914: 82.

[3] The main chronological change in archaic Rhodes is the switch to inhumation *c.* 550 B.C. (Gates 1983). Seven groups, Kinch 1914: 35–6.

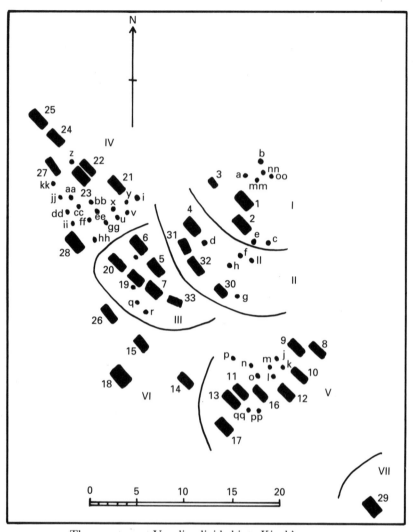

41. The cemetery at Vroulia, divided into Kinch's seven groups

only way to analyse a unique find is by unsupported direct interpretation. At Vroulia, there are several outliers. Gr. 29, stuck
out on its own on the south-east edge of the cemetery, is one of only
two child cremations (the other is gr. 3); it is the only grave with
the ashes in a jug; and the great size of the grave pit is out of
proportion with the tiny urn. Something about this child was very

special, but we will never know what. Group vi as a whole is also unusual in the wide spacing of the graves and the absence of children. It was common in Greece to place a hero's grave by the gate, and the nearest grave to the gate is gr. 18, a strange quadruple inhumation (probably all young men), which included a spear-shaft, the only evidence for weapons at Vroulia. Grs. 14, 15 and 26 are similar to those in group iii, but my feeling is that group vi was organised round gr. 18 (one of the earliest burials) – perhaps a special area for the village's war dead? But this is another direct interpretation, and I will take it no further.

DEMOGRAPHY

The next step is to look at the demography of the grave plots. Kinch said that he found men, women and children. If he had found evidence that the plots were sex-specific he would probably have said so, but his silence leaves the field open – maybe there was no evidence; maybe he missed some evidence; maybe there was in fact evidence that the plots were mixed sex, but he did not think it worth mentioning. This problem will reappear later.[4]

The pots used to hold children can be divided into four types (jug, cooking pot, hydria, amphora), but the main distinction must be between the amphoras and the rest. The other three shapes were all ordinary household vessels, but at least some of the amphoras were finer pots. Four of them (grs. e, j, r, z) were 'SOS-type' amphoras, and may have been Athenian or Euboean imports. Of the amphoras, these four and gr. d did not have grave goods, but the other six had miniature offerings. None of the other 31 child graves (counting the two cremations) had grave goods. What are we to make of this? The amphora/non-amphora distinction could be based on sex, but the ratio is 11:25. We could even it out by grouping the hydrias with the amphoras, but this would be arbi-trary; or by assuming that the amphoras were for boys and that Vroulians practised preferential female infanticide, putting the more numerous dead girls into low-grade household pots and bury-ing the less common dead boys in amphoras, usually with grave

---

[4] Demography, Kinch 1914: 90; however, as Gates notes (1983: 24), the demographic data from the early digs on Rhodes are not reliable on details.

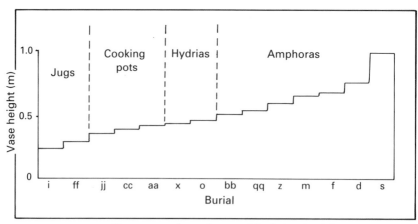

42. Pot types and pot sizes used for infant burials

goods. The bones rarely survived for sexing, so this is all speculative, and neither idea is compelling.[5]

Fig. 42 shows that there is a clear correlation between the type
and size of the pots. Kinch comments that jugs were used for 'les
plus petits enfants' and the other shapes for 'les enfants plus
grands' (1914: 40–1), so we are probably justified in seeing a link
between age at death and type of pot, with the largest (oldest)
children in amphoras with grave goods. If Kinch had recorded the
size of more of the pots in the houses we could see whether jugs
were always smaller than cooking pots, and so on, running a significance test to find the likelihood of fig. 42 being purely a chance
result. But that is not an option, so we must proceed with what we
have got. One burial, amphora gr. s, was certainly better furnished
than the others, with 11 vases, 2 clay scarabs and 2 miniature
bronze fibulas; but on the whole, the use of grave goods and types
of burial vessel seem to underline age boundaries rather than dividing children on other principles within the age groups.

An even more important line was drawn after six years, with the
transition from inhumation in a pot to cremation. Fig. 43 shows

[5] Kinch (ibid.: 37–9) divides the pots into five classes, but this seems over-fine. Skeleton: pot
size ratio, ibid.: 40. Kinch (ibid.: 43) also says that gr. m, an amphora, contained a body
aged 1–2 years. Household pots, ibid.: 37. The SOS amphoras are not in Johnston &
Jones' catalogue (1978: 113), but the only Vroulian example with a recorded height – gr. z,
at 60 cm – fits their model of changes in size (ibid.: 133). Gr. ff, a jug, may have had two
cups with it, but the attribution is doubtful (Kinch 1914: 48, n. 1). Miniature pots, Kinch
1914: 42–9. Gates (1983: 28–9) describes pot burials in other Rhodian cemeteries.

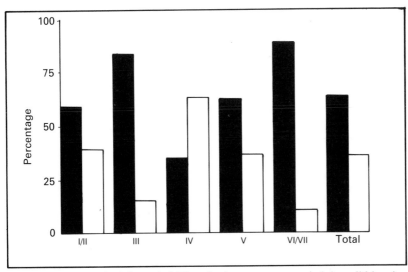

43. Proportions of adults and children in the seven groups (adults solid bars)

how the ratio between these two broad age categories varies from one plot to another. Even if we leave aside the childless group VI, the adult:child ratios vary from 6.1:1 (group I) to 0.6:1 (group IV). These are too diverse to be differences in child mortality due to living conditions. Using just about any life table for agricultural populations, the child mortality rate in area I would give these people a life expectancy at birth of around 50 years, while in area IV it would be more like 15 years. Both are very unlikely, although the ratio for the whole cemetery would give a life expectancy at birth of 25–30 years, which is what we expect. A χ^2 test revealed no strong correlation between grave groups and the age of the children. The best interpretation must be that the adult/child division was symbolised not just by the types of disposal, container and grave goods, but also by location. We cannot be dealing with straightforward 'family' grave plots: children were buried in the interstices between and within adult groups, not formally attached to them.[6]

---

[6] The child graves between groups III and IV could conceivably be attached to group III instead of IV (see fig. 41). Group III would then be 22% adult and 78% child, with group IV at 60% adult and 40% child instead of the scores shown in fig. 43; but this would not affect my argument in any way, since the imbalances would remain. The χ^2 test, see pp. 112–14 above and S. J. Shennan 1988: 65–76.

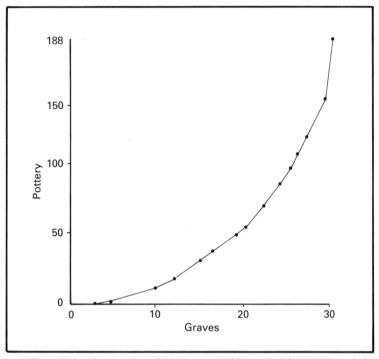

44. Cumulative frequencies of (a) pots and (b) metal objects in the adult cremations

GRAVE GOODS

Armed with these observations, I turn to the adults, starting with grave goods. The distribution of pottery was quite even, except for gr. 2, which held 23% of all vases in the adult cremations; but the distribution of metalwork was highly skewed (fig. 44). A χ^2 test produced a significant result for the distribution of grave goods between groups, but a quick glance shows that it is gr. 2 which is largely responsible. Without this grave, the significance disappears. There is a similar pattern with the child graves; the distribution of grave goods varies significantly from plot to plot, but if we leave out the wealthy gr. s the variability loses its statistical significance. We come back to the question of chapter 4: what do grave goods mean? Once again, only the context can supply answers.

Interpreting offerings in multiple tombs is usually difficult because the objects cannot easily be assigned to individual burials,

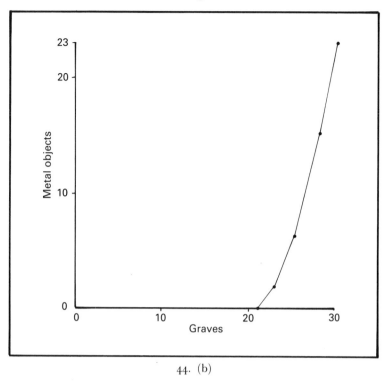

44. (b)

but here there is a striking pattern. When Kinch reports the position of finds within the graves, nearly all were associated with the first burial (table 10). Of the 30 ceramic finds with the secondary burials, 12 were pierced clay discs; only 6 of these were among the 111 ceramic finds from the primary burials. After this initial use of grave goods to start off the tomb, other burials were largely undifferentiated apart from the pierced discs. Once again, there is no point in speculating on what the discs 'meant'; we have to concede that this is unknowable, and press on with the broader pattern.

The adult pattern is like the use of grave goods with children, except that with the grown-ups age did not determine offerings in the sense of senior citizens getting ritual benefits (or at least not necessarily – again we are held back by the lack of demographic data). The richest burials were the 'oldest' in the sense that those dead had predeceased the others buried in the same tomb. This raises the crucial question of how the Vroulians decided who would

Table 10. *Grave goods with primary and secondary adult cremations at Vroulia*

	Primary deposit				Secondary deposits			
Grave	Pottery	Discs	Metal	Faience	Pottery	Discs	Metal	Faience
2	29	1	2	—	14	4	—	—
3*	2	—	—	—	—	—	—	—
4	3	1	—	—	—	—	—	—
6	9	—	3	1	—	3	—	—
7*	2	—	—	—	—	—	—	—
8	2	—	—	—	—	—	—	—
9	2	—	—	—	—	—	—	—
11	10	—	—	1	4	—	—	—
17*	8 vases, unburned, on top of ashes							
19	9	1	—	1	(all with first or second burial)			
21	3	—	—	—	—	1	—	—
22	7	—	2	—	—	4	—	—
23*	3	2	—	—	—	—	—	—
24*	6	—	—	—	—	—	—	—
25*	2	—	—	—	—	—	—	—
26*	7	—	4	—	—	—	—	—
27*	7	1	1	—	—	—	—	—
28*	1	—	—	—	—	—	—	—
31*	5	1	3	—	—	—	—	—

* Single cremation only

be buried where. It was clearly not a matter of burning the dead in any old hole. After each cremation, the tomb was filled to the surface level with earth; and for the next use, the buriers had to dig it out again, generally being quite careful to stop at the surface of the last cremation. Kinch was certain that each tomb belonged to a family, but there is no direct evidence, nor, as we saw in chapter 3, could there be. We have to argue from probabilities. The first evidence for Rhodian burial groups comes from inscribed funerary caskets, beginning around 250 B.C. Fraser (1977: 58) concludes from these that 'It is clear . . . that the family link was in this respect strongly felt and sustained.' A few inhabitants of Rhodes were starting to bury as associations (*koina*) like the Roman *collegia* (see p. 44 above) in the third century, but even these were mostly resident aliens, who might not have had a wide network of kin around them. Projecting such *koina* back onto a tiny Rhodian village around 600 B.C. will not do. I cannot see what principles other than descent and kinship could have structured cemetery space.[7]

Kinch, excited by the regularity of the settlement and its wall, saw Vroulia as a fortress guarding the best stopping point on the route from Lindos to Egypt. The grave plots might then belong to different military units, but this hypothesis is not very plausible. Kinch observed that since the wall was only 1.25 m high, it must have had a mudbrick superstructure; but this could only have been 80 cm wide. This might deter wild animals, but little else. The 'tower' is equally flimsy; and non-military sites such as Megara Hyblaea in Sicily and the so-called 'Potters' Quarter' at Corinth were being laid out in regular fashion a full century before Vroulia. In fourth-century Athens the ephebes (young men aged 18–20 years) had a regular round of the fortresses along the frontiers; however, not only is Vroulia a full three centuries earlier, but the age structure of its cemeteries would fit a 'normal' agricultural population far better than a putative garrison.[8]

A pattern begins to emerge. Age and descent are the keys to the Vroulian funerary ritual. The social structure created in it reminds me strongly of Shaw's pattern of 'ascending commemoration' in the late Roman tombstones from Altava (see pp. 162–4 above). There was a major ritual division around six years old. The separation of adults and children through different rites and even discrete cemeteries was quite common in archaic Greece, as was some kind of orientation towards the first grave in a lineage's burying area. At Athens, the mounds over seven graves in the Kerameikos dating *c.* 700–650 were superimposed to form a single large mound, and by 650 the Rundbau mound had secondary burials cut into it. At Knossos, some chamber tombs were used from the tenth century to the late seventh; and at Pithekoussai, eighth-century tombs were carefully placed to form overlapping series. But no other site compares with the Vroulian founding ancestors' near·monopoly on grave goods. Each descent group, perhaps a nuclear family along with some unmarried close kin, would begin a grave group with a large deep tomb. The first appropriate person to die received grave

[7] Refilling tombs, Kinch 1914: 55. Family tombs, ibid.: 53. Hellenistic Rhodes, Fraser 1977: 52–60; cf. Hopkins 1983: 212–17; Morris 1987: 87–91 (criticised by Humphreys (1990), but I am still not persuaded).

[8] Military interpretation, Kinch 1914: 6–7. Fortification wall, Kinch 1914: 90–7. Megara Hyblaea, Vallet et al. 1976. 'Potters' Quarter', Williams 1982. Ephebes, Pélékidis 1962.

Table 11. *Mean numbers of grave goods per burial at Ialysos, Kameiros*
and Vroulia, c. 625–575 B.C.

	Number of graves	Mean number of pots/grave	Mean number of metal objects/grave
Ialysos: cremations	27	8.0	1.0
Vase burials	7	1.4	0.7
Kameiros: cremations	6	4.7	0
Vase burials	12	5.9	1.0
Vroulia: cremations	30	1.8	0.4
Vase burials	43	0.6	0.05

Source: Ialysos and Kameiros data from Gates 1983: 76–82, periods I & II

goods, and then the tomb remained in use for a generation or so. When it was full or the descent line broke up into two or more households, another deep tomb would be dug; or if a line died out, the area would perhaps be abandoned. The best evidence comes from group I, where the floor deposit of gr. 2 seems to date around 625 B.C., while pots from the upper 20 cm should be *c.* 600. Right next to it, gr. 1 begins with an early sixth-century floor deposit. This tomb, like gr. 2, was about 90 cm deep, and was probably intended to carry on for another 30–40 years, but it was only used twice. Maybe the family died out; or maybe at this point (*c.* 575) the site was abandoned.[9]

Compared to what we find at Kameiros and Ialysos, the Vroulian grave goods are rather poor (table 11); but seen from within the local system, they were probably rather important. Table 12 compares the 'exotic' finds (metals, faience, imported pottery) from the cemetery, the settlement and the sanctuaries. There are the usual problems, such as people taking things away when they left, and the fact that one sanctuary was looted in 1905 (although Kinch notes that most of the material was recovered); but judging from the lack of even tiny sherds of broken imported vases, we should conclude that what Vroulians diverted into burials was for them considerable riches. We cannot read off wealth or power from the grave goods, but their presence does suggest that the recipient was represented as a figure deserving honour. The buriers who founded

[9] Athenian burials, Morris 1987: 129–30, 136. Knossos, see especially Brock 1957; Catling 1979. Pithekoussai, Ridgway 1984: 85–95.

Table 12. *Imported finds at Vroulia*

Area	Pottery Corinth	Pottery Athens	Cyprus	Bronze	Silver	Iron	Faience	Other
Graves								
e	—	?1	—	—	—	—	—	—
j	—	?1	—	—	—	—	—	—
p	3	—	—	—	—	—	—	—
r	—	?1	—	—	—	—	—	—
s	3	—	—	2	—	—	—	2 scarabs
z	2	—	—	—	—	—	—	—
1	2	—	—	—	—	—	—	—
2	13	—	—	2	—	—	—	—
4	1	—	—	—	—	—	—	—
6	5	—	—	3	—	—	1	—
7	1	—	—	—	—	—	—	—
8	1	—	—	—	—	—	—	—
9	1	—	—	—	—	—	—	—
11	8	—	—	—	—	—	1 bead	—
12	5	—	—	—	—	—	—	—
13	1	—	—	—	—	—	—	—
15	—	—	—	4	—	—	—	—
17	2	—	—	—	—	—	—	—
19	—	—	1	—	—	—	1	—
20	—	—	—	2	1	—	—	—
22	1	—	—	2	—	—	—	—
24	4	—	—	—	—	—	—	—
26	—	—	—	3	—	1	—	—
27	3	—	—	1	—	—	—	—
31	1	—	—	3	—	—	—	—
32	1	—	—	—	—	1	—	—
Houses								
I.2	—	—	—	—	—	—	1	—
I.3	1	—	—	—	—	—	—	—
I.4	1	—	—	—	—	—	—	—
I.6	1	—	—	—	—	—	—	—
I.8	—	—	—	—	—	—	1	—
I.12	—	—	1	—	—	—	—	—
I.18	1	—	1	—	—	—	—	—
I.27	1	—	—	—	—	—	—	—
I.28	1	—	—	—	—	—	—	—
I.32	—	1	—	—	—	—	—	—
II.7	—	—	—	1	—	—	—	—
Sanctuary A								
	—	—	—	—	—	2	—	—
Sanctuary B								
	—	—	—	2	1	2	3	—

gr. 2 and the parents of the child in gr. s bestowed special honour on their dead. Again, saying why would be speculative direct interpretation; but the fact that there were such disparities should not surprise us. There is similar variation in 'rich' objects from the houses (table 12), as well as architectural differences (see pp. 193–5 below).[10]

GRAVE SIZE

The other major variable is the size of the tombs. All of them had a length:width ratio of 2:1 to 2.5:1, but the ratios of surface area to depth are more interesting. The graves in group IV are far shallower than those in groups I–III and V. The mean ratio of area to depth in group IV is 6.4:1, compared to 2.3:1 in the other groups, and 8:1 to 10:1 at Ialysos and Kameiros. Group IV, then, seems more typical of Rhodes as a whole than the other Vroulian groups. However, there is more to it than this. In fig. 45, I have calculated the 'regression lines' which fit most accurately the scatter of points. The lines for groups I–III and V are similar, as are the correlation coefficients (r^2), which tell us what percentage of the variation in our data is explained by this simple linear correlation. Group IV is radically different from the others. The line slopes in the opposite direction, and the correlation coefficient is a meagre 3%, as compared to 27–39% for the other groups. This is particularly important: the dimensions of group IV graves are not consistent, suggesting little overall structure to this aspect of ritual behaviour. This reflects on the comparison with other Rhodian cemeteries. Group IV at first seemed more 'typical'; but in fact shallow cremation pits were used differently at Vroulia, being governed only by very loose rules of behaviour.[11]

This may seem trivial, but it is not. The depth of the tomb was determined by the number of burials intended to be made in it, *before* the first cremation took place. Making the grave 30 cm deep

[10] Ialysos/Kameiros grave goods, Gates 1983: 36–41, 76–91. Looting of the temple, Kinch 1914: 8. No kilns were found at Vroulia, and possibly all the pottery was imported from other parts of Rhodes. However, Kinch (1914: 123) also comments that no hearths or bread ovens were found, and suggests that the strength of the sea breezes made elaborate facilities unnecessary.

[11] Ialysos and Kameiros tomb depths, Gates 1983: 33–4. Even the late sixth-century chamber tombs at these sites rarely had more than 1 or 2 burials in them. Regression analysis is explained in S. J. Shennan 1988: 114–89.

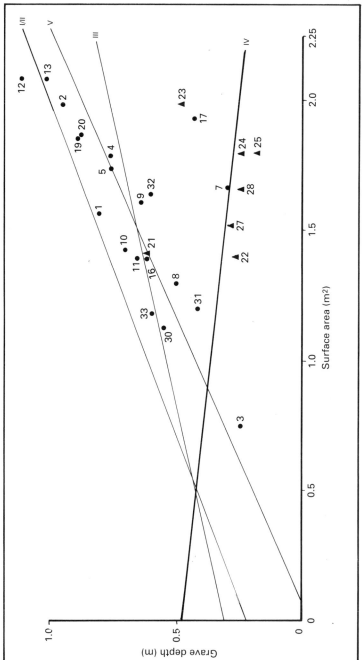

45. Regressing depth of grave on surface area. Group IV graves are marked by triangles. The formulae are: groups I and II, $\hat{y} = 0.22 + 0.28x$ $(r^2 = 27\%)$; group III, $\hat{y} = 0.31 + 0.22x$ $(r^2 = 29\%)$; group IV, $\hat{y} = 0.47 - 0.11x$ $(r^2 = 3\%)$; group V, $\hat{y} = -0.03 + 0.44x$ $(r^2 = 29\%)$.

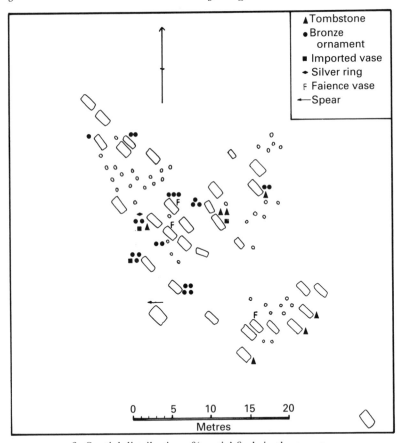

46. Spatial distribution of 'exotic' finds in the cemetery

rather than 75–90 cm deliberately ruled out the possibility of estab-
lishing a lineage tomb. So those who buried their dead in group IV,
separated from the main cemetery by a band of child graves, did so
with a very different attitude towards the symbolic expression of
descent.

How are we to explain group IV's deviation from the descent
dogma of Vroulian ritual? There is no strong correlation between
depth of grave and quantity or quality of grave goods with the
initial burial; some of the group IV graves are as rich as any others
in the cemetery (fig. 46). We are not dealing with a group of
pariahs, despite Kinch's argument (1914: 82) from the unburned
pebbles in gr. 23 that this was a criminal who had been stoned to

death. However, the few tombstones found stood over some of the deepest graves, suggesting a different sort of honour, one more oriented towards the memory of the tomb over a long period – as we should expect from people especially concerned with descent and elders. No tombstones were found in group IV.

The contrast could be explained simply in terms of settlers coming to Vroulia from different parts of Rhodes in 625, each group sticking to its own fashions. However, this ignores the contrast between both sets of Vroulian burials and what we find elsewhere; and is not really an explanation at all, since the redefinition of shallow pits as a minority rite at Vroulia inevitably means that as a ritual statement they worked differently there from the ways in which they functioned in northern Rhodes. We have to treat the Vroulian customs as a coherent functioning symbolic system rather than as a mélange of odds and ends. Alternatively, if Vroulia was an important stopping off point on the route from Lindos to Egypt,[12] the unstructured and 'descent-less' graves in group IV, separate from the main cemetery, could be mortalities from visiting ships. This is plausible, since group IV only contains 10 cremations out of a total of about 80; and it would explain why these burials were never intended to begin lineage tombs. If we found the same pattern at other sites in southern Rhodes, such contingent factors would lose their appeal; but a unique site – like a unique grave – is open to any number of direct interpretations.

THE SETTLEMENT

The houses offer a different sort of context (see fig. 47). There is obviously a distinction between rows I and II, and we can also separate small rooms with rock floors and no visible doors from larger rooms with porches and one or two doors. The former, as Kinch surmised, were probably storerooms attached to larger residential complexes. In row I we find two groups of rooms without doors (I.19–22, 29–31). Next to the second group was I.32, a much grander building with a paved floor. The stretch of wall outside I.32 seems to mark a courtyard running up to the wall extending from

---

[12] Herodotus 2.178 mentions Rhodian involvement at Naucratis, which, in spite of his dating, probably began around the time Vroulia was founded (Austin 1970: 22–33; Coulson & Leonard 1982); and two Ialysians, Telephos and Anaxanor, are known to have been serving as mercenaries in Egypt in 591 B.C. (Meiggs & Lewis 1969: no. 7).

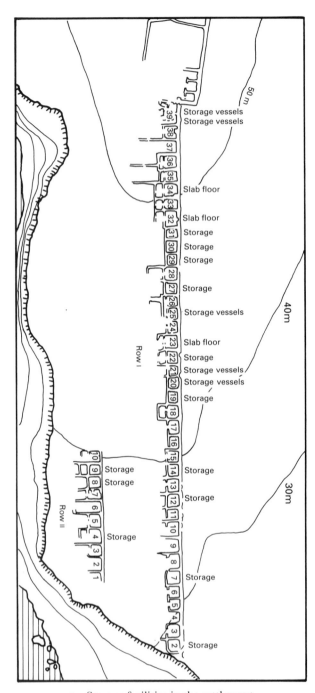

50 m

Storage vessels
Storage vessels

Slab floor

Slab floor
Storage
Storage
Storage

Storage

Storage vessels

Slab floor
Storage
Storage vessels
Storage vessels
Storage

40 m

Row I

Storage
Storage

Storage

Storage

Row II

Storage

30 m

Storage

Storage

47. Storage facilities in the settlement

the front of 1.28, making the three storerooms part of a single unit with 1.32. Twelve vases were found in 1.32, more than in any other room, including the only sherds of Attic black-figure. However, it may not be wise to rely on this, since it must be largely a result of the abandonment process. Some houses would have been emptied more thoroughly than others, and some (e.g. 1.1, 25, 39, 40) were badly eroded; and the little which survived these processes is not described consistently in the site report. The stub of a wall running south-west from the south-east corner of 1.22 was probably part of a similar courtyard, suggesting that 1.19–21 would have belonged with 1.18, which, with nine vases, was the second richest source of pottery in the settlement. Fragments of storage jars were found in the north corner of 1.22, which perhaps did not have a separate storeroom. The well-preserved 1.23 also had a paved floor, and the corridor-and-courtyard arrangement outside 1.24–6 (1.25 containing storage vessels) might mean that these three rooms were subsidiary to 1.23. Rooms 1.27–8 with their courtyard may form another unit.[13]

This sort of analysis could be extended to the whole site. There must be 15–20 units in the preserved part of the village. This suggests another argument. The 80 or so cremations represent about 40 adults burying two generations of their dead, which is roughly the population I would surmise for the published area of the site; but it is very likely that there were in fact many more houses, and more walls on the same alignment as row II are clearly visible today. The area between the rows was probably more built up, and more rooms have probably fallen off the cliff at the south-east end of row I, which ends abruptly in the middle of room 1.1. Kinch certainly thought that the settlement had a larger population than the cemetery. He wrote:

We were astonished by the small size of the cemetery, and the limited number of tombs it contained. The search for tombs in other parts of Vroulia, both around the settlement and within it, was fruitless, and we are almost certain that the cemetery we found is the only one. (Kinch 1914: 35)

This is very important, *if* we can believe it. This is a typical problem for archaeologists. Kinch's failure to indicate that he had

[13] Houses, Kinch 1914: 112–24.

only excavated part of row II is not reassuring; but we do not have an explicit statement from him that only one cemetery could be found, and Kinch was an experienced archaeologist, who had worked at Lindos for many years. We have a hard choice. We either arrogantly assume that we know better than Kinch, and reject his claim; or we run the risk of being gullible, and believe that if he could not find more graves, then they were not there.

If he was right, we have three types of adult graves, not two. First, groups I, II, III and V, cremations in deep pits with evidence of veneration for the founding ancestor; then group IV, cremations in shallow pits with less emphasis on descent; and now a group of funerals which did not end with pit graves at all. In *Burial and Ancient Society* I argued that in some areas of early Greece sections of the population were buried in ways which are very hard for excavators to find, with those whose resting places elude us generally being at the bottom end of the social structure, excluded from full membership and perhaps even from access to the land. Some support could be found for this by a desperate search through the literary sources. Rhodes traditionally had strong links with Crete in the seventh century. Thucydides (6.4.3) says they co-founded a colony at Gela in 688, and Pausanias (5.24.1–3; 6.7) that the late seventh-century Eratidai who ruled Ialysos called themselves Heraklidai. We see a similar status structure in the fifth-century Gortyn law code from Crete (*IC* 4.42), with serf-like groups called *doloi* and *woikees* distinguished from more privileged *eleutheroi*; perhaps something like this could be extended to Vroulia. But it would be grasping at straws. Pausanias lived a thousand years later; Herodotus (7.153.1) does not refer to Cretan involvement in Gela; and in any case, these stories need not imply anything about Rhodian social structure.

This is a dead end. Another approach is to compare the use of space in the settlement with the social structure evoked in the cemetery. However, the site report again presents problems. Vroulia was inhabited for 50 years, and we cannot ignore the developmental cycles of the families which grew up and died there (fig. 48). Let us imagine a newly married couple coming to Vroulia in 625; following Hesiod's advice (*WD* 695–8), our man can be aged about thirty and our woman eighteen. By 620 they would probably have a small child; by 615 probably a second, plus the husband's widowed mother moving in with them. By 605 the household would be at its

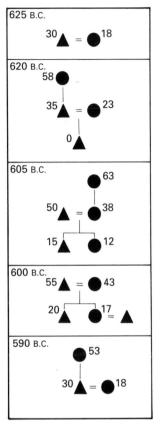

48. Hypothetical family developmental cycle at Vroulia, 625–575 B.C.

productive height, with the children in their teens and any aged dependants probably dead, but by 590 their children would probably be married and gone, the husband might well be dead, and a son might take over the household, or the widow might move away to become a dependant in someone else's *oikos*. Next door, by contrast, there might be someone like the man in Hesiod's *Theogony* (603–7), who avoided marriage and whose property was divided up by his kinsmen when he died. We cannot suppose that walls, floors and doors remained fixed through all this. Rooms would be added on, knocked through and abandoned in constantly shifting patterns. Kinch comments that the paved floors in 1.23, 32, 34 and II.4 all had sherds under them and thus belonged to a second phase of occupation, but gives no more evidence for architectural changes through time.[14]

The settlement plan, then, is only relevant to the 570s. This is important. As we have seen, the superficial uniformity of the village was broken up by detailed variations in house type and perhaps contents, just as the theme of age and descent in the cemetery was challenged by the unusual riches of grs. s and 2. But this evidence requires careful handling. A Vroulian did not come home from an 'ideological' funeral or festival to a 'real' home; the process of structuration continued in the village, at once constrained by its physical form and contributing to changing it.[15] But the dynamic element of the settlement has been lost, and thinking that we have discovered something important because none of the houses stood out as much in 575 as the wealth of gr. 2 had in 625 would surely be wrong. To return to an earlier point, grs. s and 2 are difficult to interpret because they are so unusual; the *general patterns* are more valuable.

We have to try to imagine the interaction of the various areas in Vroulia. In the cemeteries, Vroulians took part in rituals emphasising descent and the continuing influence of the founders of a lineage. There was some room for differences between families, in the use of tombstones for example, but not much. They would react to these rites with expectations shaped partly by their constant experience of the settlement space, where uniformity was even stronger. Vroulian space was not Hippodamian, creating a democratic citizen, nor that of an army camp; walking home from a cremation past the well-measured rooms backed up to the village wall, Vroulians would understand this order in terms of or in opposition to the ideal of descent created in the funeral. The paucity of the gifts given to the gods in the sanctuaries when compared to those given to the founders of new tombs could hardly fail to underline the point. We might see in this peculiar site an attempt in the rapidly changing world of the late seventh century to set up at the end of the island, if not exactly of the earth, an ideal peasant world, preserving the proper stable relations between men in spite of the disruptive forces of birth, marriage and death – age, family,

[14] Developmental cycle, Goody, ed., 1958; Elder 1978; 1987; Carter 1984. Sherds under floors, Kinch 1914: 118.
[15] Structuration and settlement space, H. L. Moore 1986.

descent, all themes which crop up in the ideologies of peasant societies all over the world, but here articulated in a remarkably powerful form.

Perhaps. It is easy to get carried away, and Vroulia illustrates another important point: the analysis of burial as ritual action yields results in direct proportion to the amount of other types of evidence available to provide a context.

In Vroulia we find a world very different from that which Greek historians can usually study. We should expect kinship and descent to be important in a small village roughly in the age of Hesiod, just as they were to be in fourth-century Athens; yet in the social structure of the *polis*, a battery of rituals acted to subordinate the individual descent group to the community as a group of citizens, along with their women and children. As we saw on pp. 150–1 above, the balance between communal and individualising rituals varied widely in archaic times, but I know of no site with such an extreme individualising emphasis as Vroulia. There is certainly nothing like it at Kameiros and Ialysos, even though wealth and grave type could vary considerably. Vroulia suggests a ritual division between town and country in archaic Rhodes – something most unusual in ancient Greece; and shows a non-citizenship social structure persisting in an isolated spot. Perhaps sites like this can help us to see the underside of classical history. Historians have learned to explore hidden worlds of rural experience by exploiting neglected kinds of evidence, such as Le Roy Ladurie's evocation from inquisitors' records of the village of Montaillou in the years around A.D. 1300. There will never be an ancient Greek Martin Guerre or Menocchio, but we do not have to depend entirely on the overwhelmingly urban literary record. The burials expand the historian's horizons; and we are in no position to ignore them.[16]

---

[16] P. Millett (1984) analyses Hesiod's peasant lifestyle; Lamberton (1988) adds important perspectives on the literary genre. Peasant families, e.g. Shanin, ed., 1971; Segalen 1986. Town, country and citizenship, Wood 1988: 101–10. Montaillou, Le Roy Ladurie 1978. Martin Guerre, Davis 1983. Menocchio, Ginzburg 1980.

CHAPTER 8

Conclusion

Cynics sometimes suggest that 'progress' in historiography is no more than a series of mutual misunderstandings, as historians rush to disprove things that others had never intended to say. In writing a methodological book like this I perhaps run even more of a risk of creating the wrong impression than I would in a more substantive work. I have argued that a kind of evidence which most ancient historians ignore is in fact a vital source; and that when historians have used it, it has generally been in the least appropriate ways. Some readers will find this annoying, incomprehensible or not worth the bother; but others, I hope, may see ways to extend their own research. I close with a summary of the points I have tried to make, but first I will set out a series of propositions which I have *not* made.

WHAT IS *NOT* BEING SAID

1. *Burials are the 'best' source*

Classicists who rely mainly on texts and those who rely mainly on archaeological evidence often act as if they were two sides in a competition, and one day an impartial observer will judge whose evidence is best and who wins the game. We have to take our evidence where we can find it; and my argument here has been that we need to combine as many genres as possible. Historians who write about community without using material evidence for rituals and archaeologists who write their monographs without reference to historical concepts both lose out. I do not believe those who say archaeology is a zero-sum game, with its value declining in direct relationship to the amount of literary evidence available. If there is a kind of evidence which renders material culture superfluous (which I very much doubt) we certainly do not have it from classical antiquity. Every kind of evidence has its own problems and gaps, and the study of burials allows us to fill in some of these in our other sources. This is particularly true of artistic evidence, which often comes from graves. Without detailed analysis of the archaeological context, we run a serious risk of misinterpreting this material; but that is not the same as saying that art history is a waste of time. Again, my argument is that different kinds of evidence need to be combined.

2. *Burials are irrelevant to religious belief*

In dwelling on the sociological side of ancient rituals, I do not want to create the impression that I think that personal, religious belief (as defined on pp. 15–16 above) has nothing to do with the formation of burials. It is self-evident that a rite of passage which eases the dead person into the afterworld is going to be shaped in terms of the actors' perceptions of the next life. But the interpretation of the material in these terms is in fact much more difficult than the kind of analyses I pursue here. On the whole, historians of classical antiquity have not joined in the debates over the meaning of the notion of 'mentality' and how we can write its history; but even if we ignore this conceptual difficulty, we have the fundamental problem that an intellectualist reading of burials cannot work without direct interpretation of symbolism (see pp. 17–21 above). The most rigorous contextual analysis will not allow us to say with much confidence that a ritual action 'means' a specific idea. In chapter 2 I ignored most interpretations of inhumation and cremation in the Roman empire rather than fighting step-by-step over the evidence, because I do not think that these theories have many points of contact with it. Yet at a certain point we *have* to make direct interpretations if we are to write what I would consider to be 'history' rather than an archaeological version of formalist literary theory. My tentative reading of the mounds of the northern provinces in the second and third centuries A.D. as symbols of resistance to Rome (p. 51) is one such case. More work on other types of resistance might allow me to reformulate the statement in more subtle ways, but it would still rest on my assessment of what went through the heads of different people when they saw a tumulus. The weakness of intellectualist approaches, though, is that they tend to rest *exclusively* on such leaps of faith.

3. *Graves are always useful*

The burial is only one part of the funeral ritual, and it may not be the most important part. If a body was cremated away from the grave, it is quite possible that grave goods were important when smashed on the pyre, but unimportant when a few bones were scooped up and thrown into a pit, taking a random shovelful of sherds with them. Analysing this material would reveal nothing about purposeful behaviour. But admitting that a type of evidence is not always useful does not mean that it is never useful. When we detect a strong pattern in the evidence – as with the placement of grave goods mainly in the first burials in each tomb at Vroulia – this demands explanation unless there is reason to think that it has been produced by post-depositional processes. Statistical methods can be particularly helpful in defining patterns. The absence of a pattern is much more problematic, and arguments from silence – whether we are talking about the Peace of Callias or late Roman inhumations – are always weaker than positive evidence.

4. *Analysis of burials explains social structure*

I have frequently spoken of rituals as 'creating' social structure. In this I dissent from what I think is the dominant view in classics, that insofar as rituals are connected to something other than belief, it is as a mirror reflecting a deeper social reality. I argued in chapter 1 that ritual action imposes order on everyday events just as much as the reverse is true; but I also dissented from the extreme position that ritual is all that there is, existing as an irreducible sphere of experience. Whenever possible, burials must be combined with written sources, iconographic evidence and other types of archaeological deposits. When this is not possible, we end up with a rather abstract model of social structure, although it is still better than not having a model at all. As I said in point 1 above, the commonsense assumption that the value of the archaeological record declines as the textual record grows could not be more wrong.

POSITIVE CONCLUSIONS

Burials are difficult to analyse and have their own problems, but they can be used to augment texts and pictures to give us a fuller understanding of one type of ritual. From this, we can develop models of ancient social structures that make far greater allowance than previous interpretations for changes through time and space, for differing perceptions of structure by different groups, and for conflicts over meaning.

The key to manipulating this evidence is the use of context. No single feature of burial practices can be separated and treated in isolation. We may start off by noticing, for example, that the dominant burial rite in the western part of the Roman empire changed from cremation to inhumation between about A.D. 150 and 300. By including different kinds of evidence, by changing the geographical scale of the system within which we study the changes, and by trying to see the rituals from different social perspectives, we are able to transform the problem. It ceases to be a technical archaeological one of accounting for a change in the graves, and becomes a more interesting, historical one of why death ritual became more homogenised across the empire just at the time when economic and political regionalism was increasing. By playing around with context we are able to acquire a wholly new kind of evidence. In chapter 1, I suggested five axes along which we can examine any particular set of burials, progressively widening the context we see them in: typology, time, contexts of deposition, space and demography. As I showed in chapter 7, in practice we do not have to move from one level of analysis to another in any predetermined order. In different situations, different approaches will work, but any persuasive study will necessarily be on a large scale. It is difficult to write a short paper analysing burial evidence, since it is precisely by its inclusiveness and the richness of the context that this kind of evidence persuades. Looking back over this book, I am more struck by what I have left out than by what I have said. I offer no extended discussion of spatial factors like the placement of cemeteries relative to settlements; nor of the use of 'special' tombs as places for continuous cult activities; nor of feasts and festivals in cemeteries. These are all fascinating subjects, which show distinct historical patterns. However, as in studies of particular bodies of evidence, it is impossible.to include everything.

Of course, I hope that the concrete interpretations in chapters 2–7 will be persuasive, or at least provocative enough to stimulate better research into the same questions, but the arguments of the book as a whole do not stand or fall by my ideas about Athenian democracy or imperial Roman society. I chose problems outside my field of specialisation – Dark Age and archaic Greece – to make another general point: that this sort of analysis is useful in *all* periods of ancient history, not just the murky days at the beginning or the end of the period canonically defined as 'the classical world'. Indeed, as I keep pointing out, the potential of burial evidence increases in direct proportion to the amount of other types of sources we have. There is more room for radical reinterpretations of late Roman Britain than of classical Athens, but the possibilities for relating ritual structures to individual action are so much greater in the latter case that they may actually make the burials more, not less, valuable to the historian. Collingwood, no stranger to archaeological materials, wrote in his famous essay on historical evidence that 'anything is evidence which is used as evidence, and no one can know what is going to be useful as evidence until he has had occasion to use it' (Collingwood 1946: 280). He was right.

Bibliographical essay

The footnotes scattered through the book provide brief references for the points made in the text, and the full details are collected in a consolidated bibliography on pp. 211–56 below. In this section, I want to suggest a few works which might be useful in more general terms. The literature on death and burial is large and rapidly expanding, so this is no more than a list of the titles which I have found most useful. I try as far as possible to provide references to recent books in English, but in a few cases the most important studies are in foreign languages.

DEATH

Greece is better served by intellectualist histories than Rome. E. Rohde's nineteenth-century classic *Psyche* (English translation, New York 1925) is still useful for the sources he presents, although his evolutionary reconstructions can be misleading. Among the best recent works are J. Bremmer, *The Early Greek Concept of the Soul* (Princeton 1983); R. Parker, *Miasma* (Oxford 1983); R. Garland, *The Greek Way of Death* (London 1985); and J.-P. Vernant, *L'individu, la mort, l'amour* (Paris 1989). I discuss some of the difficulties in interpreting archaeological evidence in these terms in 'Attitudes toward death in archaic Greece', *Classical Antiquity* 8 (1989) 296–320. The iconographic and poetic evidence is presented in a judicious balance in E. Vermeule's highly readable *Aspects of Death in Early Greek Art and Poetry* (Berkeley 1979). Fifth-century tragedy is an important source for ideas about death, but one which I have neglected in this book. The most detailed treatments are N. Loraux, *Tragic Ways of Killing a Woman* (Cambridge, Mass. 1987) and M. Rehm, *Marriage to Death* (Princeton, forthcoming), which also contains a useful summary of fifth-century Athenian rituals.

The proceedings of two conferences about death in the ancient world held on Capri in 1977 and 1987 are indispensable. The first was edited by G. Gnoli & J.-P. Vernant as *La mort, les morts, dans les sociétés anciennes* (Cambridge 1982), and contains important essays on Greek and Roman subjects, combining studies of ideas of death in literature with archaeological analyses. The second is published as *AION ArchStAnt* 10 (1988) and concentrates on Greece. Another collective volume, S. Humphreys and H. King's *Mortality and Immortality* (London 1981), contains fascinating papers on Greek literature as well as historical, archaeological and ethnographic studies from around the world. Humphreys' own contributions to this book are republished along with several other studies in her *The Family, Women and Death* (London 1983). For Rome, P. Friedländer's massive *Life and Manners under the Early Empire* (4 vols., English translation of the 8th edn, London 1908–13) and F. Cumont's *Afterlife in Roman Paganism* (New Haven 1922) and *Lux Perpetua* (Paris 1949) remain basic resources. *Jenseitsvorstellungen im Antike und Christentum* (*Jahrbuch für Antike und Christentum* Ergänzungsband 9 (1982)) and F. Hinard, ed., *La mort, les morts, et l'au-delà dans le monde romain* (Caen 1987) contain some interesting papers spanning a very wide range of approaches and sources. More anthropologically informed studies can be found in K. Hopkins, *Death and Renewal* (Cambridge 1983) ch. 4 and the papers in *AION ArchStAnt* 6 (1984).

BURIAL

There is no substitute for direct acquaintance with excavation reports, which are usually the archaeologist's equivalent of primary textual sources. However, in practice it is often necessary to begin from syntheses, if only to identify the main sites and the journals and series likely to carry further publications, and to learn some of the jargon of cemetery studies. The problem is that satisfactory syntheses of the archaeological evidence are very difficult to produce, since there is so much to be condensed. D. Kurtz & J. Boardman's *Greek Burial Customs* (London 1971) works very well by concentrating mainly on Athens between 1100 and 325 B.C. Other states and periods are less well served, although Kurtz and Boardman provide brief bibliographies, and J. Fedak's *Monumental Tombs of the Hellenistic Age* (Toronto 1990) fills part of the gap. The main Athenian cemetery on which Kurtz and Boardman base their account is the ubiquitous Kerameikos, published in the fourteen massive tomes of *Kerameikos: Ergebnisse der Ausgrabungen* (Berlin 1939–1990), with more to come. The historian's task has been made vastly easier by U. Knigge's superb summary *Der Kerameikos von Athen* (Athens 1988). Annual summaries in English of the year's work and publications in Greece appear in *Archaeological Reports*, a supplement to *JHS*. These provide the most sensible way to master the evidence, since Kurtz and Boardman's book is now twenty years old. *AR* also carries occasional reports on Italy and Turkey.

The Roman equivalent to Kurtz and Boardman is J. Toynbee's *Death and Burial in the Roman World* (London 1971). The scale of her topic – not just Rome and Etruria from 900 B.C. to A.D. 500, but also the whole of the rest of the empire – is simply unmanageable, and it is difficult to form a clear impression from this book of developments in any specific place or period. Fortunately, there are a number of more detailed studies which fill the gap. R. Reece's edited volume *Burial in the Roman World* (London 1977) is a fine collection of papers on the western empire, including areas outside the borders. However, some knowledge of German is necessary to master the most important recent studies. V. Kockel's *Die Grabbauten vor dem Herkulaner Tor* (Mainz 1983) summarises the Pompeian evidence, and M. Eisner's *Zur Typologie der Grabbauten im Suburbium Roms* (Mainz 1986) the architectural remains of the most prominent tombs at Rome. D. Boschung's *Antike Grabaltäre aus den Nekropolen Roms* (Berne 1987), F. Sinn-Henninger's *Stadtrömische Marmorurnen* (Mainz 1987) and D. Kleiner's *Roman Imperial Funerary Altars with Portraits* (Rome 1987) provide important catalogues and analyses of grave markers. S. Dyson's *Community and Society in Roman Italy* (forthcoming) ch. 6 is a fascinating treatment of the place of cemeteries in the life of Roman cities. In his article 'Neuere Literatur zu römischen Grabbauten', *Journal of Roman Archaeology* 2 (1989) 207–13, H. von Hesberg reviews the impact of these recent works; but pride of place goes to the volume which he co-edited with P. Zanker, *Römische Gräber-strasse* (Munich 1987), a magnificent collection of essays. Zanker's *The Power of Images in the Age of Augustus* (Ann Arbor 1988) is equally important, putting burial into the context of Augustus' 'cultural renewal'. It should be read in conjunction with A. Wallace-Hadrill's perceptive review in *JRS* 79 (1989) 157–64.

Just as Greek cemetery studies are dominated by the Kerameikos, Rome is ruled by Ostia and the Vatican hill. The main texts for Ostia are G. Calza, *La necropoli del Porto di Roma nell'Isola Sacra* (Rome 1940) and M. F. Squarciapino, *Scavi di Ostia 3.1: La necropoli* (Rome 1958), with a summary in R. Meiggs, *Roman Ostia* (2nd edn, Oxford 1973) 455–70. Baldassarre's recent excavations have somewhat altered the picture (see Baldassarre's and Boschung's papers in *Römische Gräberstrasse*). The original report on the Vatican excavations is badly flawed and shows a near total lack of interest in stratigraphy. The best account is J. Toynbee & J. Ward-Perkins, *The Shrine of St Peter and the Vatican Excavations* (London 1956), with a detailed account of part of the cemetery in H. Mielsch & H. von Hesberg, *Die heidnische Nekropole unter St. Peter in Rom. Die Mausoleen* A–D (Rome 1986).

RITUAL

The classic accounts of death ritual in R. Hertz, *Death and the Right Hand* (Aberdeen 1960; first published in French 1907) and A. van Gennep, *The Rites of Passage* (London 1960; first published in French 1909) are little read these days, but it is hard to understand the tradition which has shaped modern studies of rituals without them. Of the many recent works, I would single out R. Huntington & P. Metcalf's *Celebrations of Death* (Cambridge 1979), M. Bloch & J. Parry's edited *Death and the Regeneration of Life* (Cambridge 1982) and L. Danforth & A. Tsiaras' *The Death Rituals of Rural Greece* (Princeton 1982) as the best, for both their theoretical and empirical richness. J. La Fontaine's *Initiation* (London 1985) is the best modern introduction to rites of passage. G. Lewis' *Day of Shining Red* (Cambridge 1980) is unsurpassed as an introduction to the analysis of ritual symbolism. There are many studies which link symbolism to concepts of social structure. L. Hunt, ed., *The New Cultural History* (Berkeley 1989) and C. Tilley, ed., *Reading Material Culture* (Oxford 1990) provide introductions to the thought of some of the critical figures.

QUANTIFICATION

The statistical methods deployed in this book are all very simple. There are many textbooks on statistics, and some of them cater specifically for the archaeologist. C. Orton's *Mathematics in Archaeology* (London 1980) is the easiest introduction, but is very limited in scope; while S. Shennan's *Quantifying Archaeology* (New York 1988) is more difficult but is an exemplary introduction to many of the pattern-finding and testing techniques likely to be useful in burial analysis. D. H. Thomas' *Figuring Anthropology* (New York 1978) draws on a wider selection of anthropological examples, but constantly appeals to the sort of problems archaeologists face. R. Floud's *An Introduction to Quantitative Methods for Historians* (2nd edn, Cambridge 1983) is oriented more towards serial data from archival sources, but includes a number of techniques not to be found in Shennan or Hurst. More advanced students will find J. Doran & F. R. Hodson's edited book *Mathematics and Computers in Archaeology* (Edinburgh 1975), C. Ruggles & P. Rahtz's *Computer and Quantitative Methods in Archaeology 1987* (Oxford 1988: *BAR* S 393) and the periodical *Computer Applications in Archaeology* more useful. Computer programs which carry out most of the techniques an archaeologist is likely to need are now available for microcomputers, and Shennan lists the main companies. For more advanced skills, it is necessary to abandon specifically archaeological works and to consult more technical manuals.

ETHNOGRAPHIC AND HISTORICAL COMPARISONS

Comparative readings reveal both the limits and the possibilities of ancient burials. The range of choices here is enormous, but J. Goody's *Death, Property and the Ancestors* (London 1962) and M. Bloch's *Placing the Dead* (London 1971) deserve special mention. The drawback of many ethnographic studies is that they create a rather timeless atmosphere, a result of the brevity of most fieldworkers' stay among the community under study. Recent works have tried to break through this by combining participant observation with textual evidence. M. Bloch's *From Blessing to Violence* (Cambridge 1986) is a superb study of changing rituals across two centuries; and J. Glazier's 'Mbeere ancestors and the domestication of death', *Man* 19 (1984) 133–48, focuses on a shorter period but exposes more of the complexities of chronological change.

French scholars have set the pace in historical work on death. The best known is P. Ariès, whose *The Hour of Our Death* (New York 1981) and *Images of Man and Death* (New York 1985) have had enormous influence, although they are highly idiosyncratic. J. Whaley, ed., *Mirrors of Mortality* (London 1981), collects a number of papers extending or criticising Ariès' style of analysis. This methodology is extremely idealist, but other historians favour more materialist explanations. M. Vovelle's *Piété baroque et déchristianisation en Provence au XVIIIe siècle* (abr. edn, Paris 1978) seeks a middle ground. J. McManners' paper in Whaley's book discusses some of the reasons for the French historiographical interest in death. On the whole, studies of modern periods tend to be more useful when looking at intellectualist problems surrounding ancient death than at the kind of social history I have attempted in this book. D. Stannard's *The Puritan Way of Death* (Oxford 1977) and R. Etlin's *The Architecture of Death* (Cambridge, Mass. 1984) are rare exceptions. The papers collected in *Anthropological Quarterly* 62 (1989) blend topics which would conventionally be separated into 'anthropological' and 'historical' categories, and for this reason all of them – especially Jill Dubisch's on modern Greece – are worth reading.

I have not drawn much on imperial China for comparative analysis in this book, but some historians emphasise its parallels or instructive contrasts with Rome, and Chinese burial should be very interesting for Romanists. The cemeteries of the South (especially Hong Kong, the New Territories and Taiwan) have been extensively studied. M. Freedman's *Chinese Lineage and Society* (London 1966) and E. Ahern's *The Cult of the Dead in a Chinese Village* (Stanford 1973) are classics, both favouring sociological analysis. J. Watson & E. Rawski's edited volume *Death Ritual in Late Imperial and Modern China* (Berkeley 1988) may suggest possible lines of inquiry into the Roman empire. P. Ebrey, 'Cremation in Sung China', *AHR* 95 (1990) 406–28 discusses the same type of problems that I face in chapter 2 above, but from a markedly intellectualist position. For earlier periods, K. C. Chang's *Shang Civilization* (New Haven 1980) summarises some of the archaeological evidence.

THE ARCHAEOLOGY OF DEATH

The best way to learn about the potential of burial evidence is to study examples of its use, which generally means to turn to prehistory.

The classic collections of 'New Archaeology' studies of burial are J. A. Brown, ed., *Approaches to the Social Dimensions of Mortuary Practices* (New York 1971) and R. Chapman, I. Kinnes & K. Randsborg, eds., *The Archaeology of Death* (Cambridge 1981), along with A. Saxe's Ph.D. thesis, 'Social dimensions of mortuary practices' (University of Michigan 1970). S. Shennan's paper 'The social organisation at Branc', *Antiquity* 49 (1975)

279–88, J. Tainter's 'Mortuary practices and the study of prehistoric social systems', *AMT* 1 (1978) 104–41, F. Hodson's 'Quantifying Hallstatt', *Am Ant* 42 (1977) 394–412 and J. O'Shea's *Mortuary Variability* (New York 1984) also repay close study. R. W. Chapman's *Emerging Complexity* (Cambridge 1990) attempts to refute some of the post-processual criticisms of New Archaeology approaches to burial. Much of this will seem very abstract and systematised to ancient historians, but they contain valuable ideas and methods which can be deployed in more 'humanist' ways.

The 'post-New Archaeology' of the 1980s has produced a number of studies of prehistoric burial which may be more directly applicable. In terms of general ideas, some of the earliest work remains the most useful, such as M. Rowlands, 'Kinship, alliance and exchange in the European Bronze Age', in J. Barrett & R. Bradley, eds., *Settlement and Society in the British Later Bronze Age* (Oxford 1980: *BAR* 83) 15–55; R. Bradley, 'The destruction of wealth in later prehistory', *Man* 17 (1982) 108–22, and some of the papers in P. Rahtz, T. Dickinson, & L. Watts, eds., *Anglo-Saxon Cemeteries 1979* (Oxford 1980: *BAR* 82). The *New Directions in Archaeology* series has consistently published collections including papers of this type, including I. Hodder, ed., *Symbolic and Structural Archaeology* (Cambridge 1982) and *The Archaeology of Contextual Meanings* (Cambridge 1987); A. C. Renfrew & S. Shennan, eds., *Ranking, Resource and Exchange* (Cambridge 1982); D. Miller & C. Tilley, eds., *Ideology, Power and Prehistory* (Cambridge 1984); M. Spriggs, ed., *Marxist Perspectives in Archaeology* (Cambridge 1984). Paul Courbin, the wittiest (if not always the fairest) critic of the New Archaeology, points out in his *What is Archaeology?* (Chicago 1988) p. xxiii that the greatest disappointment of that school was its failure to come up with major substantive contributions. Until recently the same was true of the 'contextual' archaeology school. R. Bradley's *The Social Foundations of Prehistoric Britain* (Harlow 1984) has for long been the best attempt to apply the principles. It is now joined by Ian Hodder's ambitious *The Domestication of Europe* (Oxford 1990); but it is perhaps no coincidence that the only region to have received *two* full-length studies is Dark Age Greece (I. Morris, *Burial and Ancient Society* (Cambridge 1987); J. Whitley, *Style and Society in Dark Age Greece* (Cambridge 1991)). Classical archaeology may surprise its critics yet.

Bibliography

ABERCROMBIE, N., HILL, S., & TURNER, B. S. (1980) *The Dominant Ideology Thesis*. London.

AGACHE, R. (1975) 'La campagne à l'époque romaine dans les grandes plaines du Nord du France d'après les photographies aériennes', *ANRW* 2.4: 658–713. Berlin.

AGACHE, R. & S. (1978) 'De la recherche des paysages de l'antiquité dans le nord de la France', *Caesarodunum* 13: 149–67.

AHERN, E. (1973) *The Cult of the Dead in a Chinese Village*. Stanford.

AKURGAL, E. (1955) *Zwei Grabstelen vorklassischer Zeit aus Sinope*. Berlin (Winckelmannsprogramm 111).

ALBERTONI, M. (1983) 'La necropoli Esquilina arcaica e repubblicana', in *L'archeologia in Roma capitale tra sterro e scavo:* 140–55. Rome.

ALCOCK, L. (1971) *Arthur's Britain*. London.

ALESHIRE, S. B. (1989) *The Athenian Asklepieion*. Amsterdam.

ALEXANDRI, O. (1968) '3e ephoreia klassikon arkhaiotiton', *AD* 23.2: 33–109.

(1970) '3e ephoreia klasikon arkhaiotiton', *AD* 25.2: 40–91.

(1972) '3e ephoreia klasikon arkhaiotiton', *AD* 27.2: 22–146.

(1973/4) 'Ephoreia klasikon arkhaiotiton Attikis', *AD* 29.2: 31–181.

(1975) 'Ephoreia klasikon arkhaiotiton Attikis', *AD* 30.2: 15–48.

(1976) '3e ephoreia klasikon arkhaiotiton', *AD* 31.2: 24–61.

(1977) '3e ephoreia klasikon kai proistorikon arkhaiotiton', *AD* 32.2: 16–35.

ALFÖLDY, G. (1974) 'The crisis of the third century as seen by contemporaries', *GRBS* 15: 89–111.

(1985) *The Social History of Rome*. 3rd edn, London.

ALMAGRO, M. (1953) *Las necrópolis de Ampurias* I: *introducción y necrópolis griegas*. Barcelona.

(1955) *Las necrópolis de Ampurias* II: *necrópolis romanas y necrópolis indígenas*. Barcelona.

AMAND, M. (1960) 'Roman barrows in Belgium', in *Analecta Archaeologica. Festschrift Fritz Fremersdorf:* 69–81. Cologne.

(1965) 'Les tumules d'époque romaine dans le Norique et la Pannonie', *Latomus* 24: 614–28.

(1987) 'La réapparition de la sépulture sous tumulus dans l'empire romain', *Ant Cl* 56: 163–82.

(1988) 'La réapparition de la sépulture sous tumulus dans l'empire romain (II)', *Ant Cl* 57: 176–203.

AMANDRY, P. (1988) 'A propos de monuments de Delphes: questions de chronologie (I)', *BCH* 112: 591–610.

AMYX, D. A. (1958) 'The Attic stelai, part III', *Hesperia* 27: 163–254.

(1988) *Corinthian Vase-Painting of the Archaic Period.* 3 vols. Berkeley.

ANDREIOMENOU, A. (1985) 'La nécropole classique de Tanagra', in *La Béotie antique*: 109–30. Paris.

ANDRIKOPOULOU-STRACK, J.-N. (1986) *Grabbauten des 1. Jahrhunderts n. Chr. im Rheingebiet.* Bonn (43. Beiheft Bonner Jahrbücher).

ANDRONIKOS, M. (1968) *Totenkult.* Göttingen (*Arch Hom* Band w).

(1984) *Vergina. The Royal Tombs.* Athens.

(1987) 'Some reflections on the Macedonian tombs', *BSA* 82: 1–16.

ANGEL, J. L. (1939) 'Geometric Athenians', in R. S. Young, *Late Geometric Graves and a Seventh-Century Well*: 236–46. Princeton (*Hesperia* supp. vol. 2).

(1944) 'Greek teeth, ancient and modern', *Human Biology* 16: 283–97.

(1945) 'Skeletal material from Attica', *Hesperia* 14: 279–363.

(1964) 'Osteoporosis: thalassemia?', *AJPA* 22: 369–72.

(1966) 'Porotic hyperostosis, anemias, malarias, and marshes in the prehistoric eastern Mediterranean', *Science* 153: 760–3.

(1969) 'The bases of paleodemography', *AJPA* 30: 427–38.

(1970) 'Human skeletal remains at Karatas', *AJA* 74: 253–9.

(1971) *The People of Lerna: Analysis of a Prehistoric Aegean Population.* Princeton.

(1972) 'Ecology and population in the east Mediterranean', *WA* 4: 88–105.

(1974) 'The cultural ecology of general versus dental health', in G. Fischer, ed., *Bevölkerung Biologie*: 382–91. Stuttgart.

(1977) 'Anemias of antiquity: eastern Mediterranean', in *Porotic Hyperostosis: An Enquiry*: 1–5. Detroit.

(1978) 'Porotic hyperostosis in the eastern Mediterranean', *Medical College of Virginia Quarterly* 15: 10–16.

ANTONACCIO, C. M. (1992) 'Terraces, tombs, and the early Argive Heraion', *Hesperia* 61: 85–105.

ARAFAT, K. & MORGAN, C. (1989) 'Pots and potters in Athens and Corinth: a review', *OJA* 8: 311–46.

(Forthcoming) 'Athens, Etruria and the Heueneberg: mutual misconceptions in the study of Greek-barbarian relations', in I. Morris, ed., *Classical Greece: Ancient Histories and Modern Archaeologies.* Cambridge.

ARCE, J. (1988) *Funus Imperatorum: los funerales de los emperadores romanos.* Madrid.

ARCHONDIDOU-ARGYRI, A. (1983) 'Mimiseis protokorinthiakon angeion apo tin Rodo', *ASAA* 45: 19–29.

ARIÈS, P. (1981) *The Hour of Our Death*. Harmondsworth.
(1985) *Images of Man and Death*. New York.

ARNOLD, C. J. (1984) *Roman Britain to Saxon England*. London.

ASAD, T. (1979) 'Anthropology and the analysis of ideology', *Man* 14: 607–27.

ASHMOLE, B. (1970) 'Sir John Beazley, 1885–1970', *PBA* 56: 443–61. Reprinted in Kurtz, ed., 1985: 57–71.

AUDIN, A. (1960) 'Inhumation et incinération', *Latomus* 19: 312–22, 518–32.

AUSTIN, M. M. (1970) *Greece and Egypt in the Archaic Age*. Cambridge (*PCPhS* supp. vol. 2).

BAKER, B. J. & ARMELAGOS, G. J. (1988) 'The origin and antiquity of syphilis', *CA* 29: 703–37.

BALDASSARRE, I. (1984) 'Una necropoli imperiale romana: proposte di lettura', *AION ArchStAnt* 6: 141–9.
(1985) 'La necropoli dell'Isola Sacra. Campagne di scavo 1976–1979', *Quaderni de 'La ricerca scientifica'* 112: 262–83.
(1987) 'La necropoli dell'Isola Sacra (Porto)', in von Hesberg & Zanker, eds.: 125–38.
(1988) 'Tomba e stele nelle lekythoi a fondo bianco', *AION ArchStAnt* 10: 107–15.

BALDWIN, R. (1985) 'Intrusive burial groups in the late Roman cemetery at Lankhills, Winchester – a reassessment of the evidence', *OJA* 4: 93–104.

BAR-ADON, P. (1977) 'Another settlement of the Judaean Desert Sect at 'Ain el-Ghuweir on the Dead Sea', *BASOR* 227: 1–25.

BARLEY, M. W. & HANSON, R. P. C., eds. (1968) *Christianity in Britain, 300–700*. Leicester.

BARTEL, B. (1982) 'A historical review of ethnological and archaeological analyses of mortuary practice', *Journal of Anthropological Archaeology* 1: 32–58.
(1985) 'Comparative historical archaeology and archaeological theory', in S. L. Dyson, ed., *Comparative Studies in the Archaeology of Colonialism*: 8–37. Oxford (*BAR* S 233).

BAZANT, J. (1986) 'Entre la croyance et l'expérience: la mort sur les lécythes à fond blanc', in *Iconographie classique et identités régionales*: 34–44. Paris (*BCH* supp. vol. 14).

BEARD, M. (1985) 'Writing and ritual: a study of diversity and expansion in the Arval Acta', *PBSR* 40: 114–62.
(1987) 'A complex of times: no more sheep on Romulus' birthday', *PCPhS* 213: 1–15.
(1989) 'Acca Larentia gains a son: myths and priesthood at Rome', in

M. M. Mackenzie & C. Roueché, eds., *Images of Authority*: 41–61. Cambridge: *PCPhS* supp. vol. 16.

BEARD, M. & NORTH, J., eds. (1990) *Pagan Priests*. London.

BECK, L. A. (1985) 'Bivariate analysis of trace elements in bone', *JHE* 14: 493–502.

BECKER, E. (1973) *The Denial of Death*. New York.

BELLAH, R. N. (1967) 'Civil religion in America', *Daedalus* 96: 1–21.

BELLAH, R. N., MADSEN, R., SULLIVAN, W. M., SWIDLER, A., & TIPTON, S. M. (1985) *Habits of the Heart: Individualism and Commitment in American Life*. New York.

BENNETT, D. O. (1988) ' "The poor have much more money": changing socio-economic relations in a Greek village', *JMGS* 6: 117–34.

BENNIKE, P. (1985) *Palaeopathology of Danish Skeletons: A Comparative Study of Demography, Disease and Injury*. Copenhagen.

BÉRARD, C. (1970) *Eretria III: L'héröon à la porte de l'ouest*. Berne.

BÉRARD, C., ed. (1989) *A City of Images*. Princeton.

BERNAL, M. (1987) *Black Athena 1: The Fabrication of Ancient Greece, 1785–1985*. London.

BERNHARDT, R. (1985) *Polis und römische Herrschaft in der späten Republik*. Berlin.

BIERSACK, A. (1989) 'Local knowledge, local history: Geertz and beyond', in Hunt, ed.: 72–96.

BIESANTZ, H. (1965) *Die Thessalischen Grabreliefs. Studien zur nordgriechischen Kunst*. Mainz.

BINFORD, L. R. (1968) 'Archeological perspectives', in L. R. & S. R. Binford, eds., *New Perspectives in Archeology*: 5–32. Chicago.

(1971) 'Mortuary practices: their study and their potential', in Brown, ed.: 6–29. Reprinted in L. R. Binford, *An Archeological Perspective*: 208–43. New York, 1972.

(1981) 'Archaeology and the "Pompeii premise" ', *Journal of Anthropological Research* 37: 195–208.

(1982) 'Meaning, inference and the material record', in A. C. Renfrew & S. Shennan, eds., *Ranking, Resource and Exchange*: 160–3. Cambridge.

(1987) 'Data, relativism and archaeological science', *Man* 22: 391–404.

BISEL, S. C. (1980) 'A pilot study in aspects of human nutrition in the ancient eastern Mediterranean', Ph.D. thesis, University of Minnesota.

(1987) 'Human bones at Herculaneum', *Rivista di Studi Pompeii* 1: 123–9.

(1988) 'Nutrition in first-century Herculaneum', *Anthropologie* 26: 61–6.

BISEL, S. C., & ANGEL, J. L. (1985) 'Health and nutrition in Mycenaean Greece', in N. C. Wilkie & W. D. E. Coulson, eds., *Contributions to Aegean Archaeology*: 197–210. Minneapolis.

BLEGEN, C. W., PALMER, H., & YOUNG, R. S. (1964) *Corinth* XIII: *The North Cemetery*. Princeton.

BLOCH, M. (1971) *Placing the Dead*. London.

(1977) 'The past and the present in the present', *Man* 12: 278–92.

(1982) 'Death, women and power', in Bloch & Parry, eds.: 211–30.

(1983) *Marxism and Anthropology*. Oxford.

(1986) *From Blessing to Violence*. Cambridge.

(1987) 'The ritual of the royal bath in Madagascar', in Cannadine & Price, eds.: 271–97.

BLOCH, M., & PARRY, J., eds. (1982) *Death and the Regeneration of Life*. Cambridge.

BOARDMAN, J. (1984) 'Signa tabulae priscae artis', *JHS* 104: 161–3.

(1987) 'Silver is white', *RA*: 279–95.

(1988a) 'Dates and doubts', *AA*: 423–5.

(1988b) 'Trade in Greek decorated pottery', *OJA* 7: 27–33.

(1988c) 'The trade figures', *OJA* 7: 371–3.

(1988d) 'Sex differentiation in grave vases', *AION ArchStAnt* 10: 171–9.

(1989) *Athenian Red Figure Vases: The Classical Period*. London.

BOATWRIGHT, M. T. (1985) 'The "Ara Ditis-*ustrinum*" of Hadrian in the western Campus Martius, and other problematic Roman *ustrina*', *AJA* 89: 485–97.

(1987) *Hadrian and the City of Rome*. Princeton.

BOCQUET-APPEL, J.-P., & MASSET, C. (1982) 'Farewell to paleodemography', *JHE* 11: 321–33.

BODDINGTON, A. (1987) 'From bones to population: the problem of numbers', in Boddington et al., eds.: 180–97.

BODDINGTON, A., GARLAND, A. N., & JANAWAY, R. C., eds. (1987) *Death, Decay and Reconstruction: Approaches to Archaeology and Forensic Science*. Manchester.

BODEL, J. (Forthcoming) *Graveyards and Groves: A Study of the Lex Lucerina*. To appear as *AJAH* 10.1 (1985).

BOMMELAER, J. F. (1986) 'Sur le monument des Néréides et sur quelques principes de l'analyse architecturale', *BCH* 110: 249–71.

BONI, G. (1907) 'I. Roma. Esplorazione del Forum Ulpium', *NSc*: 361–427.

BORELLI, L. V., D'AMBROSIO, A., & DE ACRO, S. (1983) *La necropoli di Porta Nocera*. Milan.

BORZA, E. (1990) *In the Shadow of Olympus*. Princeton.

BOSCHUNG, D. (1987a) 'Die Republikanischen und Frühkaiserzeitlichen Nekropolen vor den Toren Ostias', in von Hesberg & Zänker, eds.: 111–24.

(1987b) *Antike Grabaltäre aus den Nekropolen Roms*. Berne.

BOSWELL, J. (1988) *The Kindness of Strangers*. New York.

BOUSQUET, J. (1971) 'Circonscription des Pays de Loires', *Gallia* 29: 249–54.

BOWERSOCK, G. (1969) *Greek Sophists in the Roman Empire*. Oxford.

BOWMAN, L. (1959) *The American Funeral: A Study in Guilt, Extravagance and Sublimity*. Washington DC. Reprinted 1973, Westport, Connecticut.

BOWRA, C. M. (1957) 'Asius and the old-fashioned Samians', *Hermes* 85: 391–401.

BRADEEN, D. W. (1969) 'The Athenian casualty lists', *CQ* 19: 145–59.
    (1974) *The Athenian Agora* XVII. *Inscriptions: The Funerary Monuments*. Princeton.

BRADLEY, R. (1982) 'The destruction of wealth in later prehistory', *Man* 17: 108–22.
    (1984) *The Social Foundations of Prehistoric Britain*. London.

BRADLEY, R., & GORDON, K. (1988) 'Human skulls from the River Thames, their dating and significance', *Antiquity* 62: 503–9.

BRÄUER, G., & FRICKE, R. (1980) 'Zur Phänomenologie osteoporotischer Veränderungen bei Bestehen systematischer hämatologischen Affektionen', *Homo* 31: 198–211.

BREITINGER, E. (1939) 'Die Skelette aus den submykenischen Gräbern', in W. Kraiker & K. Kübler, *Kerameikos* I: 233–55. Berlin.

BREITSPRECHER, U. (1987) *Zum Problem der geschlechtsspezifischen Bestattungen in der römischen Kaiserzeit*. Oxford (*BAR* S 376).

BREMMER, J. (1983) *The Early Greek Concept of the Soul*. Princeton.

BRIJDER, H. A. G., ed. (1984) *Ancient Greek and Related Pottery*. Amsterdam (Allard Pierson Series 5).

BROCK, J. K. (1957) *Fortetsa*. Cambridge (*BSA* supp. vol. 2).

BROMMER, F. (1985) *Griechische Weihegaben und Opfer*. Berlin.

BROOKS, D. A. (1986) 'The evidence for continuity in British towns in the fifth and sixth centuries', *OJA* 5: 77–102.
    (1988) 'The case for continuity in fifth-century Canterbury re-examined', *OJA* 7: 99–114.

BROTHWELL, D. (1981) *Digging Up Bones*. London.
    (1986) *The Bog Man and the Archaeology of People*. London.

BROWN, J. A., ed. (1971) *Approaches to the Social Dimensions of Mortuary Practices*. New York (Memoirs of the Society for American Archaeology 25).

BROWN, P. (1981) *The Cult of the Saints*. Chicago.
    (1987) 'Late antiquity', in P. Veyne, ed., *A History of Private Life* I: 235–312. Cambridge, Massachusetts.

BRÜCKNER, A. (1909) *Der Friedhof am Eridanos bei der Hagia Triada zu Athen*. Berlin.
    (1910) 'Kerameikos-Studien', *AM* 35: 183–234.

BRÜCKNER, A., & PERNICE, E. (1893) 'Ein attischer Friedhof', *AM* 18: 73–191.

BRULET, R., & COULON, G. (1977) *La nécropole gallo-romaine de la Rue Perdue à Tournai*. Louvain.

BRUNEAU, P., et al. (1970) *Exploration archéologique de Délos* XXVII. *L'îlot de la maison des comédiens*. Paris.

BRUNS-ÖZGAN, C. (1987) *Lykische Grabreliefs des 5. und 4. Jhs. v. Chr.* Tübingen (*Ist Mitt* Beiheft 33).

BRUSH, K. (1988) 'Gender and mortuary analysis in pagan Anglo-Saxon archaeology', *Archaeological Review from Cambridge* 7: 76–89.

BRUSIN, G. (1941) *Nuovi monumenti sepolcrali di Aquileia*. Rome.

BUCHET, L. (1978) 'La nécropole gallo-romaine et mérovingienne de Frénouville (Calvados). Étude anthropologique', *Archéologie Médiévale* 8: 5–53.

BUGH, G. R. (1982) 'Introduction of the *katalogeis* of the Athenian cavalry', *TAPhA* 113: 23–32.

(1988) *The Horsemen of Athens*. Princeton.

BUIKSTRA, J. E. (1981) 'Mortuary practices, palaeodemography and palaeopathology: a case study from the Koster site (Illinois)', in Chapman et al., eds.: 123–32.

BUIKSTRA, J. E., & KONIGSBERG, L. W. (1985) 'Paleodemography: critiques and controversies', *American Anthropologist* 97: 136–33.

BUONOCORE, M. (1984) *Schiavi e liberti dei Volusi Saturnini: le inscrizioni del colombario sulla Via Appia antica*. Rome.

BURKERT, W. (1983) *Homo Necans*. Berkeley.

(1985) *Greek Religion*. Berkeley.

(1987) *Ancient Mystery Cults*. Cambridge, Massachusetts.

BURN, L. (1985) 'Honey pots: three white-ground cups by the Sotades Painter', *AntK* 28: 93–105.

BURR THOMPSON, D. (1954) 'Three centuries of Hellenistic terracottas', *Hesperia* 23: 72–107.

(1960) 'The house of Simon the shoemaker', *Archaeology* 13: 234–40.

BURROWS, R. M., & URE, P. N. (1907/8) 'Excavations at Rhitsóna in Boeotia', *BSA* 14: 226–318.

BURTON, A. (1989) 'Looking forward from Ariès? Pictorial and material evidence for the history of childhood and family life', *Continuity & Change* 4: 203–29.

CAHILL, N. (1988) 'Tas Kule: a Persian period tomb near Phokaia', *AJA* 92: 481–501.

CALDWELL, J., CALDWELL, C., & CALDWELL, B. (1987) 'Anthropology and demography: the mutual reinforcement of speculation and research', *CA* 28: 25–46.

CALLAGHAN, P. J., & JONES, R. E. (1985) 'Hadra hydriae and central Crete: a fabric analysis', *BSA* 80: 1–17.

CALLIGAS, P. G. (1988) 'Hero-cult in Early Iron Age Greece', in Hägg et al., eds.: 229–34.

CALZA, G. (1928) 'Ostia', *NSc* 1928: 133–75.

(1940) *La necropoli del Porto di Roma nell'Isola Sacra*. Rome.

CAMBI, N. (1987) 'Salona und seine Nekropolen', in von Hesberg & Zanker, eds.: 251–79.

CANNADINE, D. (1981) 'War and death, grief and mourning in modern Britain', in Whaley, ed.: 187–242.

CANNADINE, D., & PRICE, S., eds. (1987) *Rituals of Royalty*. Cambridge.

CANNON, A. (1989) 'The historical dimension in mortuary expressions of status and sentiment', *CA* 30: 437–58.

CARPENTER, R., & BON, A. (1936) *Corinth* III.2. *The Defences of the Lower Town*. Cambridge, Massachusetts.

CARRATELLI, G. P. (1961/2) 'Supplemento epigrafico cirenaico II: Cirene', *ASAA* 39/40: 273–375.

CARRINGTON SMITH, J. (1982) 'A Roman chamber tomb on the south-east slopes of Monasteriaki Kephala, Knossos', *BSA* 77: 255–93.

CARTER, A. T. (1984) 'Household histories', in R. Netting, R. Wilk & E. Arnould, eds., *Households: Comparative and Historical Studies of the Domestic Group*: 44–83. Berkeley.

CARTER, H., & MACE, A. C. (1977) *The Discovery of the Tomb of Tutankhamen*. New York. Based on a first edition of 1923.

CARTLEDGE, P. A. (1977) 'Hoplites and heroes: Sparta's contribution to the technique of ancient warfare', *JHS* 97: 11–28.

(1979) *Sparta and Lakonia*. London.

(1985) 'The Greek religious festivals', in P. E. Easterling & J. V. Muir, eds., *Greek Religion and Society*: 98–127. Cambridge.

CARTLEDGE, P. A. & SPAWFORTH, A. (1989) *Hellenistic and Roman Sparta: A Tale of Two Cities*. London/New York.

CATLING, H. W. (1979) 'Knossos, 1978', *AR 1978/9*: 43–8.

(1989) 'Archaeology in Greece, 1988–89', *AR 1988–1989*: 3–116.

CAVANAGH, W. G. (1987) 'Cluster analysis of Mycenaean chamber tombs', in R. Laffineur, ed., *Thanatos. Les coutumes funéraires en Égée à l'Age du Bronze*: 161–9. Liège (*Aegeum* 1).

CAVANAGH, W. G., & MEE, C. B. (1978) 'The re-use of earlier tombs in the LH IIIC period', *BSA* 73: 31–44.

(1990) 'The location of Mycenaean chamber tombs in the Argolid', in R. Hägg and G. Nordquist, eds., *Celebrations of Death and Divinity in the Bronze Age Argolid*: 55–64. Stockholm.

CAYTON, H. (1980) 'Some contributions from the written sources', *East Anglian Archaeology* 9: 303–14.

CHAMPION, T. C., ed. (1989) *Centre and Periphery*. London.

CHANG, K. C. (1980) *Shang Civilization*. New Haven.

CHANTRAINE, H. (1980) ' "Doppelbestattungen" römischer Kaiser', *Historia* 29: 71–85.

CHAPMAN, R. W. (1990) *Emerging Complexity*. Cambridge.

CHAPMAN, R. W., KINNES, I., RANDSBORG, K., eds. (1981) *The Archaeology of Death*. Cambridge.

CHAPMAN, R. W., & RANDSBORG, K. (1981) 'Perspectives on the archaeology of death', in Chapman et al., eds.: 1–24.

CHARITONIDES, S. I. (1958) 'Anaskaphi klassikon taphon para tin Pla-
teian Syndagmatos', *AE* 1958: 1–152.

CHARLES, R.-P. (1958) 'Étude anthropologique des nécropoles d'Argos,
contribution à l'étude des populations de la Grèce antique', *BCH* 82:
258–313.

(1963) *Étude anthropologique des nécropoles d'Argos, contribution à l'étude des
populations de la Grèce antique*. Paris (*Études péloponnésiennes* 3).

CHARTIER, R. (1985) 'Text, symbols, and Frenchness', *JMH* 57: 982–
95.

(1989) 'Le monde comme représentation', *Annales ESC* 44: 1505–20.

CHERRY, D. F. (1989) 'Soldiers' marriages and recruitment in Upper
Germany and Numidia', *AHB* 3: 128–30.

CHILDE, V. G. (1942) *What Happened in History*. Harmondsworth.

(1945) 'Directional changes in funerary practices during 50,000 years',
Man (1st ser.) 45: 13–19.

CHRISTIE, N. J. (1989) 'The archaeology of Byzantine Italy: a synthesis of
recent research', *Journal of Mediterranean Archaeology* 2: 249–93.

CLAIRMONT, C. (1970) *Gravestone and Epigram*. Mainz.

(1981) 'New evidence for a polyandrion in the *Demosion Sema* of Athens?', *JHS* 101: 132–4.

(1983) *Patrios Nomos. Public Burial at Athens During the Fifth and Fourth
Centuries B.C.* 2 vols. Oxford (*BAR* 161).

CLARKE, G. (1975) 'Popular movements and late Roman cemeteries', *WA*
7: 46–56.

(1978) Review of Kraskovská 1976 and Martin-Kilcher 1976, *Britannia*
9: 510–12.

(1979) *The Roman Cemetery at Lankhills*. Oxford (*Winchester Studies* 2).

CLAUSS, M. (1973) 'Probleme der Lebensalterstatistiken aufgrund
römischer Grabinschriften', *Chiron* 13: 395–417.

COALE, A. J., & DEMENEY, P. (1983) *Regional Model Life Tables and Stable
Populations*. 2nd edn. New York.

COARELLI, F. (1979) 'Fregellae e la colonizzazione latina nella valle del
Liri', *Archeologia Laziale* 2: 197–204.

COHEN, I. J. (1987) 'Structuration theory and social *praxis*', in A. Giddens
& J. Turner, eds., *Social Theory Today*: 273–308. Stanford.

COLE, S. G. (1980) 'New evidence for the mysteries of Dionysus', *GRBS*
21: 223–38.

COLLINGWOOD, R. G. (1946) *The Idea of History*. Oxford.

COLLIS, J. (1977a) 'Pre-Roman burial rites in north-western Europe', in
Reece, ed.: 1–13.

(1977b) 'Owslebury (Hants.) and the problem of burials on rural settlements', in Reece, ed.: 26–34.

(1984) *The European Iron Age*. London.

CONDON, K., CHARLES, D. K., CHEVERUD, J. M., & BUIKSTRA, J. (1986) 'Cementum annulation and age deterioration in homo sapiens', *AJPA* 74: 321–30.

CONNOR, W. R. (1971) *The New Politicians of Fifth-Century Athens*. Princeton.

(1987) 'Tribes, festivals, and processions; civic ceremonial and political manipulation in Archaic Greece', *JHS* 107: 40–50.

(1988a) ' "Sacred" and "secular". *Hiera kai hosia* and the classical Athenian concept of the state', *Anc Soc* 19: 161–88.

(1988b) 'Early Greek land warfare as symbolic expression', *P & P* 119: 3–29.

(1989a) 'The new classical humanities and the old', in P. Culham, L. Edmunds & A. Smith, eds., *Classics: A Profession and Discipline in Crisis?*: 25–38. Lanham, Maryland.

(1989b) 'City Dionysia and Athenian democracy', *C & M* 40: 7–32.

CONOPHAGOS, C. (1980) *Le Laurium antique*. Athens.

COOK, B. F. (1968/9) 'A dated Hadra vase in the Brooklyn Museum', *Brooklyn Museum Annual* 10: 115–38.

COOK, R. M. (1934) 'Fikellura pottery', *BSA* 34: 1–98.

(1958) Review of Schiering 1957, in *Gnomon* 30: 71–2.

(1972) *Greek Painted Pottery*. 2nd edn. London.

(1987) ' "Artful crafts": a commentary', *JHS* 107: 169–71.

(1989) 'The Francis-Vickers chronology', *JHS* 109: 164–70.

CORMACK, S. (1989) 'A mausoleum at Ariassos, Pisidia', *Anat St* 39: 29–40.

COULSON, W. D. E., & LEONARD, A. (1982) 'Investigations at Naukratis and environs, 1980 and 1981', *AJA* 86: 361–80.

COUPEL, P., & DEMARGNE, P. (1969) *Fouilles de Xanthos* III. *Le monument des néréides: l'architecture*. Paris.

COURBIN, P. (1988) *What Is Archaeology?* Chicago.

COVENTRY, L. (1989) 'Philosophy and rhetoric in the *Menexenus*', *JHS* 109: 1–15.

CRAWFORD, M. H., ed. (1983) *Sources for Ancient History*. Cambridge.

CROSBY, A. W. (1986) *Biological Imperialism: The Biological Expansion of Europe, 900–1900*. Cambridge.

CRUWYS, E. (1989) 'Tooth wear and the archaeologist', in Roberts et al., eds.: 151–66.

CUMONT, F. (1922) *Afterlife in Roman Paganism*. New Haven.

(1942) *Recherches sur le symbolisme funéraire des romains*. Paris.

(1949) *Lux Perpetua*. Paris.

CUNNINGTON, P., & LUCAS, C. (1964) *Costumes for Births, Marriages and Deaths*. London.

CURL, J. S. (1972) *The Victorian Celebration of Death*. London.

(1982) *The Egyptian Revival: An Introductory Study of a Recurring Theme in the History of Taste*. London.

D'AGOSTINO, B. (1989) 'Image and society in archaic Etruria', *JRS* 79: 1–10.

D'AMBROSIO, A., & DE CARO, S. (1987) 'La necropoli di Porta Nocera. Campagna di scavo 1983', in von Hesberg & Zanker, eds.: 199–226.

DAMSGAARD-MADSEN, A. (1988) 'Attic funeral inscriptions. Their use as historical sources and some preliminary results', in *Studies in Ancient History and Numismatics Presented to Rudi Thomsen:* 55–68. Åarhus.

DANFORTH, L., & TSIARAS, A. (1982) *The Death Rituals of Rural Greece.* Princeton.

DARNTON, R. (1986) 'The symbolic element in history', *JMH* 58: 218–34.

DAUX, G. (1958) 'Chronique des fouilles ... en 1957', *BCH* 82: 644–830.

DAVARAS, K. (1985) 'Romaïko nekrotapheio Agiou Nikolaou', *AE* 1985: 130–216.

DAVIES, G. (1977) 'Burial in Italy up to Augustus', in Reece, ed.: 13–19.

DAVIES, J. K. (1971) *Athenian Propertied Families, 600–300 B.C.* Oxford.
   (1978) *Democracy and Classical Greece.* London.
   (1981) *Wealth and the Power of Wealth in Classical Athens.* New York.

DAVIS, N. Z. (1983) *The Return of Martin Guerre.* Princeton.

DAY, J. W. (1989) 'Rituals in stone: early Greek epigrams and monuments', *JHS* 109: 16–28.

DE BLOIS, L. (1984) 'The third-century crisis and the Greek elite in the Roman empire', *Historia* 33: 358–77.

DEGRASSI, A. (1962) 'Nerva funeraticum plebi urbanae instituit', in A. Degrassi, *Scritti vari di antichità* I: 697–702. Rome.

DE LAET, S. J., VAN DOORSELAER, A., SPITAELS, P., & THEON, H. (1972) *La nécropole gallo-romaine de Blicquy.* Ghent (Diss. Arch. Gand. 14).

DEMAND, N. (1982) *Thebes in the Fifth Century.* London.

DEMOUGEOT, E. (1972) 'Stèles funéraires d'une nécropole de Lattes', *Revue archéologique Narbonnaise* 5: 49–116.

DEMPSEY, D. (1975) *The Way We Die.* New York.

DE NIRO, M. J., SHOENINGER, M. J., & HASTDORF, C. A. (1985) 'Effect of heating on the stable carbon and nitrogen isotope ratios of bone collagen', *JAS* 12: 1–7.

DENNISON, J. (1979) 'Citrate analysis as a means of determining the sex of human skeletal material', *Archaeology and Physical Anthropology in Oceania* 14: 136–43.

DE POLIGNAC, F. (1984) *La naissance de la cité grecque.* Paris.

DETIENNE, M. (1979) *Dionysos Slain.* Baltimore.

DEUEL, L. (1977) *The Memoirs of Heinrich Schliemann.* New York.

DE VAUX, R. (1973) *Archaeology and the Dead Sea Scrolls.* London.

DE VISSCHER, F. (1963) *Le droit des tombeaux romains.* Milan.

DIERKENS, A. (1986) 'La tombe privilégiée (IVe-VIIIe siècles) d'après les trouvailles en Belgique actuelle', in Duval & Picard, eds.: 47–56.

DONLAN, W. (1980) *The Aristocratic Ideal in Ancient Greece.* Lawrence, Kansas.

D'ONOFRIO, A. M. (1982) '*Korai* e *kouroi* funerari attici', *AION ArchStAnt* 4: 135–70.

(1988) 'Aspetti e problemi del monumento funerario attico arcaico', *AION ArchStAnt* 10: 83–96.

DORAN, J., & HODSON, F. R. (1975) *Mathematics and Computers in Archaeology*. Edinburgh.

DOUGLAS, M. (1966) *Purity and Danger*. London.

(1970) *Natural Symbols*. London. Reissued Harmondsworth, 1973.

DOWN, A., & RULE, M. (1971) *Chichester Excavations* I. Chichester.

DRERUP, H. (1969) *Griechische Baukunst in geometrischer Zeit*. Göttingen (*Arch Hom* O).

DROESSLER, J. (1981) *Craniometry and Biological Distance*. Evanston, Illinois (Center for American Archeology Research Series 1).

DUBISCH, J. (1989) 'Death and social change in Greece', *AQ* 62: 189–200.

DUMAS, F. (1975) *Le tombeau de Childeric*. Rouen.

DUNCAN-JONES, R. (1990) *Structure and Scale in the Roman Economy*. Cambridge.

DUVAL, N. (1986) ' "L'inhumation privilégiée" en Tunisie et en Tripolitaine', in Duval & Picard, eds.: 25–42.

DUVAL, Y. (1982) *Loca sanctorum Africae. Le culte des martyrs en Afrique du IVe au VIIe siècle*. 2 vols. Rome.

DUVAL, Y., & PICARD, J.-C., eds. (1986) *L'inhumation privilégiée du IVe au VIIIe siècle en occident*. Paris: Boccard.

DYGGVE, E. (1953) 'L'origine del cimitero entro la cinta della città', *Studi Bizantini e Neoellenici* 8: 137–41.

DYSON, S. (Forthcoming) *Community and Society in Roman Italy*.

DZIERZYKRAY-ROGALSKI, T. (1980) 'Paleopathology of the Ptolemaic inhabitants of Dakleh oasis (Egypt)', *JHE* 9: 71–4.

EARLE, T. K., & PREUCEL, R. W. (1987) 'Processual archaeology and the radical critique', *CA* 28: 501–38.

EBREY, P. (1990) 'Cremation in Sung China', *AHR* 95: 406–28.

ECK, W. (1984) 'Senatorial self-representation: developments in the Augustan period', in F. Millar & E. Segal, eds., *Caesar Augustus. Seven Aspects*: 129–67. Oxford.

(1986) 'Inschriften aus der vatikanischen Nekropole unter St. Peter', *ZPE* 65: 245–93.

(1987) 'Römische Grabinschriften. Aussageabsicht und Aussagefähigkeit im funerären Kontext', in von Hesberg & Zanker, eds.: 61–83.

(1988) 'Aussagefähigkeit epigraphischer Statistik und die Bestattung von Sklaven im kaiserzeitlichen Rom', in Kneissl & Losemann, eds.: 130–9.

(1989) 'Inschriften und Grabbauten in der Nekropole unter St. Peter', in G. Alföldy, ed., *Vom frühen Griechentum bis zur römischen Kaiserzeit*: 55–89. Wiesbaden.

ECKSTEIN, F. (1958) 'Die attischen Grabmälergesetze', *JdI* 73: 18–29.

EISNER, M. (1986) *Zur Typologie der Grabbauten im Suburbium Roms.* Mainz (*Röm Mitt*, Ergänzungsheft 26).

ELDER, G. H. (1978) 'Family history and the life course', in T. Hareven, ed., *Transitions: The Family and the Life Course in Historical Perspective*: 17–64. New York.

(1987) 'Families and lives: some developments in life-course studies', in T. Hareven & A. Plakans, eds., *Family History at the Crossroads*: 179–200. Princeton.

ELIAS, M. (1980) 'The feasibility of dental strontium analysis for diet assessment of human populations', *AJPA* 53: 1–4.

ELLIOTT SMITH, G., & WOOD JONES, F. (1910) 'Report on the human remains', *Archaeological Survey of Nubia. Report of 1907–1908*: 11.

ELLIS, S. P., & HUMPHREY, J. (1988) 'Interpretation and analysis of the cemetery', in J. Humphrey, ed., *The Circus and a Byzantine Cemetery at Carthage*: 325–36. Ann Arbor.

ENGELS, D. (1980) 'The problem of female infanticide in the Graeco-Roman world', *CP* 75: 112–20.

(1984) 'The use of historical demography in ancient history', *CQ* 34: 386–93.

ENSOLI, S. (1987) *L'Heróon di Dexileos nel Ceramico di Atene.* Rome.

ESMONDE CLEARY, A. S. (1989) *The Ending of Roman Britain.* London.

ETLIN, R. (1984) *The Architecture of Death.* Cambridge, Massachusetts.

EVANS, J. (1987) 'Graffiti and evidence of literacy and pottery use in Roman Britain', *ArchJ* 144: 191–204.

EVANS-PRITCHARD, E. E. (1951) *Kinship and Marriage Among the Nuer.* Oxford.

FAGERSTRÖM, K. (1988a) *Greek Iron Age Architecture: Developments through Changing Times.* Göteborg (*SIMA* 81).

(1988b) 'Finds, function and plan: a contribution to the interpretation of Iron Age Nichoria in Messenia', *Op Ath* 17: 33–50.

FALKNER, T. M., & DE LUCE, J., eds. (1989) *Old Age in Greek and Latin Literature.* Albany, New York.

FARRELL, J. J. (1980) *Inventing the American Way of Death, 1830–1920.* Philadelphia.

FEDAK, J. (1990) *Monumental Tombs of the Hellenistic Age.* Toronto.

FELL, C. (1956) 'Roman burials found at Arbury Road, Cambridge, 1952', *Proceedings of the Cambridge Antiquarian Society* 49: 13–23.

FELLMANN, R. (1956) *Das Grab des Lucius Munatius Plancus bei Gaeta.* Munich.

FELTEN, F. (1976) 'Weissgrundige Lekythen aus dem Athener Kerameikos', *AM* 91: 77–113.

FÉVRIER, P.-A. (1978) 'Le culte des morts dans les communautés chrétiennes durant le IIIe siècle', in *Atti del IX° congresso internazionale di archeologia cristiana*: 258–311. Rome.

(1986) 'Tombes privilégiées en Mauretaine et Numidie', in Duval & Picard, eds.: 13–23.

FÉVRIER, P.-A., & GASPARY, A. (1966/7) 'La nécropole orientale de Sétif', *Bulletin d'archéologie algérienne* 2: 11–93.

FÉVRIER, P.-A., & GUÉRY, R. (1980) 'Les rites funéraires de la nécropole orientale de Sétif', *Antiquités africaines* 15: 91–124.

FILOW, B. D. (1934) *Die Grabhügelnekropole bei Duvanlij in Südbulgarien*. Sofia.

FINLEY, M. I. (1975) *The Use and Abuse of History*. London. Reissued 1986. (1985) *Democracy Ancient and Modern*. 2nd edn. London.

FISHWICK, D. (1978) 'The development of provincial ruler worship in the western Roman empire', *ANRW* 2.16.1: 1,201–53. Berlin. (1988) *The Imperial Cult in the Latin West* I. Leiden.

FITTSCHEN, K. (1979) 'Sarkophage römischer Kaisermoder vom Nutzen der Porträtsforschung', *JdI* 94: 578–93.

FLOUD, R. (1983) *An Introduction to Quantitative Methods for Historians*. 2nd edn. London.

FOLEY, A. (1988) *The Argolid 800–600 B.C. An Archaeological Survey*. Göteborg (*SIMA* 80).

FORNACIARI, G., & MALLEGNI, F. (1980) 'Iperostosi porotica verosimilmente talassemica in due scheletri rinvenuti in un gruppo di tombe del III secolo a.C. di San Giovenale (Viterbo)', *Quaderni Scienza Antropologica* 4: 21–50.
(1986) 'Si un gruppo di inumati della necropoli di Cornus', in *L'archeologia Romana e Altomedievale nell' Oristanese*: 213–29. Taranto (Mediterraneo Tardoantico e Medievale, Scavi e Richerche 3).

FORNACIARI, G., MALLEGNI, F., BERTINI, D., & NUTI, V. (1981) 'Cibra orbitalia and elemental bone iron in the Punics of Carthage', *Ossa* 8: 63–77.

FORNARA, C. W. (1983) *Translated Documents of Greece and Rome* I: *Archaic Times to the End of the Peloponnesian War*. 2nd edn. Cambridge.

FORNARI, F. (1917) 'Via Caelimontana', *NSc* 1917: 174–9.

FOSTER, J. (1986) *The Lexden Tumulus*. Oxford (*BAR* 156).

FOUCAULT, M. (1972) *The Archaeology of Knowledge*. New York. (1980) *Power/Knowledge*. New York.

FRANCIS, E. D., & VICKERS, M. J. (1981) 'Leagros *kalos*', *PCPhS* 207: 97–136.
(1983) '*Signa priscae artis*: Eretria and Siphnos', *JHS* 103: 49–67.
(1988) 'The Agora revisited: Athenian chronology *c*. 500–450 B.C.', *BSA* 83: 143–67.

FRASCHETTI, A. (1984) 'Morte dei "principi" ed "eroi" della famiglia di Augusto', *AION ArchStAnt* 6: 151–89.

FRASER, P. M. (1977) *Rhodian Funerary Monuments*. Oxford.

FRASER, P. M., & RÖNNE, T. (1957) *Boeotian and West Greek Tombstones*. Lund.

FREEDMAN, M. (1966) *Chinese Lineage and Society: Fukien and Kwangtung.* London.

FREND, W. H. C. (1984) *The Rise of Christianity.* London.

FREYTAG GEN. LÖRINGHOFF, B. VON (1976) 'Archaische und klassische Grabfunde auf dem Hang nördlich der "Eckterrasse" im Kerameikos', *AM* 91: 31–61.

FRIED, M. N., & FRIED, M. H. (1980) *Transitions: A Study of Four Rituals in Eight Cultures.* New York.

FRIEDLÄNDER, P. (1908–13) *Life and Manners under the Early Empire.* English translation, 8th edn. 4 vols. London. Reissued 1909–28.

FRONING, H. (1980) 'Die ikonographische Tradition der kaiserzeitlichen mythologischen Sarkophagreliefs', *JdI* 95: 322–41.

FROST, F. (1984) 'The Athenian military before Cleisthenes', *Historia* 33: 283–94.

FURET, F. (1983) 'Beyond the *Annales*', *JMH* 55: 389–410.

FURLEY, W. D. (1981) *Studies in the Use of Fire in Ancient Greek Religion.* New York.

GABELMANN, H. (1979) *Römische Grabbauten der frühen Kaiserzeit.* Stuttgart.
(1987) 'Römische Grabbauten der Nordprovinzen im 2. und 3. Jh. n. Chr.', in von Hesberg & Zanker, eds.: 291–308.

GALLAGHER, C. (1990) 'Marxism and the new historicism', in Veeser, ed.: 37–48.

GALLANT, T. W. (1982) 'Agricultural systems, land tenure and the reforms of Solon', *BSA* 77: 111–24.
(1985) *A Fisherman's Tale.* Ghent (*MIGRA* supp. vol. 7).
(1989) 'Crisis and response: risk-buffering behavior in Hellenistic Greek communities', *JIH* 19: 393–413.

GALLIOU, P. (1989) *Les tombes romaines d'Armorique.* Paris.

GARLAND, A. N. (1988) 'Contributions to palaeohistory', in E. A. Slater & J. O. Tate, eds., *Science and Archaeology, Glasgow 1987* II: 321–8. 2 vols. Oxford (*BAR* 196).
(1989) 'Microscopy of fossil bones', *Applied Geochemistry* 4: 215–29.

GARLAND, A. N., & JANAWAY, R. C. (1989) 'The taphonomy of inhumation burials', in Roberts et al., eds.: 15–37.

GARLAND, A. N., JANAWAY, R. C., & ROBERTS, C. A. (1988) 'A study of the decay processes of human skeletal remains from the parish church of the Holy Trinity, Rothwell, Northamptonshire', *OJA* 7: 235–52.

GARLAND, R. S. J. (1982) 'A first catalogue of Attic peribolos tombs', *BSA* 77: 125–76.
(1985) *The Greek Way of Death.* London.
(1989) 'The well-ordered corpse: an investigation into the motives behind Greek funerary legislation', *Bulletin of the Institute of Classical Studies* 36: 1–15.
(1990) *The Greek Way of Life.* London.

GARNSEY, P. (1970) *Social Status and Legal Privilege in the Roman Empire.* Oxford.

(1974) 'Aspects of the decline of the urban aristocracy in the Empire', *ANRW* 2.1: 229–52.

(1988) *Famine and Food Supply in the Graeco-Roman World.* Cambridge.

(1989) 'Infant health and upbringing in antiquity', in P. Garnsey, ed., 'Food, health and culture in classical antiquity': 50–67. Cambridge: Faculty of Classics Working Papers no. 1.

GARNSEY, P., & MORRIS, I. (1989) 'Risk and the *polis*', in P. Halstead & J. O'Shea, eds., *Bad Year Economics*: 98–105. Cambridge.

GARNSEY, P., & SALLER, R. P. (1987) *The Roman Empire: Economy, Society and Culture.* London.

GATES, C. (1983) *From Cremation to Inhumation: Burial Practices at Ialysos and Kameiros during the Mid-Archaic Period, ca. 625–525 B.C.* Los Angeles (University of California at Los Angeles Institute of Archaeology, Occasional Paper 11).

GAUTHIER, P. (1971) 'Les *xenoi* dans les textes athéniens dans la seconde moitié du Ve siècle av. J-C.', *REG* 84: 44–79.

(1985) *Les cités grecques et leurs bienfaiteurs.* Paris (*BCH* supp. vol. 15).

GEARY, P. (1979) 'L'humiliation des saints', *Annales ESC* 34: 27–42.

GEDDES, A. G. (1987) 'Rags and riches: the costume of Athenian men in the fifth century', *CQ* 37: 307–31.

GEERTZ, C. (1973) *The Interpretation of Cultures.* New York.

(1980) *Negara: The Theatre State in Nineteenth-Century Bali.* Princeton.

GEJVALL, N. G., & HENSCHEN, F. (1968) 'Two late skeletons with malformations and close family relationship from ancient Corinth', *Op Ath* 8: 179–93.

GELLNER, E. (1958) 'Time and theory in social anthropology', *Mind* 67: 182–202.

(1983) *Nations and Nationalism.* Oxford.

(1985) *Relativism and the Social Sciences.* Cambridge.

(1988) *Plough, Sword and Book.* Chicago.

GIBBON, G. (1989) *Explanation in Archaeology.* Oxford.

GIDDENS, A. (1976) 'Introduction', in Weber 1976: vii–xxvi.

(1984) *The Constitution of Society.* Oxford.

(1987) *The Nation-State and Violence.* Oxford.

GILL, D. W. J. (1986) 'Classical Greek fictile imitations of precious metal vases', in Vickers, ed.: 9–30.

(1987a) 'Two new silver shapes from Semibratny (Seven Brothers' Tumuli)', *BSA* 82: 47–53.

(1987b) 'An Attic lamp in Reggio: the largest batch notation outside Athens?', *OJA* 6: 121–5.

(1987c) 'METRU.MENECE: an Etruscan painted inscription on a mid-fifth-century BC red-figure cup from Populonia', *Antiquity* 61: 82–7.

(1988a) 'Expressions of wealth: Greek art and society', *Antiquity* 62: 735–43.

(1988b) 'The temple of Aphaia on Aegina: the date of the reconstruction', *BSA* 83: 169–77.

(1988c) ' "Trade in Greek decorated pottery": some corrections', *OJA* 7: 369–70.

(1991) 'Pots and trade: space fillers or *objets d'art?*', *JHS* 111: 29–47.

GILL, D. W. J., & VICKERS, M. J. (1989) 'Pots and kettles', *RA*: 297–303.

(1990) 'Reflected glory: pottery and precious metal in classical Greece', *JdI* 105: 1–30.

GINZBURG, C. (1980) *The Cheese and the Worms: The Cosmos of a Sixteenth-Century Miller*. Baltimore.

GLAZIER, J. (1984) 'Mbeere ancestors and the domestication of death', *Man* 19: 133–47.

GLEDHILL, J. (1988) 'Introduction: the comparative analysis of social and political transitions', in J. Gledhill, B. Bender & M. T. Larsen, eds., *State and Society*: 1–29. London.

GNOLI, G., & VERNANT, J.-P., eds. (1982) *La mort, les morts, dans les sociétés anciennes*. Cambridge.

GOLDEN, M. (1988) 'Did the ancients care when their children died?', *G & R* 35: 152–63.

(1990a) *Children and Childhood in Classical Athens*. Baltimore.

(1990b) 'Chasing change in Roman childhood', *AHB* 4: 90–4.

GOLDHILL, S. (1987) 'The Great Dionysia and civic ideology', *JHS* 107: 58–76. Revised version in Winkler & Zeitlin, eds., 1990: 97–129.

(1988) 'Battle narrative and politics in Aeschylus' *Persae*', *JHS* 108: 189–93.

GOLDSTEIN, L. (1981) 'One-dimensional archaeology and multi-dimensional people: spatial organisation and mortuary analysis', in Chapman, Kinnes & Randsborg, eds.: 53–69.

GOMME, A. W. (1933) *The Population of Athens in the Fifth and Fourth Centuries B.C.* Oxford.

(1945) *An Historical Commentary on Thucydides* I. Oxford.

GONZALEZ, J. (1986) 'The Lex Irnitana: a new copy of the Flavian municipal law', *JRS* 76: 147–243.

GOODMAN, A. H., & ARMELAGOS, G. J. (1989) 'Infant and child morbidity and mortality risks in archaeological populations', *WA* 21: 225–43.

GOODY, J. R. (1961) 'Religion and ritual – the definitional problem', *British Journal of Sociology* 12: 142–64.

(1962) *Death, Property and the Ancestors*. London.

GOODY, J. R., ed. (1958) *The Developmental Cycle in Domestic Groups*. Cambridge.

GORDON, R. L. (1975) 'Franz Cumont and the doctrines of Mithraism', in J. R. Hinnells, ed., *Mithraic Studies* I: 215–48. 2 vols. Manchester.

(1990a) 'From Republic to Principate: priesthood, religion and ideology', in Beard & North, eds.: 177–98.

(1990b) 'Religion in the Roman empire: the civic compromise and its limits', in Beard & North, eds.: 233–55.

GORER, G. (1965) *Death, Grief and Mourning in Contemporary Britain*. London.

GOWLETT, J. A. J., HEDGES, R. E. M., & LAW, I. A. (1989) 'Radiocarbon accelerator (AMS) dating of Lindow Man', *Antiquity* 63: 71–9.

GREEN, C. J. S. (1977) 'The significance of plaster burials for the recognition of Christian cemeteries', in Reece, ed.: 46–53.

(1982) 'The cemetery of a Romano-British community at Poundbury', in Pearce, ed.: 61–76.

GRMEK, M. D. (1989) *Diseases in the Ancient Greek World*. Baltimore.

GRUEN, E. S. (1990) *Studies in Greek Culture and Roman Policy*. Leiden.

GRUPE, G. (1988) 'The impact of choice of bone samples on trace element data in excavated human skeletons', *JAS* 15: 123–9.

GSELL, A. (1901) *Monuments de l'Algérie* II. 2 vols. Paris.

GUYON, J. (1983) 'Le décor des cimetières chrétiens de Rome au tournant du IVe siècle: réflet ou miroir d'une "nouvelle société"?', in E. Frézouls, ed., *Crise et renouveau dans les provinces européennes de l'Empire (milieu du IIIe siècle-milieu du IVe siècle ap. J-C.)*: 49–61. Strasbourg.

(1986) 'L'inhumation privilégiée dans un cimetière romain au IVe siècle: l'exemple de la nécropole "Aux deux Lauriers"', in Duval & Picard, eds.: 173–87.

HAAS, J. (1981) 'Class conflict and the state in the New World', in G. D. Jones & R. R. Kautz, eds., *The Transition to Statehood in the New World*: 80–102. Cambridge.

HABENSTEIN, R. W., & LAMERS, W. M. (1955) *History of American Funeral Directing*. Milwaukee.

HACHLILI, R., & KILLEBREW, A. (1983) 'Jewish funerary customs during the Second Temple Period, in the light of the excavations at the Jericho necropolis', *PEQ* 115: 109–32.

HÄGG, R., MARINATOS, N., & NORDQUIST, G. C., eds. (1988) *Early Greek Cult Practice*. Stockholm.

HAHN, J., & LEUNISSEN, P. (1990) 'Statistical method and inheritance of the consulate under the early Roman Empire', *Phoenix* 44: 60–81.

HAMMOND, M. (1957) 'Composition of the Senate, A.D. 68–235', *JRS* 47: 74–81.

HAMMOND, N. G. L. (1990) *The Macedonian State*. Oxford.

HAMMOND, N. G. L., & GRIFFITH, G. T. (1979) *A History of Macedonia* II. Oxford.

HANSEN, M. H. (1983) 'Political activity and the organization of Attica in the fourth century B.C.', *GRBS* 24: 227–38.

(1988) *Three Studies in Athenian Demography*. Copenhagen (Royal Danish

Academy of Science and Letters, Historisk-filosofike Meddelelser 56).

(1989a) *Was Athens a Democracy?* Copenhagen (Royal Danish Academy of Science and Letters, Historisk-filosofike Meddelelser 59).

(1989b) 'Demos, ekklesia and dikasterion. A reply to Martin Ostwald and Josiah Ober', *C & M* 40: 101–6.

(1989c) 'On the importance of institutions in an analysis of Athenian democracy', *C & M* 40: 107–13.

HARMAN, M., MOLLESON, T., & PRICE, J. L. (1981) 'Burials, bodies and beheadings in Romano-British and Anglo-Saxon cemeteries', *Bulletin British Museum (Natural History, Geology)* 35: 145–88.

HARRIS, M. (1974) *Cows, Pigs, Wars and Witches*. New York.

(1985) *Good to Eat*. New York. Reprinted as *The Sacred Cow and the Abominable Pig*. New York, 1989.

HARRIS, W. V. (1980) 'Towards a study of the Roman slave trade', in J. H. D'Arms & E. D. Kopff, eds., *Roman Seaborne Commerce*: 117–40. Rome (*MAAR* 36).

(1982) 'The theoretical possibility of extensive infanticide in the Graeco-Roman world', *CQ* 32: 114–16.

HASELGROVE, C. (1984) 'Warfare and its aftermath as reflected in the precious metal coinage of Belgic Gaul', *OJA* 3: 81–105.

(1987) 'Culture process on the periphery: Belgic Gaul and Rome during the late Republic and early Empire', in Rowlands et al., eds.: 104–24.

HASELGROVE, S. (1979) 'Romano-Saxon attitudes', in P. J. Casey, ed., *The End of Roman Britain*: 4–13. Oxford (*BAR* 71).

HATT, J.-J. (1951) *La tombe gallo-romaine*. Paris.

HÄUSLER, H. (1980) *Das Denkmal als Garant des Nachruhms: eine Studie zu einem Motif in lateinischen Inschriften*. Munich (*Zetemata* 75).

HELDEJÜRGEN, H. (1981) 'Frühkaiserzeitliche Sarkophage in Griechenland', *JdI* 96: 413–35.

HENDERSON, J. (1989) 'Pagan Saxon cemeteries: a study of the problems of sexing by grave goods and bones', in Roberts et al., eds.: 77–83.

HENGEN, O. P. (1971) 'Cribra orbitalia: pathogenesis and probable etiology', *Homo* 22: 57–75.

HERMAN, G. (1987) *Ritualised Friendship and the Greek City*. Cambridge.

HERRMANN, B., & BERGFELDER, T. (1978) 'Über den diagnostischen Wert des sogenannten Geburtstrauma am Schambein bei der Identifikation', *Zeitschrift Rechtsmedizin* 81: 73–8.

HERTZ, R. (1960) *Death and the Right Hand*. Aberdeen. First published in French, 1907.

HILLER, H. (1975) *Ionische Grabreliefs der ersten Hälfte des 5. Jhs. v. Chr.* Tübingen (*Ist Mitt* Beiheft 12).

HILLSON, S. (1986) *Teeth*. Cambridge.

(1989) 'Teeth: some current developments in research', in Roberts et al., eds.: 129–49.

HINARD, F., ed. (1987) *La mort, les morts et l'au-delà dans le monde romain.* Caen.

HIRSCHON, R. (1983) 'Women, the aged and religious activity: oppositions and complementarity in an urban locality', *JMGS* 1: 113–30.

HOBSBAWM, E. (1987) *The Age of Empire, 1875–1914.* London.
(1990) *Nations and Nationalism since 1780.* Cambridge.

HODDER, I. (1979) 'Economic and social stress and material culture', *Am Ant* 44: 446–54.
(1982a) 'Theoretical archaeology: a reactionary view', in Hodder, ed.: 1–16.
(1982b) *The Present Past.* London.
(1982c) *Symbols in Action.* Cambridge.
(1984) 'Burials, houses, women and men in the European Neolithic', in Miller & Tilley, eds.: 51–68.
(1985) 'Post-processual archaeology', *AMT* 8: 1–26.
(1986) *Reading the Past.* Cambridge.
(1987a) 'The contextual analysis of symbolic meanings', in Hodder, ed.: 1–10.
(1987b) 'The meaning of discard: ash and domestic space in Baringo', in S. Kent, ed., *Method and Theory for Activity Area Research*: 424–48. New York.
(1988) 'Material culture text and social change', *PPS* 54: 67–75.
(1989) 'Writing archaeology: site reports in context', *Antiquity* 63: 268–74.
(1990) *The Domestication of Europe.* Oxford.

HODDER, I., ed. (1982) *Symbolic and Structural Archaeology.* Cambridge.
(1987) *The Archaeology of Contextual Meanings.* Cambridge.

HODDER, I., BINFORD, L., & STONE, N. (1988) 'Archaeology and theory', *Man* n.s. 23: 373–6.

HODGES, R. (1989) *The Anglo-Saxon Achievement.* London.

HODSON, F. (1977) 'Quantifying Hallstatt', *Am Ant* 42: 394–412.

HOEPFNER, W. (1973) 'Das Grabmonument des Pythagoras aus Selymbria', *AM* 88: 145–63.

HOEPFNER, W., & SCHWANDNER, E.-L. (1986) *Haus und Stadt im klassischen Griechenland.* Munich.

HOFFMANN, G. (1988) 'La jeune fille et la mort: quelques stèles à épigramme', *AION ArchStAnt* 10: 73–82.

HOFFMANN, H. (1977) *Sexual and Asexual Pursuit.* London (Royal Anthropological Institute of Great Britain and Ireland, Occasional Paper 34).
(1986) 'From Charos to Charon: some notes on the human encounter with death in Attic red-figure vase painting', *Visible Religion* 4/5: 173–94.

(1988) 'Why did the Greeks need imagery? An anthropological approach to the study of Greek vase painting', *Hephaistos* 9: 143–62.

(1989) '*Aletheia*: the iconography of death/rebirth in three cups by the Sotades Painter', *Res* 17/18: 69–88.

HOLLOWAY, R. R. (1966) 'The tomb of Augustus and the princes of Troy', *AJA* 70: 171–3.

HOOD, M. S. F., & SMYTH, D. (1981) *Archaeological Survey of the Knossos Area*. London (*BSA* supp. vol. 12).

HOPKINS, K. (1966) 'On the probable age structure of the Roman population', *Population Studies* 20: 245–64.

(1983) *Death and Renewal*. Cambridge.

(1987) 'Graveyards for historians', in Hinard, ed.: 113–26.

HOPPER, R. J. (1949) 'Addenda to *Necrocorinthia*', *BSA* 44: 162–257.

HOROWITZ, S., ARMELAGOS, G. D., & WACHTER, K. (1988) 'On generating birth rates from skeletal populations', *AJPA* 76: 189–96.

HOUSTON, M. G. (1947) *Ancient Greek, Roman and Byzantine Costume*. London.

HUBERT, F. (1963) *Cimetière du Parc de l'Hotel de Ville à Tournai*. Brussels (*Arch Belg* 68).

HUGHES, D., & PARSONS, P. J. (1984) *Oxyrhynchus Papyri* 52. London.

HÜLSEN, C. (1889) 'Antichità di Monte Citorio', *Röm Mitt* 4: 41–64.

HUMPHREYS, S. C. (1980) 'Family tombs and tomb cult in ancient Athens: tradition or traditionalism?', *JHS* 100: 96–126. Reprinted in Humphreys 1983: 90–120.

(1983) *The Family, Women and Death*. London.

(1986) 'Kinship patterns in the Athenian courts', *GRBS* 27: 57–91.

(1987) 'Law, custom and culture in Herodotus', *Arethusa* 20: 211–20.

(1988) 'The discourse of law in archaic and classical Greece', *Law and History Review* 6: 465–93.

(1990) Review of Morris 1987, *Helios* 17: 263–8.

HUMPHREYS, S. C., & KING, H., eds. (1981) *Mortality and Immortality*. London.

HUNT, L. (1986) 'French history in the last twenty years: the rise and fall of the *Annales* paradigm', *Journal of Contemporary History* 21: 209–24.

(1989) 'Introduction: history, culture and text', in Hunt, ed.: 1–24.

HUNT, L., ed. (1989) *The New Cultural History*. Berkeley.

HUNTINGTON, R., & METCALF, P. (1979) *Celebrations of Death*. Cambridge.

HURWIT, J. (1989) 'The Kritios Boy: discovery, reconstruction, and date', *AJA* 93: 41–80.

IRION, P. E. (1968) *Cremation*. Philadelphia.

JACKSON, K. T. (1989) *Silent Cities: The Evolution of the American Cemetery*. New York.

JACKSON, R. (1988) *Doctors and Diseases in the Roman Empire*. London.

(1990) 'Roman doctors and their instruments: recent research into ancient practice', *JRA* 3: 5–27.

JACOB, J. (1899) 'The dying of death', *Fortnightly Review* 72: 264–9.

JACOBS, B. (1987) *Griechische und Persische Elemente in der Grabkunst Lykiens zur Zeit der Achämenidenherrschaft.* Göteborg (*SIMA* 78).

JACOBY, F. (1944) 'GENESIA: a forgotten festival of the dead', *CQ* 38: 65–75.

JAMESON, M. H. (1977/8) 'Agriculture and slavery in classical Athens', *CJ* 73: 122–45.

(1988a) 'Sacrifice and animal husbandry in Classical Greece', in Whittaker, ed.: 87–119.

(1988b) 'Sacrifice and ritual: Greece', in M. Grant & R. Kitzinger, eds., *Civilization of the Ancient Mediterranean. Greece and Rome* II: 959–79. New York.

(1989) Review of Pesando 1987, in *AJA* 91: 478–9.

(1990a) 'Private space and the Greek city', in O. Murray & S. Price, eds., *The Greek City from Homer to Alexander*: 169–93. Oxford.

(1990b) 'Domestic space in the Greek city-state', in S. Kent, ed., *Domestic Architecture and the Use of Space*: 92–113. Cambridge.

JASTRZEBOWSKA, E. (1981) *Untersuchungen zum christlichen Totenmahl aufgrund der Monumente des 3. und 4. Jahrhunderts unter der Basilika des hl. Sebastian in Rom.* Frankfurt (Europäische Hochschulschriften: Reihe 38 – Archäologie: Bd 2).

JEFFERY, L. H. (1962) 'The inscribed gravestones of archaic Attica', *BSA* 57: 115–53.

JESSUP, R. F. (1959) 'Barrows and walled cemeteries in Roman Britain', *JBAA*, 3rd series, 22: 1–32.

(1962) 'Roman barrows in Britain', in *Hommages à Albert Grenier* II (*Collections Latomus* 58): 853–67.

JOHANSEN, K. F. (1923) *Les vases sicyoniens.* Copenhagen.

(1951) *The Attic Grave-Reliefs of the Classical Period.* Copenhagen.

JOHANSEN, O. S., GULLIKSEN, S., & NYDAL, R. (1986) 'Delta 13C and diet: analysis of Norwegian human skeletons', *Radiocarbon* 28: 754–61.

JOHNSON, A., & EARLE, T. (1987) *The Evolution of Human Societies: From Foraging Group to Agrarian State.* Stanford.

JOHNSTON, A. W. (1979) *Trademarks on Greek Vases.* Warminster.

JOHNSTON, A. W., & JONES, R. E. (1978) 'The "SOS" amphora', *BSA* 73: 103–41.

JOHNSTON, D. (1988) *The Roman Law of Trusts.* Oxford.

JOHNSTONE, S. (1989) 'Social relations, rhetoric, ideology: the people's power and the Athenian courts'. Ph.D. thesis, University of Chicago.

JONES, A. H. M. (1964) *The Later Roman Empire.* 3 vols. Oxford. Reissued in 2 vols., Baltimore, 1987.

JONES, J. E. (1975) 'Town and country houses of Attica in classical times', *MIGRA* 1: 63–144.

JONES, J. E., SACKETT, L. H., & GRAHAM, A. J. (1962) 'The Dema house in Attica', *BSA* 57: 75–114.

JONES, J. E., GRAHAM, A. J., & SACKETT, L. H. (1973) 'An Attic country house below the Cave of Pan at Vari', *BSA* 68: 355–452.

JONES, R. F. J. (1975) 'The Romano-British farmstead and cemetery at Lynch Farm, near Peterborough', *Northamptonshire Archaeology* 10: 94–137.

(1977) 'A quantitative approach to Roman burial', in Reece, ed.: 20–5.

(1981) 'Cremation and inhumation – change in the third century', in A. King & M. Henig, eds., *The Roman West in the Third Century* I: 15–19. 2 vols. Oxford (*BARS* 109).

(1984a) 'The cemeteries of Roman York', in P. V. Addyman & V. E. Black, eds., *Archaeological Papers from York for W. M. Barley*: 34–42. York.

(1984b) 'The Roman cemeteries of Ampurias reconsidered', in T. F. C. Blagg, R. F. J. Jones & S. J. Keay, eds., *Papers in Iberian Archaeology* I: 237–65. 2 vols. Oxford (*BARS* 193).

(1984c) 'Death and distinction', in T. F. C. Blagg & A. King, eds., *Military and Civilian in Roman Britain*: 219–25. Oxford (*BAR* 136).

(1987) 'Burial customs of Rome and the provinces', in J. Wacher, ed., *The Roman World* II: 812–31. 2 vols. London.

JONES, W. H. S. (1909) *Malaria and Greek History*. Manchester.

JORDAN, T. G. (1982) *Texas Graveyards: A Cultural Legacy*. Austin, Texas.

JOUFFROY, H. (1986) *La construction publique en Italie et dans l'Afrique romaine*. Strasburg.

KAEMPF-DIMITRIADOU, S. (1986) 'Ein attisches Staatsgrabmal des 4. Jhs. v. Chr.', *AntK* 29: 23–36.

KARAGIORGA-STATHAKOPOULOU, TH. (1978) '3e ephoreia proistorikon kai klasikon arkhaiotiton', *AD* 33.2: 10–42.

(1979) '3e ephoreia proistorikon kai klasikon arkhaiotiton', *AD* 34.2: 11–37.

KAROUZOS, C. J. (1951) 'An early classical disc relief from Melos', *JHS* 71: 96–110.

KARP, I. (1986) 'Agency and social theory: a review of Anthony Giddens', *American Ethnologist* 13: 131–7.

KATZ, D., & SUCHEY, J. M. (1986) 'Age determination of the male os pubis', *AJPA* 69: 427–35.

KELLY, R. C. (1974) *Etoro Social Structure. A Study in Structural Contradiction*. Ann Arbor.

KERAMOPOULLOS, A. D. (1934/5) 'Epigraphai ek Voiotias', *AE* chronika: 1–16.

KERTZER, D. (1988) *Ritual, Politics and Power*. New Haven.

KERTZER, D. I., & SALLER, R. P., eds. (1991) *The Family in Italy from Antiquity to the Present*. New Haven.

KEY, P. J. (1983) *Craniometric Relationships among Plains Indians*. Knoxville, Tennessee.

KINCH, F. K. (1914) *Fouilles de Vroulia (Rhodes)*. Copenhagen.

KING, A. (1990) *Roman Gaul and Germany*. Berkeley.

KING, A., & HENIG, M., eds. (1981) *The Roman West in the Third Century*. Oxford (*BAR* S 109).

KIRSCHBAUM, E. (1959) *The Tombs of St Peter and St Paul*. New York.

KJELDSEN, K., & ZAHLE, J. (1976) 'A dynastic tomb in central Lycia: new evidence for the study of Lycian architecture and history in the classical period', *Acta Archaeologica* 47: 29–46.

KLEINER, D. E. E. (1977) *Roman Group Portraiture: The Funerary Reliefs of the Late Republic and Early Empire*. New York.

(1983) *The Monument of Philopappos in Athens*. Rome.

(1987) *Roman Imperial Funerary Altars with Portraits*. Rome.

(1988) 'Roman funerary art and architecture: observations on the significance of recent studies', *JRA* 1: 115–19.

KLEPINGER, L. L. (1984) 'Nutritional assessment from bone', *Ann Rev Anth* 13: 75–96.

KNEISSL, P., & LOSEMANN, V., eds. (1988) *Alte Geschichte und Wissenschaftsgeschichte. Festschrift für Karl Christ*. Darmstadt.

KNIGGE, U. (1972) 'Untersuchungen bei den Gesandtenstelen im Kerameikos zu Athen', *AA*: 584–629.

(1980) 'Der Rundbau am Eridanos', in *Kerameikos* XII: *Rundbauten im Kerameikos*: 57–94. Berlin.

(1988) *Der Kerameikos von Athen*. Athens.

KOCH, G., & SICHTERMANN, H. (1982) *Römische Sarkophage*. Munich.

KOCKEL, V. (1983) *Die Grabbauten vor dem Herkulaner Tor in Pompeji*. Mainz.

(1985) 'Archäologische Funde und Forschungen in den Vesuvstädten I', *AA*: 495–571.

(1986) 'Archäologische Funde und Forschungen in den Vesuvstädten II', *AA*: 443–569.

KOETHE, H. (1939) 'Römerzeitliche Grabhügel des Trierer Landes und seiner Nachbargebiete', *Trierer Zeitschrift* 14: 113–53.

KOKULA, G. (1984) *Marmorlutrophoren*. Mainz (*AM* Beiheft 10).

KOLENDO, J. (1981) 'La répartition des places aux spectacles et la stratification sociale dans l'empire romain', *Ktema* 6: 301–15.

KOMLOS, J. (1990) 'Height and social status in eighteenth-century Germany', *JIH* 20: 607–21.

KONDOLEON, N. (1962) 'The gold treasure of Panagurishte', *Balkan Studies* 3: 185–200.

KONSTAN, D. (1985) 'The politics of Aristophanes' *Wasps*', *TAPhA* 115: 27–46.

KOUMANOUDES, S., & MILLER, S. G. (1971) 'Inscriptiones Graecae, II² 1477 and 3046 rediscovered', *Hesperia* 40: 448–57.

KOVACSCOVICS, W. (1990) *Kerameikos* XIV: *Die Eckterrasse.* Berlin.

KRAMER, L. S. (1989) 'Literature, criticism and historical imagination', in Hunt, ed.: 97–128.

KRANIOTI, L., & ROZAKI, V. (1979) 'Aigina', *A D* 34.2: 68–70.

KRASKOVSKA, L. (1976) *The Roman Cemetery at Gerulata Rusovce, Czechoslovakia.* Oxford (*B A R* S 10).

KRAUTHEIMER, R. (1980) *Rome: Profile of a City, 312–1308.* Princeton.

(1983) *Three Christian Capitals.* Princeton.

KÜBLER, K. (1973) 'Eine archaische Grabanlage vor dem Heiligen Tor und ihre Deutung', *A A*: 172–93.

(1976) *Kerameikos* VII.1. Berlin.

KÜBLER-ROSS, E. (1970) *On Death and Dying.* London.

KUPER, A. (1983) *Anthropology and Anthropologists.* 2nd edn. London.

KURTZ, D. C. (1975) *Athenian White Lekythoi.* Oxford.

(1984) 'Vases for the dead, an Attic selection, 750–400 B.C.', in Brijder, ed.: 314–28.

KURTZ, D. C., ed. (1985) *Beazley and Oxford.* Oxford.

KURTZ, D. C., & BOARDMAN, J. (1971) *Greek Burial Customs.* London.

KYRIELEIS, H. (1988) 'Offerings of the "common man" in the Heraion at Samos', in Hägg et al., eds.: 215–21.

LA CAPRA, D. (1983) *Rethinking Intellectual History.* Ithaca, New York.

(1985) *History and Criticism.* Ithaca, New York.

LA FONTAINE, J. S. (1985) *Initiation.* Manchester.

LALLO, J., ARMELAGOS, G. J., & MENSFORTH, R. P. (1977) 'The role of diet, disease and physiology in the origin of porotic hyperostosis', *Human Biology* 49: 471–83.

LAMBERG-KARLOVSKY, C. G., ed. (1989) *Archaeological Thought in America.* Cambridge.

LAMBERT, J. B., SIMPSON, S. V., BUIKSTRA, J. E., & CHARLES, D. K. (1984) 'Analysis of soil associated with Woodland burials', in J. B. Lambert, ed., *Archaeological Chemistry* III: 97–113. 3 vols. Washington DC.

LAMBERTON, R. (1988) *Hesiod.* New Haven.

LAMBRINOUDAKIS, V. (1988) 'Veneration of ancestors in Geometric Naxos', in Hägg et al., eds.: 235–46.

LANCASTER, O. (1984) *The Littlehampton Saga.* London.

LANCIANI, R. (1888) *Ancient Rome in the Light of Recent Discoveries.* London.

LANE, C. (1981) *The Rites of Rulers.* Cambridge.

LANE, R. A., & SUBLETT, A. J. (1972) 'Osteology of social organization: residence pattern', *Am Ant* 37: 186–201.

LARKIN, E. (1972) 'The devotional revolution in Ireland: 1850–75', *A H R* 77: 625–52.

LARSEN, C. S. (1987) 'Bioarchaeological interpretations of subsistence economy and behavior from human skeletal remains', *A M T* 10: 339–445.

LATTIMORE, R. (1962) *Themes in Greek and Latin Epitaphs.* Urbana, Illinois.

LAUBENHEIMER, F. (1987) 'Incinération et inhumation dans l'occident romain', *DHA* 13: 361–2.

LAWRENCE, A. W., & TOMLINSON, R. A. (1983) *Greek Architecture.* 3rd edn. Harmondsworth.

LAZARIDES, D. (1966) 'Arkhaiotites kai mnimeia Attikis kai nison', *AD* 21.2: 90–107.

LE GALL, J. (1980/1) 'La sépulture des pauvres à Rome', *Bulletin de la société nationale des Antiquaires de France*: 148–63.

LE ROY LADURIE, E. (1971) *Times of Feast, Times of Famine.* New York. (1978) *Montaillou.* New York.

LEACH, E. R. (1976) *Culture and Communication.* Cambridge. (1979) 'Discussion', in B. C. Burnham & J. Kingsbury, eds., *Space, Hierarchy and Society*: 119–24. Oxford (*BARS* 59).

LEACH, E. W. (1982) 'Patrons, painters and patterns', in B. Gold, ed., *Literary and Artistic Patronage in Ancient Rome:* 135–73. London.

LEE, F., & MAGILTON, J. (1989) 'The cemetery of the hospital of St James and St Mary Magdalene, Chichester – a case study', *WA* 21: 273–82.

LEECH, R. (1981) 'The excavation of a Romano-British farmstead and cemetery on Bradley Hill, Somerton, Somerset', *Britannia* 12: 177–252.

LEEK, F. F. (1979) 'The dental history of the Manchester mummies', in A. R. David, ed., *Manchester Museum Mummy Project*: 65–77. Manchester.

LEGLAY, M. (1971) 'Circonscription de Rhône-Alpes', *Gallia* 29: 407–45.

LERNER, J. C. (1975) 'Changes in attitude toward death: the widow in Great Britain in the early 20th century', in B. Schoenberg, I. Gerber, A. Weiner, A. Kitscher, D. Peretz & A. Carr, eds., *Bereavement: Its Psychosocial Aspects.* New York.

LÉVI-STRAUSS, C. (1953) 'Social structure', in A. L. Kroeber, ed., *Anthropology Today*: 524–53. Chicago. Reprinted in C. Lévi-Strauss, *Structural Anthropology*: 277–345, New York, 1968.

LEWIS, D. M. (1966) 'After the profanation of the Mysteries', in E. Badian, ed., *Ancient Society and Institutions: Studies ... V. Ehrenberg*: 177–91. Oxford. (1986) 'Temple inventories in ancient Greece', in Vickers, ed.: 71–81.

LEWIS, G. (1980) *Day of Shining Red.* Cambridge.

LIEBESCHUETZ, J. H. W. G. (1979) *Continuity and Change in Roman Religion.* Oxford.

LINDERS, T. (1988) *Comptes et inventaires dans la cité grecque.* Neuchâtel.

LINTOTT, A. (1982) *Violence, Civil Strife and Revolution in the Classical City, 750–330 B.C.* London.

LISSARRAGUE, F. (1988) 'La stèle avant le lettre', *AION ArchStAnt* 10: 97–105.

LIVERSIDGE, J. (1973) *Britain in the Roman Empire.* London.

LLOYD, C. (1986) *Explanation in Social History.* Stanford.

LORAUX, N. (1982) 'Mourir devant Troie, tomber pour Athènes: de la gloire du héros à l'idée de la cité', in Gnoli & Vernant, eds.: 27–43.
(1986) *The Invention of Athens*. Cambridge, Massachusetts.
(1987) *Tragic Ways of Killing a Woman*. Cambridge, Massachusetts.

LORDKIPANIDZE, O. (1971) 'La civilisation de l'ancienne Colchide aux Ve–IVe siècles', *RA*: 259–88.

MACAULAY, D. (1979) *Motel of the Mysteries*. Boston.

MACDONALD, J. (1977) 'Pagan religions and burial practices in Roman Britain', in Reece, ed.: 35–8.

MCDONALD, W. A., COULSON, W. D. E., & ROSSER, J. J. (1983) *Excavations at Nichoria in South-west Greece* III. Minneapolis.

MACFARLANE, A. (1986) *Marriage and Love in England: Modes of Reproduction 1300–1840*. Oxford.

MCGRAIL, S. (1989) 'The shipment of traded goods and of ballast in antiquity', *OJA* 8: 353–8.

MCKECHNIE, P. (1989) *Greeks outside the Polis in the Fourth Century B.C.* London.

MCKINLEY, J. I. (1989) 'Cremations: expectations, methodologies and realities', in Roberts et al., eds.: 65–76.

MCMANNERS, J. (1981a) *Death and the Enlightenment*. Oxford.
(1981b) 'Death and the French historians', in Whaley, ed.: 106–30.

MACMULLEN, R. (1963) *Soldier and Civilian in the Later Roman Empire*. Cambridge, Massachusetts.
(1981) *Paganism in the Roman Empire*. New Haven.
(1982) 'The epigraphic habit in the Roman Empire', *AJPh* 103: 233-46.
(1984a) *Christianizing the Roman Empire, A.D. 100-400*. New Haven.
(1984b) 'The legion as a society', *Historia* 33: 440-56.
(1986a) '"What difference did Christianity make?"', *Historia* 35: 322-43.
(1986b) 'Frequency of inscriptions in Roman Lydia', *ZPE* 65: 237–8.
(1987) 'Late Roman slavery', *Historia* 36: 359–82.
(1988) *Corruption and the Decline of Rome*. New Haven.

MCNEILL, W. H. (1976) *Plagues and Peoples*. New York.

MCWHIRR, A., VINER, L., & WELLS, C., eds. (1982) *Romano-British Cemeteries at Cirencester*. Cirencester (*Cirencester Excavations* 2).

MAKARONAS, CH. (1963) 'Taphoi para to Derveni Thessalonikis' *A D* 18.3: 193-6.

MALLEGNI, F., FORNACIARI, G., & PALMIERI, S. (1980/1) 'I resti umani di Vada (IV–V secolo d.C.) e di Rosignano Solvay (IV secolo d.C.)', in *Studi sul Territorio Livornese*: 219–51. Livorno.

MALLWITZ, A. (1980) 'Das Staatsgrab am 3. Horos', in *Kerameikos* XII: *Rundbauten im Kerameikos*: 99–125. Berlin.
(1981) 'Kritisches zur Architektur Griechenlands im 8. und 7. Jh.', *AA*: 599–642.

MANCHESTER, K. (1984) 'Tuberculosis and leprosy in antiquity: an interpretation', *Medical History* 28: 162–73.

MANCHESTER, K., & ROBERTS, C. (1989) 'The palaeopathology of leprosy in Britain – a review', *WA* 21: 265–72.

MANCINI, G. (1913) 'Le recenti scoperti di antichità a Monte Citorio', *Studi Romani. Rivista di archeologia e storia* 1: 3–15.

MANN, J. C. (1985) 'Epigraphic consciousness', *JRS* 75: 204–6.

MANVILLE, B. (1990) *The Origins of Citizenship in Ancient Athens*. Princeton.

MARCILLET-JAUBERT, J. (1968) *Les inscriptions d'Altava*. Paris (Publications de la faculté des lettres et sciences humaines d'Aix-en-Provence, n.s. 65).

MARCUS, G., & FISCHER, M. (1986) *Anthropology as Cultural Critique*. Chicago.

MARTIN, D. L., GOODMAN, A. H., & ARMELAGOS, G. J. (1985) 'Skeletal pathologies as indicators of quality and quantity of diet', in R. I. Gilbert & J. H. Miekle, eds., *The Analysis of Prehistoric Diets*: 227–79. Orlando, Florida.

MARTIN, P. (1971) 'Le monument des néréides et l'architecture funéraire', *RA*: 327–37.

MARTIN-KILCHER, S. (1976) *Das römische Gräberfeld von Curroux im Berner Jura*. Basel (Basler Beiträge zur Ur- und Frühgeschichte 2).

MAURIN, J. (1984) '*Funus* et rites de séparation', *AION ArchStAnt* 6: 191–208.

MAYS, S. (1989) 'Human bone strontium analysis in the investigation of palaeodiets: a case-study from a British Anglo-Saxon site', in Roberts et al., eds.: 215–33.

MAZARAKIS AINIAN, A. (1985) 'Contribution à l'étude de l'architecture religieuse grecque des Ages Obscurs', *Ant Cl* 54: 5–48.

(1987) 'Geometric Eretria', *AntK* 30: 3–24.

(1988) 'Early Greek temples: their origin and function', in Hägg et al., eds.: 105–19.

MEE, C. B., & CAVANAGH, W. G. (1984) 'Mycenaean tombs as evidence for social and political organisation', *OJA* 3.3: 45–64.

MEEKS, W. (1983) *The First Urban Christians: The Social World of the Apostle Paul*. New Haven.

MEIGGS, R. (1973) *Roman Ostia*. 2nd edn. Oxford.

MELTZER, D. J., FOWLER, D. D., & SABLOFF, J. E., eds. (1986) *American Archaeology Past and Future*. Washington DC.

MERKELBACH, R. (1989) 'Zwei neue Orphisch-Dionysische Totenpässe', *ZPE* 76: 15–16.

MERRIFIELD, R. (1987) *The Archaeology of Ritual and Magic*. London.

MERTENS, J., & REMY, H. (1972) *La nécropole antique sous l'église St-Quentin à Tournai*. Brussels (*Arch Belg* 137).

MEYER, E. (1988) 'Literacy, literate practice, and the law in the Roman empire, A.D. 100–600', unpublished Ph.D. thesis, Yale University.

(1990) 'Explaining the epigraphic habit in the Roman empire', *JRS* 80: 74–96.

MEYER, R. E. (1989) *Cemeteries and Gravemarkers: Voices of American Culture.* Ann Arbor.

MICHELS, R. (1915) *Political Parties. A Sociological Study of the Oligarchical Tendencies of Modern Democracy.* Glencoe, Illinois. Reprinted New York, 1962.

MIELSCH, H., & VON HESBERG, H. (1986) *Die heidnische Nekropole unter St. Peter in Rom. Die Mausoleen A-D.* Rome.

MILLAR, F. (1983) 'Epigraphy', in Crawford, ed.: 80–136.

MILLER, D. (1985) *Artefacts as Categories.* Cambridge.

(1989) 'The limits of dominance', in D. Miller, M. Rowlands & C. Tilley, eds., *Domination and Resistance*: 63–79. London.

MILLER, D., & TILLEY, C., eds. (1984) *Ideology, Power and Prehistory.* Cambridge.

MILLER, S. G. (1979) *Two Groups of Thessalian Gold.* Berkeley (UCal Class Stud 18).

(1982) 'Macedonian tombs: their architecture and architectural decoration', in B. Barr-Sharrar & E. Borza, eds., *Macedonia and Greece in Late Classical and Early Hellenistic Times*: 152–69. Washington DC.

(1986) 'An elaborate pin of Illyrian type from Thessaly', *AntK* 29: 37–42.

MILLETT, M. (1986) 'An early Roman burial tradition in central southern England', *OJA* 5: 63–8.

(1990) *The Romanization of Britain.* Cambridge.

MILLETT, P. (1984) 'Hesiod and his world', *PCPhS* 210: 84–115.

(1989) 'Patronage and its avoidance in classical Athens', in A. Wallace-Hadrill, ed., *Patronage in Ancient Society*: 15–47. London.

MILOJCIC, V. (1960) 'Ausgrabungen in Thessalien Herbst 1959', AA: 150–78.

MITFORD, J. (1963) *The American Way of Death.* London.

MOCSY, A., ed. (1981) *Die spätrömische Festung und das Gräberfeld von Tokod.* Budapest.

MOESCH, R. M. (1988) 'Le mariage et la mort sur les loutrophores', *AION ArchStAnt* 10: 117–39.

MØLLER-CHRISTENSEN, V. (1966) 'Evidence of tuberculosis, leprosy and syphilis in antiquity and the middle ages', *Proceedings of the XIX International Congress on the History of Medicine (Basel, 1964)*: 229–37. Basel.

MOLLESON, T. (1981) 'What the bones tell us', in Humphreys & King, eds.: 15–32.

MOORE, H. L. (1986) *Space, Text and Gender: An Anthropological Study of the Marakwet of Kenya.* Cambridge.

MOORE, J. A., SWEDLUND, A. C., & ARMELAGOS, G. J. (1975) 'The use of life tables in palaeodemography', *Am Ant* 40: 57–70.

MOORE, R. I. (1987) *The Formation of a Persecuting Society.* Oxford.

MORGAN, C. A. (1990) *Athletes and Oracles: The Transformation of Olympia and Delphi in the Eighth Century B.C.* Cambridge.

MORGAN, G. (1982) 'Euphiletos' house: Lysias 1', *TAPh A* 112: 115–23.

MORRIS, I. (1986a) 'The use and abuse of Homer', *Cl Ant* 5: 81–138.

(1986b) 'Gift and commodity in archaic Greece', *Man* 21: 1–17.

(1987) *Burial and Ancient Society: The Rise of the Greek City State*. Cambridge.

(1988) 'Tomb cult and the "Greek renaissance": the past in the present in the eighth century B.C.', *Antiquity* 62: 750–61.

(1989a) 'Attitudes toward death in archaic Greece', *Cl Ant* 8: 296–320.

(1989b) 'Circulation, depostion and the formulation of the Greek Iron Age', *Man* 24: 502–19.

(1991) 'The archaeology of ancestors: the Saxe/Goldstein hypothesis revisited', *Cambridge Archaeological Journal* 1: 147–69.

MOSSÉ, C. (1962) *La fin de la démocratie athénienne*. Paris.

MOULINIER, L. (1952) *Le pur et l'impur dans la pensée et la sensibilité des Grecs jusqu'à la fin du IVe siècle avant J-C*. Paris.

MROZEK, S. (1973) 'A propos de la répartition chronologique des inscriptions latines dans le Haut-Empire', *Epigraphica* 35: 113–18.

(1984) 'Munificentia privata im Bauwesen und Lebensmittelverteilungen in Italien während des Prinzipates', *ZPE* 57: 233–40.

(1988) 'A propos de la répartition chronologique des inscriptions latines dans le Haut-Empire', *Epigraphica* 50: 61–4.

MUNZ, F. R. (1970) 'Die Zahnfunde aus der griechischen Nekropole von Pithekoussai auf Ischia', *AA*: 425–75.

MURRAY, O. (1988) 'Death and the symposion', *AION ArchStAnt* 10: 239–57.

MUSSCHE, H. (1975) 'Thorikos in archaic and classical times', in H. Mussche, P. Spitaels & F. Goemaere-De Poerck, eds., *Thorikos and Laurion in Archaic and Classical Times*: 45–61. Ghent (*MIGRA* 1).

NASH, E. (1968) *Picture Dictionary of Ancient Rome* II. 2 vols. 2nd edn. New York.

NEEDLEMAN, L., & NEEDLEMAN, D. (1985) 'Lead poisoning and the decline of the Roman Aristocracy', *EMC/CV* 29: 62–94.

NEEFT, C. W. (1987) *Protocorinthian Subgeometric Aryballoi*. Amsterdam (Allard Pierson Series 7).

NEGEV, A. (1986) *Nabataean Archaeology Today*. New York.

NEVILLE, G. K. (1989) 'The sacred and the civic: representations of death in the town ceremony of Border Scotland', *AQ* 62: 155–73.

NICOLAI, V. F. (1986) 'Sepolture privilegiate nelle catacombe del Lazio', in Duval & Picard, eds.: 193–203.

NIELSEN, T. H., BJERSTRUP, L., HANSEN, M. H., RUBINSTEIN, L., & VESTERGARD, T. (1989) 'Athenian grave monuments and social class', *GRBS* 30: 411–20.

NOCK, A. D. (1932) 'Cremation and burial in the Roman empire', *HTR* 25: 321–59, reprinted in Nock 1972: 277–307.

(1946) 'Sarcophagi and symbolism', *AJA* 50: 140–70, reprinted in Nock 1972: 606–41.

(1972) *Essays on Religion and the Ancient World*, ed. Z. Stewart. 2 vols. Oxford.

NORTH, J. (1976) 'Conservatism and change in Roman religion', *PBSR* 30: 1–12.

(1989) 'Religion in Republican Rome', *CAH* VII.2: 573–624. Cambridge.

NOVICK, P. (1988) *That Noble Dream: The 'Objectivity Question' and the American Historical Profession*. Cambridge.

OBER, J. (1989a) 'Models and paradigms in ancient history', *AHB* 3: 134–7.

(1989b) *Mass and Elite in Democratic Athens*. Princeton.

(1989c) 'The nature of Athenian democracy', *CP* 84: 322–34.

(1991) 'Aristotle's political sociology: class, status, and order in the *Politics*', in C. Lord & D. O'Connor, eds., *Essays on the Foundations of Aristotelian Political Science*. Berkeley: 112–35.

OBER, J., & STRAUSS, B. (1990) 'Drama, political rhetoric, and the discourse of Athenian democracy', in Winkler & Zeitlin, eds.: 237–70.

OHLY, D. (1965) 'Kerameikos-Grabung. Tätigkeitsbericht 1956–1961', *AA*: 277–375.

ORTALLI, J. (1987) 'La Via dei Sepolcrali di Sarsina. Aspetti funzionali, formali e sociali', in von Hesberg & Zanker, eds.: 155–82.

ORTNER, D. J., & PUTSCHAR, W. G. U. (1981) *Identification of Pathological Conditions in Human Skeletal Remains*. Washington DC. (Smithsonian Contributions to Anthropology 28).

ORTNER, S. (1984) 'Theory in anthropology since the sixties', *Comparative Studies in Society and History* 26: 126–66.

ORTON, C. (1980) *Mathematics in Archaeology*. London.

OSBÒRNE, J. (1984) 'Death and burial in sixth-century Rome', *EMC/CV* 28: 291–9.

(1985) 'The Roman catacombs in the Middle Ages', *PBSR* 53: 278–328.

OSBORNE, M. J. (1988) 'Attic epitaphs – a supplement', *Anc Soc* 19: 5–60.

OSBORNE, R. G. (1985a) 'Law in action in classical Athens', *JHS* 105: 40–58.

(1985b) 'Buildings and residence on the land in classical and Hellenistic Greece: the evidence of epigraphy', *BSA* 80: 119–28.

(1988) 'Death revisited, death revised: the death of the artist in archaic and classical Greece', *Art History* 11: 1–16.

(1989) 'A crisis in archaeological history? The seventh century B.C. in Attica', *BSA* 84: 297–322.

O'SHEA, J. (1981) 'Social configurations and the archaeological study of mortuary practices: a case study', in Chapman et al., eds.: 39–52.

(1984) *Mortuary Variability*. New York.

OSTWALD, M. (1986) *From Popular Sovereignty to the Sovereignty of Law. Law, Society and Politics in fifth-century Athens.* Berkeley.

O'SULLIVAN, E., WILLIAMS, S. A., & CURZON, M. E. J. (1989) 'Dental caries and stress in English archaeological child populations', in Roberts et al., eds.: 167–74.

PACKER, J. E. (1967) 'Housing and population in imperial Rome and Ostia', *JRS* 57: 80–95.

PADER, E.-J. (1982) *Symbolism, Social Relations and the Interpretation of Mortuary Remains.* Oxford (*BAR* S 110).

PAIDOUSSIS, M., & SBAROUNIS, C. (1975) 'A study of the cremated bones from the cemetery at Perati', *Op Ath* 11: 129–60.

PALGI, P., & ABRAMOVICH, A. (1984) 'Death: a cross-cultural perspective', *Ann Rev Anth* 13: 385–417.

PALMER, H. (1964) 'The classical and Roman periods', in Blegen et al.: 65–327.

PARKER, R. (1983) *Miasma. Pollution and Purification in Early Greek Religion.* Oxford.

PARKER PEARSON, M. (1982) 'Mortuary practices, society and ideology: an ethnoarchaeological case study', in Hodder, ed.: 99–113.

  (1984) 'Economic and ideological change: cyclical growth in the pre-state societies of Jutland', in Miller & Tilley, eds.: 69–92.

  (1989) 'Beyond the pale: barbarian social dynamics in western Europe', in J. C. Barrett, A. P. Fitzpatrick & L. Macinnes, eds., *Barbarians and Romans in North-West Europe*: 198–226. Oxford (*BAR* S 471).

PARMEGGIANI, G. (1985) 'Voghenza, necropoli: analisi di alcuni aspetti del rituale funerario', in *Voghenza. Una necropoli di età romana nel territorio Ferrarese.* Ferrara.

PARTNER, N. F. (1986) 'Making up lost time: writing on the writing of history', *Speculum* 61: 90–117.

PATE, D., & BROWN, K. A. (1985) 'Stability of bone strontium in the geochemical environment', *JHE* 14: 483–91.

PAYNE, H. (1931) *Necrocorinthia.* Oxford.

PEARCE, S. M., ed. (1982) *The Early Church in Western Britain and Ireland.* Oxford (*BAR* 102).

PECORA, V. (1990) 'The limits of local knowledge', in Veeser, ed.: 243–76.

PEEK, W. (1955) *Griechische Versinschriften* I: *Grab Epigramme.* Berlin.

PÉLÉKIDIS, C. (1962) *Histoire de l'éphébie attique des origines à 31 devant J-C.* Paris.

PELLETIER, A. (1988) 'Découvertes archéologiques et histoire de Vienne (France) de 1972 à 1987', *Latomus* 47: 34–52.

PERGOLA, P. (1983) 'La région dite des "Flavii Aurelii" dans la catacombe de Domitille', *MEFRA* 95: 201–43.

  (1986) 'Sépultures privilégiées de la catacombe de Domitille à Rome', in Duval & Picard, eds.: 185–7.

PESANDO, F. (1987) *Oikos e ktisis. La casa greca in età classica.* Perugia.
PETRAKOS, V. (1976) 'Anaskaphi Rhamnoundos', *Praktika*: 5–60.
(1977a) 'Anaskaphi Rhamnoundos', *Praktika*: 3–22.
(1977b) '2nd ephoreia klasikon kai proistorikon arkhaiotiton', *AD* 32.2: 36–43.
(1978) 'Anaskaphi Rhamnoundos', *Praktika*: 1–16.
(1979) 'Anaskaphi Rhamnoundos', *Praktika*: 1–25.
(1982) 'Anaskaphi Rhamnoundos', *Praktika*: 127–62.
PETROPOULOU, A. (1988) 'The interment of Patroklos (*Iliad* 23.252–57)', *AJPh* 109: 482–95.
PICKARD-CAMBRIDGE, A. W. (1968) *The Dramatic Festivals of Athens.* 2nd edn. Oxford. Revised by J. Gould & D. M. Lewis. Reprinted with addenda 1988.
PILET, C. (1980) *La Nécropole de Frénouville.* 3 vols. Oxford (*BAR* S 83).
PINE, V. R. (1975) *Caretaker of the Dead: The American Funeral Director.* New York.
PINSKY, V., & WYLIE, A., eds. (1989) *Critical Traditions in Contemporary Archaeology.* Cambridge.
PINZA, G. (1914) 'Le vicende della zona Esquilina fino ai tempi di Augusto', *Bulletino della Commissione Archeologica Communale in Roma* 42: 117–75.
PIPPIDI, D. M., ed. (1976) *Assimilation et résistance à la culture gréco-romaine dans le monde ancien.* Bucharest & Paris.
PLASSART, A. (1958) 'Inscriptions de Thespies', *BCH* 82: 107–67.
PLATNER, S. B., & ASHBY, T. (1929) *A Topographical Dictionary of Rome.* Oxford.
POLACCO, J. (1982) 'Théâtre, société, organisation de l'état', in *Théâtre et spectacles dans l'antiquité*: 5–15. Strasbourg.
POLITI, N. (1953/4) 'Dyo epitymvia epigrammata ex Amorgou', *AE* part B: 24–9.
POLLOCK, L. (1983) *Forgotten Children: Parent–Child Relations from 1500 to 1900.* Cambridge.
POLSON, C. J., & MARSHALL, T. K. (1972) *The Disposal of the Dead.* 3rd edn. London.
POPE, M. (1988) 'Thucydides and democracy', *Historia* 37: 276–96.
POPHAM, M. R., CALLIGAS, P. G., & SACKETT, L. H. (1989) 'Further excavation of the Toumba cemetery at Lefkandi, 1984 and 1986', *AR* 1988–1989: 117–29.
POPHAM, M. R., TOULOUPA, E., & SACKETT, L. H. (1982) 'The hero of Lefkandi', *Antiquity* 56: 169–74.
POWELL, M. L. (1985) 'The analysis of dental wear for dietary reconstruction', in R. I. Gilbert & J. H. Miekle, eds., *The Analysis of Prehistoric Diets*: 307–38. New York.
(1988) *Health and Status in Prehistory.* Washington DC.

PRAG, A. J. N. W. (1989) 'Reconstructing King Midas: a first report', *Anat St* 39: 159–66.

(1990) 'Reconstructing King Philip II: the "nice" version', *AJA* 94: 237–47.

PRAG, A. J. N. W., MUSGRAVE, H. H., & NEAVE, R. A. H. (1984) 'The skull from tomb II at Vergina: King Philip II of Macedon', *JHS* 104: 60–78.

PRICE, S. R. F. (1984) *Rituals and Power: The Roman Imperial Cult in Asia Minor*. Cambridge.

(1987) 'From noble funerals to divine cult: the consecration of Roman emperors', in Cannadine & Price, eds.: 56–105.

PRITCHETT, W. K. (1953) 'The Attic stelai, part I', *Hesperia* 22: 225–99.

(1956) 'The Attic stelai, part II', *Hesperia* 25: 178–328.

(1961) 'Five new fragments of the Attic stelai', *Hesperia* 30: 23–9.

(1985a) *Studies in Ancient Greek Topography* v. Berkeley (UCal Class Stud 31).

(1985b) *The Greek State at War* IV. Berkeley.

PURCELL, N. (1987) 'Tomb and suburb', in von Hesberg & Zanker, eds.: 25–41.

RADCLIFFE-BROWN, A. (1952) *Structure and Function in Primitive Society*. London.

RAGON, M. (1983) *The Space of Death: A Study of Funerary Architecture, Decoration, and Urbanism*. Charlottesville, Virginia.

RAHTZ, P. (1986) 'Sub-Roman cemeteries in Somerset', Barley & Hanson, eds.: 193–5.

(1977) 'Late Roman cemeteries and beyond', in Reece, ed.: 53–64.

(1987) 'The Protestant cemetery, Rome', *Opuscula Romana* 16: 149–67.

RAHTZ, P., DICKINSON, T., & WATTS, L., eds. (1980) *Anglo-Saxon Cemeteries 1979*. Oxford (*BAR* 82).

RALEGH RADFORD, C. A. (1968) 'The archaeological background on the continent', in Barley & Hanson, eds.: 19–36.

RANSDBORG, K. (1989) 'The archaeology of the visual: burials past and present', *Dialoghi di Archeologia* 7: 85–96.

RAWSON, E. (1987) '*Discrimina ordinum*: the *lex Julia theatralis*', *PBSR* 55: 83–104.

READER, R. (1974) 'New evidence for the antiquity of leprosy in early Britain', *JAS* 1: 205–7.

REBER, K. (1988) 'Aedificia Graecorum: zu Vitruvs Beschreibung des griechischen Hauses', *AA*: 653–66.

REECE, R., ed. (1977) *Burial in the Roman World*. London (CBA Research Report 22).

(1982) 'Bones, bodies, and dis-ease', *OJA* 1: 347–58.

REESE, D. S. (1989) 'Faunal remains from the altar of Aphrodite Ourania, Athens', *Hesperia* 58: 63–70.

REHM, M. (Forthcoming) *Marriage to Death.*

RENFREW, A. C. (1974) 'Beyond a subsistence economy', in C. B. Moore, ed., *Reconstructing Complex Societies*: 69–95. New York (*BASOR* supp. vol. 20).

RENFREW, A. C., & CHERRY, J. F., eds. (1986) *Peer Polity Interaction and the Development of Socio-cultural Complexity.* Cambridge.

RENFREW, A. C., & SHENNAN, S. J., eds. (1982) *Ranking, Resource and Exchange.* Cambridge.

REUSSER, C. (1987) 'Gräberstrassen in Aquileia', in von Hesberg & Zanker, eds.: 239–49.

REYNAULD, J.-F., & JANNET-VALLET, M. (1986) 'Les inhumations privilégiées à Lyon et à Vienne', in Duval & Picard, eds.: 97–107.

RHODES, P. J. (1981) *A Commentary on the Aristotelian* Athenaion Politeia. Oxford.

(1985) *The Athenian Empire.* Oxford (*G & R* 'New Studies in the Classics' 17).

(1986) 'Political activity in classical Athens', *JHS* 106: 132–44.

RHODES, R. (1987) 'Early Corinthian architecture and the origins of the Doric order', *AJA* 91: 477–80.

RHOMAIOS, K. A. (1951) *O Makedonikos Taphos tis Verginas.* Athens. (Etaireia Makedonikon Spoudon 14).

RICHARD, J.-C. (1978) 'Recherches sur certains aspects du culte impérial: les funérailles des empereurs aux deux premiers siècles de notre ère', *ANRW* 2.16.2: 1125–7.

RICHARDSON, R. (1988) *Death, Dissection and the Destitute.* London.

RICHMOND, I. (1950) *Archaeology and the Afterlife in Pagan and Christian Imagery.* Oxford.

RICHTER, G. M. A. (1961) *The Archaic Gravestones of Attica.* London.

(1968) *Korai, Archaic Greek Maidens.* London.

(1970) *Kouroi, Archaic Greek Youths.* 3rd edn. London.

RIDER, B. L. (1964) *Ancient Greek Houses.* Chicago.

RIDGWAY, D. (1984) *L'alba della Magna Grecia.* Rome.

(1989) 'Archaeology in Sardinia and South Italy 1983–88', *AR 1988–1989*: 130–47.

RIVET, A. L. F. (1988) *Gallia Narbonensis: Southern Gaul in Roman Times.* London.

ROBERTS, C. A. (1986) 'Palaeopathology: cottage industry or interacting discipline?', in J. Bintliff & C. Gaffney, eds., *Archaeology at the Interface*: 110–28. Oxford (*BAR S* 300).

ROBERTS, C. A., LEE, F., & BINTLIFF, J., eds. (1989) *Burial Archaeology: Current Research, Methods and Developments.* Oxford (*BAR* 211).

ROBERTSON, M. (1975) *A History of Greek Art.* 2 vols. Oxford.

(1985) 'Beazley and Attic vase painting', in Kurtz, ed.: 19–30.

ROBERTSON, N. (1983) 'The collective burial of fallen soldiers at Athens, Sparta and elsewhere', *EMC/CV* 27: 78–92.

ROBINSON, D. M. (1942) *Excavations at Olynthus* XII. *Necrolynthia*. Baltimore.

ROBINSON, D. M., & GRAHAM, A. J. (1938) *Excavations at Olynthus* XI. *The Hellenic House*. Baltimore.

ROBINSON, H. S. (1962) 'Excavations at Corinth, 1960', *Hesperia* 31: 95–133.

RODWELL, W. (1982) 'From mausoleum to minster: the early development of Wells Cathedral', in Pearce, ed.: 49–59.

ROGERS, J., WALDRON, T., DIEPPE, P., & WATT, I. (1987) 'Arthropathies in palaeopathology: the basis of probable classification', *JAS* 14: 179–93.

ROHDE, E. (1966) *Psyche*. 8th edn. New York. German original 1890. Translation first published 1925.

ROSS, A., & ROBINS, D. (1989) *The Life and Death of a Druid Prince*. New York.

ROSTOVTZEFF, M. I. (1953) *Social and Economic History of the Hellenistic World*. 2nd edn, revised by P. M. Fraser. 3 vols. Oxford.

ROUSE, W. D. (1902) *Greek Votive Offerings*. Cambridge.

ROUSSELLE, A. (1988) *Porneia: On Desire and the Body in Antiquity*. Oxford.

ROWLANDS, M. J. (1980) 'Kinship, alliance and exchange in the European Bronze Age', in J. Barrett & R. Bradley, eds., *The British Later Bronze Age* I: 15–55. 2 vols. Oxford (*BAR* 82).

ROWLANDS, M. J., LARSEN, M., & KRISTIANSEN, K., eds. (1987) *Centre and Periphery in the Ancient World*. Cambridge.

ROYMANS, N. (1983) 'The North Belgic Tribes in the 1st century B.C.: a historical-anthropological perspective', in R. Brandt & J. Slofstra, eds., *Roman and Native in the Low Countries: Spheres of Interaction*: 43–69. Oxford (*BAR* S 184).

RUGGLES, C. L. N., & RAHTZ, P., eds. (1988) *Computer and Quantitative Methods in Archaeology 1987*. Oxford (*BAR* S 393).

RUMPF, A. (1933) 'Zu den klazomenischen Denkmälern', *JdI* 48: 55–83.

RUNIA, L. T. (1987) *The Chemical Analysis of Prehistoric Bones*. Oxford (*BAR* S 363).

RUSCHENBUSCH, E. (1978) *Untersuchungen zu Staat und Politik im Griechenland vom 7. bis 4. Jh. v. Chr.* Bamberg.

(1979) *Athenische Innenpolitik im 5. Jahrhundert v. Chr.: Ideologie oder Pragmatismus?* Bamberg.

RYAN, M. (1989) 'The American parade: representations of the nineteenth-century social order', in Hunt, ed.: 131–53.

SAHLINS, M. (1981) *Historical Metaphors and Mythical Realities*. Ann Arbor.

ST-ROCH, P. (1981) 'La région centrale du cimetière de Damase et des saints Marc et Marcelline', *RivArchCrist* 57: 209–51.

(1983) 'Enquête "sociologique" sur le cimetière dit "Coemeterium sanctorum Marci et Marcelliani Damasique"', *RivArchCrist* 59: 411–23.

(1986) 'Un cubicule important dans le cimetière de Damase et des saints Marc et Marcelline', in Duval & Picard, eds.: 189–91.

STE CROIX, G. E. M. DE (1981) *The Class Struggle in the Ancient Greek World.* London.

SAKELLARAKIS, Y., & SAPOUNA-SAKELLARAKI, E. (1981) 'Drama of death in a Minoan temple', *National Geographic Magazine* 159: 205–22.

SALLARES, R. (1991) *Ecology of the Ancient Greek World.* London.

SALLER, R. P. (1986) '*Patria potestas* and the stereotype of the Roman family', *Continuity & Change* 1: 15–20.

(1987) 'Men's age at marriage and its consequences in the Roman family', *CP* 82: 21–34.

(1988) '*Pietas*, obligation and authority in the Roman family', in Kneissl & Losemann, eds.: 393–410.

(1991) 'Roman heirship strategies: in principle and in practice', in Kertzer & Saller, eds.: 26–47.

(Forthcoming) 'Orders, classes and status in early imperial Rome', *CAH* XI²: ch. 26. Cambridge.

SALLER, R. P., & SHAW, B. D. (1984) 'Tombstones and Roman family relations in the principate: civilians, soldiers and slaves', *JRS* 74: 124–56.

SALMON, J. (1984) *Wealthy Corinth.* Oxford.

SAMSON, C., & BRANIGAN, K. (1987) 'A new method of estimating age at death from fragmentary and weathered bone', in Boddington et al., eds.: 101–8.

SAMSON, R. (1989) 'Rural slavery, inscriptions, archaeology and Marx', *Historia* 38: 99–110.

SANDISON, A. T. (1980) 'Diseases in ancient Egypt', in A. & E. Cockburn, eds., *Mummies, Disease, and Ancient Cultures*: 29–44. Cambridge.

SATTENSPIEL, L., & HARPENDING, H. (1983) 'Stable populations and skeletal age', *Am Ant* 48: 489–98.

SAXE, A. A. (1970) 'Social dimensions of mortuary practices', Ph.D. thesis, University of Michigan.

SCHEID, J. (1984) 'Contra facere: renversements et déplacements dans les rites funéraires', *AION ArchStAnt* 6: 117–39.

SCHIERING, W. (1957) *Werkstätten orientalisierender Keramik auf Rhodos.* Berlin.

SCHIFFER, M. (1987) *Formation Processes of the Archaeological Record.* Albuquerque, New Mexico.

SCHILARDI, D. U. (1968) 'Anaskaphai para tis Irias Pylas kai topographika provlimata tis periokhis', *AE* Chronika: 8–52.

(1975) 'Anaskaphai para ta Makra Teikhi kai i oinokhoi tou Tavrou', *AE*: 66–149.

SCHILD-XENIDOU, W. (1972) 'Boiotische Grab- und Weihreliefs archaischer und klassischer Zeit', Ph.D. thesis, Munich.

SCHLÖRB-VIERNEISEL, B. (1964) 'Zwei klassische Kindergräber im Kerameikos', *AM* 79: 85–104.
(1966) 'Eridanos-Nekropole I. Gräber und Opferstelle hS 1–204', *AM* 81: 4–111.

SCHMALTZ, B. (1983) *Griechische Grabreliefs*. Darmstadt.

SCHNEIDER, D. M. (1966) 'Some muddles in the models: or, how the system really works', in M. Banton, ed., *The Relevance of Models for Social Anthropology*. London.

SCHNITZER, G. (1934) 'Minucio Felice e la cremazione', *Religio* 10: 32–44.

SCHOENINGER, M. J., & DE NIRO, M. J. (1982) 'Carbon isotope ratios of apatite from fossil bone cannot be used to reconstruct diets of animals', *Nature* 217: 577–8.

SCHOENINGER, M. J., DE NIRO, M. J., & TAUBER, H. (1983) 'Stable nitrogen isotope ratios of bone collagen reflect marine and terrestrial components of prehistoric human diet', *Science* 220: 1381–3.

SCHULLER, W. (1974) *Die Herrschaft der Athener im Ersten Attischen Seebund*. Berlin.

SCHWIDETZKY, I. (1978) 'Anthropologie der Dürrnberger Bevölkerung, Beitrag', in L. Pauli, ed., *Der Dürrnberg bei Hallein* III: 541–81. 3 vols. Munich.

SCOBIE, A. (1986) 'Slums, sanitation and morality in the Roman world', *Klio* 68: 399–433.

SEALEY, R. (1967) *Essays in Greek Politics*. New York.

SEALY, J. C., & VAN DER MERWE, N. J. (1985) 'Isotope assessment of Holocene human diets in the southwestern Cape, South Africa', *Nature* 315: 138–40.

SEGALEN, M. (1986) *Historical Anthropology of the Family*. Cambridge.

SHANIN, T., ed. (1971) *Peasants and Peasant Societies*. Harmondsworth.

SHANKS, M., & TILLEY, C. (1987) *Social Theory and Archaeology*. Oxford.

SHAPIRO, H. A. (1989) *Art and Cult under the Tyrants in Athens*. Mainz.

SHAW, B. D. (1982a) 'Social science and ancient history: Keith Hopkins *in partibus infidelium*', *Helios* 9: 17–57.
(1982b) 'The Elders of Christian Africa', in P. Brind'Amour, ed., *Mélanges offerts à R. P. Etienne Gareau*: 207–26. Ottawa (special edition of *Cahiers des études anciennes*).
(1984) 'Latin funerary epigraphy and family life in the later Roman empire', *Historia* 33: 457–97.
(1987a) 'The family of late antiquity: the experience of Augustine', *P & P* 115: 3–51.
(1987b) 'The age of Roman girls at marriage: some reconsiderations', *JRS* 77: 30–46.
(1991) 'The cultural meaning of death', in Kertzer & Saller, eds.: 66–90.

SHEAR, T. L., JR. (1969) 'The Athenian Agora: excavations of 1968', *Hesperia* 38: 382–417.

(1973) 'The Athenian Agora: excavations of 1971', *Hesperia* 42: 121–79.

(1975) 'The Athenian Agora: excavations of 1973–1974', *Hesperia* 44: 331–74.

(1978) 'Tyrants and buildings in archaic Athens', in *Athens Comes of Age From Solon to Salamis* 1–19. Princeton.

SHENNAN, S. E. (1975) 'The social organization at Branc', *Antiquity* 49: 279–88.

SHENNAN, S. J. (1988) *Quantifying Archaeology*. Edinburgh.

(1989) 'Archaeology as archaeology or as anthropology?', *Antiquity* 63: 831–5.

SHIPLEY, G. (1988) *A History of Samos, 800–188 B.C.* Oxford.

SILLEN, A., & SMITH, P. (1984) 'Weaning patterns are reflected in strontium–calcium ratios of juvenile skeletons', *JAS* 11: 237–45.

SILVERMAN, E. K. (1990) 'Clifford Geertz: toward a more "thick" understanding?', in Tilley, ed.: 121–59.

SINN-HENNINGER, F. (1987) *Stadtrömische Marmorurnen*. Mainz.

SKINSNES, O. K. (1975) 'An ancient Briton adds to the story of leprosy', *International Journal of Leprosy* 44: 387–9.

SMADJA, E. (1985) 'L'empereur et les dieux en Afrique romaine', *DHA* 11: 541–55.

SMITH, P., BAR-YOSEF, O., & SILLEN, A. (1984) 'Archaeological and skeletal evidence for dietary change during the late Pleistocene/early Holocene in the Levant', in M. N. Cohen & J. G. Armelagos, eds., *Palaeopathology at the Origins of Agriculture*: 101–36. Orlando, Florida.

SMITH, P., BLOOM, R. A., & BERKOWITZ, J. (1984) 'Diachronic trends in humeral cortical thickness of Near Eastern populations', *JHE* 13: 603–11.

SMITH, P., & PERETZ, B. (1986) 'Hypoplasia and health status: a comparison of two lifestyles', *Human Evolution* 1: 1–10.

SMITH, P., & TAU, S. (1978) 'Dental pathology in the period of the Roman empire: a comparison of two populations', *Ossa* 5: 35–41.

SMITH, R. R. R. (1987) 'The imperial reliefs from the Sebasteion at Aphrodisias', *JRS* 77: 88–138.

(1988a) 'Philorhomaioi: portraits of Roman client rulers in the Greek East in the 1st century B.C.', *Quaderni de 'La ricerca scientifica'* 116: 493–7.

(1988b) '*Simulacra Gentium*: the *ethne* from the Sebasteion at Aphrodisias', *JRS* 78: 50–77.

SNODGRASS, A. M. (1971) *The Dark Age of Greece*. Edinburgh.

(1977) *Archaeology and the Rise of the Greek State*. Cambridge.

(1980) *Archaic Greece: The Age of Experiment*. London.

(1986) 'Interaction by design: the Greek city-state', in Renfrew & Cherry, eds.: 47–58.

(1987) *An Archaeology of Greece*. Berkeley.

(1988) 'The archaeology of the hero', *AION ArchStAnt* 10: 19–26.

SOFAER, J. A., SMITH, P., & KAYE, E. (1986) 'Affinities between contemporary and skeletal Jewish and non-Jewish groups based on tooth morphology', *AJPA* 70: 265–75.

SOKOLOWSKI, F. (1969) *Lois sacrées des cités grecques*. Paris (Ecole française d'Athènes: Travaux et Mémoires 9).

SOURVINOU-INWOOD, C. (1987) 'Images grecques de la mort: représentations, imaginaire, histoire', *AION ArchStAnt* 9: 145–58.

SPERBER, D. (1975) *Rethinking Symbolism*. Cambridge.

SPITAELS, P. (1978) 'Insula 3. Tower compound 1', in *Thorikos VII, 1970/1971*: 39–110. Ghent.

SPRIGGS, M., ed. (1984) *Marxist Perspectives in Archaeology*. Cambridge.

SQUARCIAPINO, M. F. (1958) *Scavi di Ostia* 3.1: *La necropoli*. Rome.

STAHL, M. (1987) *Aristokraten und Tyrannen im archaischen Athen*. Stuttgart.

STAMBAUGH, J. (1988) *The Ancient Roman City*. Baltimore.

STANNARD, D. (1977) *The Puritan Way of Death*. Oxford.

STAVROPOULLOS, PH. D. (1938) 'Ieratiki oikia en Zostiri tis Attikis', *AE*: 1–31.

STEARNS, P. N. (1985) 'Social history and history: a progress report', *Journal of Social History* 19: 319–34.

STEINBOCK, R. T. (1976) *Palaeopathological Diagnosis and Interpretation*. Springfield, Illinois.

STEINHAUER, G. (1982) 'Erevna khorou Aerodromiou Spaton', *Praktika*: 123–6.

STILLWELL, R. (1932) 'The temple of Apollo', in H. N. Fowler & R. Stillwell, *Corinth* I: 115–34. Cambridge, Massachusetts.

STIRLAND, A. (1989) 'Physical anthropology: the basic bones', in Roberts et al., eds.: 51–63.

STONE, L. (1977) *The Family, Sex and Marriage in England 1500–1800*. London.

STRAUSS, B. (1986) *Athens after the Peloponnesian War*. Ithaca, New York. (Forthcoming) 'Ritual, social drama and politics in classical Athens', to appear in *AJAH*.

STRONG, D. (1966) *Greek and Roman Gold and Silver Plate*. London. (1976) *Roman Art*. London.

STUART-MACADAM, P. (1985) 'Porotic hyperostosis: representative of a childhood condition', *AJPA* 66: 391–8.
(1987) 'Porotic hyperostosis: new evidence to support the anaemia theory', *AJPA* 74: 521–6.

STUPPERICH, R. (1977) 'Staatsbegräbnis und Privatgrabmal im klassischen Athen'. Ph.D. thesis, Münster: Westfälische Wilhelms-Universität.

SVENBRO, J. (1988) 'L'épitaphe de Mnésithéos: sur la lecture de l'inscription funéraire', *AION ArchStAnt* 10: 63–71.

SYMEONOGLOU, S. (1985) *The Topography of Thebes*. Princeton.

SZILAGYI, J. (1961) 'Beiträge zur Statistik der Sterblichkeit in den westeuropäischen Provinzen des römischen Imperiums', *AArchHung* 13: 125–55.

(1962) 'Beiträge zur Statistik der Sterblichkeit in der Illyrischen Provinzgruppe und in Norditalien (Gallia Padana)', *AArchHung* 14: 297–396.

(1963) 'Die Sterblichkeit in den Städten Mittel- und Süd-Italiens sowie in Hispanien (in der römischen Kaiserzeit)', *AArchHung* 15: 129–224.

(1965) 'Die Sterblichkeit in den nordafrikanischen Provinzen I', *AArchHung* 17: 309–34.

(1966) 'Die Sterblichkeit in den nordafrikanischen Provinzen II', *AArchHung* 18: 235–77.

(1967) 'Die Sterblichkeit in den nordafrikanischen Provinzen III', *AArchHung* 19: 25–59.

TAINTER, J. R. (1975) 'Social inference and mortuary practices: an experiment in numerical classification', *WA* 7: 1–15.

(1978) 'Mortuary practices and the study of prehistoric social systems', *AMT* 1: 105–41.

(1980) 'Behavior and status in a Middle Woodland mortuary population from the Illinois valley', *Am Ant* 45: 308–13.

TAUBER, H. (1981) '13C evidence for dietary habits of prehistoric man in Denmark', *Nature* 292: 332–7.

TAYLOR, L. J. (1989) '*Bás InEirinn*: cultural constructions of death in Ireland', *AQ* 62: 175–87.

TAYLOR, L. R. (1961) 'Freedmen and freeborn in the epitaphs of Rome', *AJPh* 82: 113–32.

THALMANN, R. (1978) *Urne oder Sarg? Auseinandersetzungen um die Einführung der Feuerbestattung im 19. Jh.* Berne.

THEMELIS, P. G. (1973/4) 'Anavyssos', *AD* 29.2: 108–10.

(1982) 'Kaiadas', *AAA* 15: 183–201.

THEOCHARIS, D. (1960) 'Thessalia', *AD* 16 chronika: 167–86.

THOMAS, D. H. (1978) *Figuring Anthropology.* New York.

THOMAS, R. (1989) *Oral Tradition and Written Record in Classical Athens.* Cambridge.

THOMPSON, J. B. (1984) *Studies in the Theory of Ideology.* Oxford.

TILLEY, C. (1989) 'Excavation as theatre', *Antiquity* 63: 275–80.

(1990) 'Claude Lévi-Strauss: structuralism and beyond', in Tilley, ed.: 3–81.

TILLEY, C., ed. (1990) *Reading Material Culture.* Oxford.

TIZZONI, M. (1985) 'The late Iron Age in Lombardy', in C. Malone & S. Stoddart, eds., *Papers in Italian Prehistory IV: The Cambridge Conference*, part III. *Patterns in Protohistory*: 37–68. 4 vols. Oxford. (*BAR* S 245).

TODD, S. (1987) 'Factions in early fourth-century Athens?', *Polis* 7: 32–49.

TOEWS, J. E. (1987) 'Intellectual history after the linguistic turn', *AHR* 92: 879–907.

TOHER, M. (1986) 'The tenth table and the conflict of the orders', in K. Raaflaub, ed., *Social Struggles in Archaic Rome*: 301–26. Berkeley.

TOMLINSON, R. A. (1976) *Greek Sanctuaries*. London.

TOYNBEE, J. M. C. (1927) 'A Roman sarcophagus at Pawlowsk and its fellows', *JRS* 17: 14–27.

(1971) *Death and Burial in the Roman World*. London.

TOYNBEE, J. M. C., & WARD-PERKINS, J. (1956) *The Shrine of St Peter and the Vatican Excavations*. London.

TRIGGER, B. G. (1989) *A History of Archaeological Thought*. Cambridge.

TROTTER, M., & GLESER, G. (1958) 'A re-evaluation of estimation of stature taken during life and of long bones after death', *AJPA* 16: 79–124.

TSANTSANOGLOU, K., & PARASSOGLOU, G. M. (1987) 'Two gold lamellae from Thessaly', *Ellenika* 38: 3–16.

TULLY, J. (1988) 'The pen is a mighty sword: Quentin Skinner's analysis of politics', in J. Tully, ed., *Meaning and Context: Quentin Skinner and His Critics*: 7–25. Princeton.

TURCAN, R. (1958) 'Origines et sens de l'inhumation à l'époque impériale', *REA* 60: 323–47.

(1978) 'Les sarcophages romains et le problème du symbolisme funéraire', *ANRW* 2.16.2: 1,700–35. Berlin.

TURNER, F. M. (1989) 'Why the Greeks and not the Romans in Victorian Britain?', in G. Clarke, ed., *Rediscovering Hellenism*: 61–81. Cambridge.

UBELAKER, D. H. (1984) *Human Skeletal Remains*. 2nd edn. Chicago.

UCKO, P. J. (1969) 'Ethnography and the archaeological interpretation of funerary remains', *WA* 1: 262–90.

ULLRICH, H. (1975) 'Estimation of fertility by means of pregnancy and childbirth alterations at the pubis, the ilium and the sacrum', *Ossa* 2: 25–39.

UTERMOHLE, C. J., & ZAGURA, S. L. (1982) 'Intra- and interobserver error in craniometry: a cautionary tale', *AJPA* 57: 303–10.

VAGLIERI, D. (1907) 'Roma', *NSc* 1907: 503–47.

VALLET, G., VILLARD, F., & AUBERSON, P. (1976) *Mégara Hyblaea* I. *Le quartier de l'agora archaïque*. Rome.

VAN ANDEL, T., & RUNNELS, C. (1987) *Beyond the Acropolis*. Stanford.

VAN CROMBRUGGEN, H. (1926) 'Les nécropoles gallo-romaines de Tongres', *Helinium* 2: 36–51.

VAN DER LEEUW, S., & TORRENCE, R., eds. (1989) *What's New? A Closer Look at the Process of Innovation*. London.

VAN DOORSELAER, A. (1967) *Les nécropoles d'époque romaine en Gaule septentrionale*. Ghent (Diss Arch Gand 10).

VAN GENNEP, A. (1960) *The Rites of Passage*. London. First published in French, 1909.

VAN GERVEN, D., & ARMELAGOS, G. (1983) ' "Farewell to paleodemography"? Rumors of its death have been greatly exaggerated', *JHE* 12: 353–60.

VAN STRATEN, F. T. (1981) 'Gifts for the gods', in H. S. Versnel, ed., *Faith, Hope and Worship*: 65–151. Leiden.

VEDDER, U. (1985) *Untersuchungen zur plastischen Ausstattung attischer Grabanlagen des 4. Jhs. v. Chr.* Frankfurt.

(1988) 'Frauentod-Kriegertod im Spiegel der attischen Grabkunst des 4. Jhs. v. Chr.', *AM* 103: 161–91.

VEESER, H. A., ed. (1990) *The New Historicism*. London.

VERDELIS, N. M. (1951) 'Anaskaphikai erevnai en Thessalia', *Praktika*: 129–63.

(1955) 'Anaskaphai Pharsalou', *Praktika*: 140–6.

VÉRHILHAC, A.-M. (1978) *Paides aoroi: poésie funéraire* I. Athens (Pragmateiai tis Akadimias Athinon 41).

VERMEULE, E. (1979) *Aspects of Death and Burial in Early Greek Poetry and Art*. Berkeley.

VERNANT, J.-P. (1980) *Myth and Society in Ancient Greece*. London.

(1989a) 'At man's table: Hesiod's foundation myth of sacrifice', in M. Detienne & J.-P. Vernant, eds., *The Cuisine of Sacrifice among the Greeks*: 21–86. Chicago.

(1989b) 'Dim body, dazzling body', in M. Feher, ed., *Fragments for a History of the Human Body* I: 18–37. 3 vols. New York.

(1989c) *L'individu, la mort, l'amour*. Paris.

VEYNE, P. (1978) 'La famille et l'amour sous le Haut-Empire romain', *Annales ESC* 33: 35–63.

VICKERS, M. J. (1984) 'The influence of exotic materials on Attic whiteground pottery', in Brijder, ed.: 88–97.

(1985) 'Artful crafts: the influence of metalwork on Athenian painted pottery', *JHS* 105: 108–28.

(1985/6) 'Imaginary Etruscans: changing perceptions of Etruria since the fifteenth century', *Hephaistos* 7/8: 153–68.

(1986) 'Silver, copper and ceramics in ancient Athens', in Vickers, ed.: 137–51.

(1987) 'Value and simplicity: eighteenth-century taste and the study of Greek vases', *P & P* 116: 98–137.

VICKERS, M. J., ed. (1986) *Pots and Pans*. Oxford (Oxford Studies in Islamic Art 3).

VIERNEISEL, K. (1963) 'Kerameikos-Grabung', *AD* 18.2: 27–30.

(1964a) 'Die Ausgrabungen im Kerameikos 1963', *AD* 19.2: 38–42.

(1964b) 'Die Grabung in der Nekropole 1962', *AA*: 420–62.

VOGEL, L. (1973) *The Column of Antoninus Pius*. Cambridge, Massachusetts.

VON BURG, K. (1987) *Heinrich Schliemann: For Gold or Glory?* London.

VON HESBERG, H. (1987a) 'Planung und Ausgestaltung der Nekropolen Roms im 2. Jh. n. Chr.', in von Hesberg & Zanker, eds.: 43–60.

(1987b) ' "La grotta nella Via Salaria". Ein Ziegelgrab antoninischer Zeit in Rom', *JdI* 102: 391–411.

(1989) 'Neuere Literatur zu römischen Grabbauten', *JRA* 2: 207–13.

VON HESBERG, H., & PFANNER, M. (1988) 'Ein augusteisches Columbarium im Park der Villa Borghese', *JdI* 103: 465–87.

VON HESBERG, H., & ZANKER, P., eds. (1987) *Römische Gräberstrasse*. Munich (Bayerische Akademie der Wissenschaften, Philosophisch-Historische Klasse, Abhandlungen. Neue Folge 96).

VOVELLE, M. (1990) *Ideologies and Mentalities*. Chicago.

WACHSMUTH, D. (1975) 'Weihungen', *Kleine Pauly* 5: 1,355–9. Berlin.

WAELKENS, M. (1982) 'Hausähnliche Gräber in Anatolien vom 3. Jht. v. Chr. bis in die Römerzeit', in D. Papenfuss & D. M. Strocka, eds., *Palast und Hütte*: 421–45. Mainz.

WAHL, C. W. (1959) 'The fear of death', in H. Feifel, ed., *The Meaning of Death*: 26–7. London.

WAIT, G. A. (1985) *Ritual and Religion in Iron Age Britain*. 2 vols. Oxford (*BAR* 149).

WAKEMAN, F. (1988) 'Mao's remains', in Watson & Rawski, eds.: 254–88.

WALBANK, M. (1982) 'The confiscation and sale by the *poletai* in 402/1 B.C. of the property of the Thirty Tyrants', *Hesperia* 51: 74–98.

WALDRON, T. (1983) 'On the post-mortem accumulation of lead by the skeletal tissues', *JAS* 10: 35–40.

(1987a) 'The relative survival of the human skeleton: implications for palaeopathology', in Boddington et al., eds.: 55–64.

(1987b) 'The potential of analysis of chemical constituents of bone', in Boddington et al., eds.: 149–59.

(1988) 'The exposure of some Romano-British populations to lead', *Anthropologie* 26: 67–73.

WALKER, L. (1984) 'Population and behaviour: the deposition of human remains', in B. W. Cunliffe, ed., *Danebury: An Iron Age Hillfort in Hampshire*: 442–63. London (CBA Research Report 52).

WALKER, R. L., JOHNSON, J. R., & LAMBERT, P. M. (1988) 'Age and sex biases in the preservation of human skeletal remains', *AJPA* 76: 183–8.

WALKER, S. (1983) 'Women and housing in classical Greece', in A. Cameron & A. Kuhrt, eds., *Images of Women in Antiquity*: 81–91. London.

(1985) *Memorials to the Roman Dead*. London.

WALKER, S., & CAMERON, A., eds. (1989) *The Greek Renaissance in the Roman Empire*. London.

WALL, S. M., MUSGRAVE, J. H., & WARREN, P. M. (1986) 'Human bones from a Late Minoan ıb house at Knossos', *BSA* 81: 333–88.

WALLACE-HADRILL, A. (1988) 'The social structure of the Roman house', *PBSR* 43: 43–97.

(1989) 'Rome's cultural revolution', *JRS* 79: 157–64.

WARWICK, R. (1968) 'The skeletal remains', in Wenham, ed.: 113–76.

WATERS, K. H. (1985) *Herodotos the Historian.* London.

WATSON, J. (1988) 'The structure of Chinese funerary rites', in Watson & Rawski, eds.: 3–19.

WATSON, J. L., & RAWSKI, E., eds. (1988) *Death Ritual in Late Imperial and Modern China.* Berkeley.

WATSON, P. J., & FOTIADIS, M. (1990) 'The razor's edge: symbolic-structuralist archaeology and the expansion of archaeological inference', *American Anthropologist* 92: 613–29.

WAUGH, E. (1948) *The Loved Ones.* London.

WAYWELL, G. (1980) 'Mausolea in south-west Asia Minor', *Yayla* 3: 4–11.

WEBER, M. (1976 (1904/5)) *The Protestant Ethic and the Spirit of Capitalism.* London.

WEISS, K. M. (1972) 'On the systematic bias in skeletal sexing', *AJPA* 37: 239–50.

(1973) *Demographic Models for Anthropology.* New York (Society for American Archaeology, Memoirs vol. 27).

WELLS, C. (1973) 'A palaeopathological rarity in a skeleton of Roman date', *Medical History* 17: 399–400.

(1981) 'Report on three series of Romano-British cremations and four inhumations from Skeleton Green', in C. Partridge, ed., *Skeleton Green: Late Iron Age and Romano-British Site:* 227–304. London (*Britannia* monograph 2).

(1982) 'The human burials', in McWhirr et al., eds.: 135–202.

WELLS, P. (1984) *Farms, Villages and Cities.* Ithaca, New York.

WELSKOPF, E. (1974) 'Soziale Gruppen- und Typenbegriffe. Klasse, Stand, Privatmann, Individualität – Hellenen und Barbaren, Polis und Territorialstaat', in Welskopf, ed., IV: 2, 141–76.

WELSKOPF, E., ed. (1974) *Hellenische Poleis.* 4 vols. Berlin.

WELTER, G. (1938) *Aigina.* Berlin.

WENHAM, L. P. (1968) *The Romano-British Cemetery at Trentholme Drive, York.* London.

WEST, M. L. (1983) *The Orphic Poems.* Oxford.

WESTELL, W. P. (1931). 'A Romano-British cemetery at Baldock, Herts.', *ArchJ* 88: 247–301.

WHALEY, J., ed. (1981) *Mirrors of Mortality.* London.

WHIMSTER, R. (1970) *Burial Practices in Iron Age Britain.* 2 vols. Oxford (*BAR* 90).

WHITE, H. (1987) *The Content of the Form: Narrative Discourse and Historical Representation.* Baltimore.

WHITEHEAD, D. (1975) 'Aristotle the metic', *P C Ph S* 201: 94–9.
(1983) 'Competitive outlay and community profit: *philotimia* in democratic Athens', *C & M* 34: 55–74.
(1986) *The Demes of Attica*. Princeton.

WHITEHOUSE, D. (1985) 'Raiders and invaders: the Roman campagna in the first millennium A.D.', in C. Malone & S. Stoddart, eds., *Papers in Italian Prehistory* IV: *The Cambridge Conference*, part IV. *Classical and Medieval Archaeology*: 207–13. 4 vols. Oxford (*B A R* S 245).

WHITLEY, A. J. M. (1988) 'Early states and hero cults: a reappraisal', *J H S* 108: 173–82.
(1991) *Style and Society in Dark Age Greece*. Cambridge.

WHITTAKER, C. R., ed. (1988) *Pastoral Economies in Classical Antiquity*. Cambridge (*P C Ph S* supp. vol. 14).

WHITTAKER, D. K., & STACK, M. V. (1984) 'The lead, cadmium and zinc content of some Romano-British teeth', *Archaeometry* 26: 37–42.

WHYTE, M. K. (1988) 'Death in the People's Republic of China', in Watson & Rawski, eds.: 289–316.

WIEDEMANN, T. (1989) *Adults and Children in the Roman Empire*. New Haven.

WIGHTMAN, E. (1985) *Gallia Belgica*. London.

WILLEMSEN. F. (1977) 'Zu dem Lakedämoniergrab im Kerameikos', *A M* 92: 117–57.

WILLIAMS, C. K. (1982) 'The early urbanization of Corinth', *A S A A* 60: 9–21.

WILLIAMSON, C. (1987) 'A Roman law from Narbonne', *Athenaeum* 65: 173–89.

WILSON, D. R. (1968) 'An early Christian cemetery at Ancaster', in Barley & Hanson, eds.: 197–9.

WING, E. S., & BROWN, A. B. (1970) *Paleonutrition*. New York.

WINKLER, J. J., & ZEITLIN, F., eds. (1990) *Nothing to Do with Dionysos?* Princeton.

WOOD, E. M. (1988) *Peasant-Citizen and Slave: The Foundations of Athenian Democracy*. London.

WORKSHOP OF EUROPEAN ANTHROPOLOGISTS (1980) 'Recommendations for age and sex diagnoses of skeletons', *J H E* 9: 517–49.

WREDE, H. (1978) 'Die Ausstattung stadtrömischer Grabtempel und der Übergang zur Körperbestattung', *Rom Mitt* 85: 411–33.
(1987) 'Monumente der antikaiserlich philosophischen Opposition', *Jd I* 102: 379–90.
(1989) 'Die Opera de' pili von 1542 und das Berliner Sarkophagcorpus. Zur Geschichte von Sarkophagforschung, Hermeneutik und klassischer Archäologie', *Jd I* 104: 373–414.

WYLIE, A. (1985) 'The reaction against analogy', *A M T* 8: 63–111.
(1989) 'The interpretive dilemma', in Pinsky & Wylie, eds.: 18–27.

YENGOYAN, A. (1985) 'Digging for symbols: the archaeology of everyday material life', *PPS* 51: 329–34.

YOUNG, B. (1984) *Quatres cimetières mérovingiens de l'Est de France.* Oxford (*BAR* S 306).

(1986) 'Quelques réflexions sur les sépultures privilégiées, leur contexte et leur évolution surtout dans la Gaule de l'Est', in Duval & Picard, eds.: 69–88.

YOUNG, R. S. (1951a) 'An industrial district of ancient Athens', *Hesperia* 20: 135–288.

(1951b) 'Sepulturae intra urbem', *Hesperia* 20: 67–134.

(1964) 'The Geometric period', in Blegen et al., eds.: 13–49.

ZACHARIADOU, O., KYRIAKOU, D., & BAZIOTOPOULOU, E. (1985) 'Sostiki anaskaphi ston anisopedo komvo Lenormant-Konstandino-poleos', *AAA* 18: 39–50.

ZANKER, P. (1975) 'Grabreliefs römischer Freigelassener', *JdI* 90: 267–315.

(1988) *The Power of Images in the Age of Augustus.* Ann Arbor.

ZIOLKOWSKI, J. (1981) *Thucydides and the Tradition of Funeral Speeches at Athens.* New York.

ZUNTZ, G. (1971) *Persephone.* Oxford.

Index

Abascantus, 41
Aegina, 145
Aeschines, 126
Africa, Roman province, 48, 54, 161, 164, 171
age, 27, 72–81, 141, 158, 181–3
Agrippa, funeral of, 11
Alcibiades, 119
Alexandria, 50, 53
Alföldy, G., 7
Altava, 164, 187
Ambrose, 171–2
Amorgos, 120 n. 22
amphitheatres, 11–12
Ampurias, 51, 64–5
analogy, 23
Anavyssos, 18
Andocides, 118, 119
Angel, J. L., 74–6, 90, 93–8
Anglo-Saxons, 89
Ano Voula, 120 n. 22, 135
Antoninus Pius, 56
Apollodorus, 125–6
Aquileia, 50, 67
archaeological invisibility, 195–6
Argos, 26–7, 71, 79, 151
Ariès, P., 40
Aristophanes: *Clouds*, 151; *Ecclesiazusae*, 125; *Knights*, 151; *Wasps*, 126; *Wealth*, 119–20, 125
Aristotle: *Nicomachean Ethics*, 103, 148; *Poetics*, 3; *Rhetoric*, 4
Arles, 50
Armoricum, 51
army, Roman, 83, 161–2, 165
Arras, 173
arthritis, 93–4
Arval Brethren, 12, 55
Athens, excavations: Agora, 120, 121; Benaki St., 116 n. 16; Kerameikos, 78–80, 111–18, 130–6, 149, 187, 206; Lenormant St., 132 n. 5; Madytou St.,

116 n. 16; Olymbiou St., 116 n. 16; Panepistimiou St., 116–17, 132 n. 5; Peiraios St., 116 n. 16, 132 n. 5; Pnyx, 52; Sapphous St., 116; Syndagma Square, 111–18, 135, 137, 139; Veikou St., 116 n. 16
Attic stelai, 119
Audin, A., 32, 56
Augustine, 171
Augustus, 43–4, 46, 51, 56, 160
Aylesford–Swarling Culture, 47

Balbinus, 56
Baldock, 66
barbarian burials, 88, 171
Bartel, B., 14
Beard, M., 12
Beazley J. D., 108–10, 152
Bernal, M., 37
Binford, L. R., 22
Birdlip, 48
Bisel, S., 95, 98
Blicquy, 49–50
Bloch, M., 8
Boardman, J., 89
Boatwright, M., 56
Bocquet-Appel, J.-P., 73
Boddington, A., 73
Bodel, J., 42
Boeotia, 145, 151
Bonn, 172
Bradley, R., 149
Bradley Hill, 66, 87, 89
Breitsprecher, U., 90
Britain, Roman, 48–51, 62, 66, 71, 93, 161, 162, 171
Brittany, 88
Brown, P., 172–3
Buikstra, J., 73
Burkert, W., 20 n. 25
burying groups, 185–7

259